INDIA ISRAEL

Engagement, Defence and Security Ties

INDIA ISRAEL
Engagement, Defence and Security Ties

Gurudutt Patil

HOW
ACADEMICS
an imprint of Highlyy Publishing LLP

ISBN: 978-93-95522-34-2 (Hardback)
First Published : 2023

Cataloging in Publication Data--DK
Courtesy: D.K. Agencies (P) Ltd. <docinfo@dkagencies.com>

Patil, Gurudutt, 1986- author.
India Israel : engagement, defence and security ties / Gurudutt Patil.
pages cm
ISBN 9789395522342 (hardback)

1. India--Foreign relations--Israel. 2. Israel--Foreign relations--India. 3. India--Military relations--Israel. 4. Israel--Military relations--India. I. Title.

LCC DS450.I75P38 2023 | DDC 327.5405694 23

Published by : HOW ACADEMICS
an imprint of Highlyy Publishing LLP

Correspondence Address : 4/30 A II Floor, Double Storey Buildings
Vijay Nagar, Delhi-110009
Editorial: +91 9811026449
Sales : +91 9999953412
Email: info@howacademics.com
Website: www.howacademics.com

Preface

India and Israel's relationship is a relatively recent development in international diplomacy. Despite their vast geographical distance, both nations share a deep cultural and historical connection that dates back several centuries. The two countries established formal diplomatic relations in 1992, and since then, their partnership has only grown stronger.

"India Israel Engagement, Defence and Security Ties" delves into the history, politics, and economics of this unique relationship between India and Israel. The book offers a detailed analysis of the strategic, military, and technological cooperation between the two nations, which has helped foster a mutually beneficial partnership. It also explores the factors that have shaped the trajectory of this relationship, including geopolitical considerations, strategic interests, and shared values.

Through this book, the authors explore how India and Israel have developed a shared understanding of their respective geopolitical and strategic interests. They have formed a solid alliance that has stood the test of time, despite various political and economic challenges.

With contributions from renowned scholars and experts in the field, this book provides an in-depth analysis of the various aspects of India-Israel bonhomie. It is a must-read for anyone interested in understanding the dynamics of this rapidly evolving relationship and the implications it holds for the region and beyond.

Contents

Chapter 1

The Past and Future of Israel and India

The Zionists and India

Since its start at the end of the 19th century, the Zionist movement (Jewish nationalism) has been focused on finding legitimacy and acceptance. The early Zionists did more than just build facts in the ancient homeland, the Land of Israel. They also worked hard to get international support for the Zionist cause. This was the beginning of a Jewish national home in what was then called Palestine. It was mostly aimed at the most important countries in Europe and the Ottoman Empire, which ruled Palestine at the time. Asia was not on the Zionists' list of places to talk to at first. A lot of Asian countries, including those in West Asia, were ruled by European colonists. With the exception of Japan, most Asian countries didn't have much of an impact on the rest of the world. Also, unlike in Europe and the US, the Jewish communities in Asia were small and didn't have much political power.

But since the 1930s, India has been getting more attention. The country was ruled by the British, but there was a growing movement of people who didn't like that. This movement, which Mohandas Gandhi led, became a cause célèbre all over the world. Zionist leaders saw parallels between their own fight for independence and the Indian fight for freedom, and they were very sympathetic to the Indian cause. David Ben Gurion, who would become Prime Minister of Israel, had a lot of respect for Gandhi. He said that Gandhi was a "great leader" who led an unprecedented fight for freedom against the world's strongest empire. Ben Gurion also admired how much he stressed nonviolence. Zionist leaders of all political stripes kept saying things like this even after it was known that Gandhi didn't like Zionism.

The Hebrew version of Gandhi's autobiography came out in 1945, while Jawaharlal Nehru's was translated in 1941. Other books about India came out around the same time, which shows that people in general are interested in the country.

The Zionist movement tried to get in touch with Gandhi, Nehru, and other Indian National Congress (INC) leaders to make them aware of Jewish goals. These attempts didn't go very well. Jews were seen by the Congress leadership as a religious group that didn't have any national rights. This was the same way that Muslims in India were seen. Due to their lack of knowledge about Jews and Judaism, that leadership ignored the historical ties between Jews and their home country.

Even though the Zionists thought of themselves as progressives, they were often seen as tools and allies of British colonialism. On the other hand, the Arabs in Palestine were seen as natives and allies in the fight against British rule. Also, the Zionists' desire for a split between Jews and Arabs in the Land of Israel was not acceptable in the political situation of India. Because of this, most of the political class in India, which was heavily influenced by Gandhi and Nehru, became against Zionist goals in Palestine.

Also, the political situation on the ground meant that people had to be careful when dealing with Zionists. The Hindu leaders and the British government in India and London both thought that the Muslims in India were very concerned about what was going on in Palestine. This made the Indian nationalist movement less likely to support the goals of Jewish nationalists. India, like most of Asia, didn't have a strong connection to the Bible and didn't understand why the Zionists wanted to start their own country.

After India joined the United Nations Special Committee on Palestine, Zionists worked harder to change how India felt about Zionism (UNSCOP). Still, India was the leader of the minority report that was against partition and the idea of putting a Jewish state next to an Arab one. At that time, it was not politically correct in India to split up the country based on "religious" lines. In November 1947, Nehru told the Indian delegation to the UN to vote against the UN partition resolution, which the UN General Assembly (UNGA) eventually passed 33 to 11. As a result, the Arabs of Palestine and the Arab states did not agree with the UN's decision and went to war with the new country of Israel.

To the dismay of Zionist leaders, India's early and deep dislike of Zionism lasted for years and barely changed when Israel was founded in 1948, just one year after India got its independence. The Zionist movement was not able to show the Indian government that it was more than just a culturally Western movement with political ties to Western interests.

India's Recognition of Israel

India's recognition of Israel in 1950 was a significant event in the history of both nations. Prior to this, India had not recognized Israel as a sovereign state and had maintained diplomatic relations with Arab countries. However, India's recognition of Israel marked a turning point in its foreign policy, and the two countries have since developed strong ties in various fields.

India's stance on the Israel-Palestine conflict has been shaped by its historical ties with the Arab world and its support for the Palestinian cause. India played a significant role in the establishment of the State of Israel in 1948 when it voted in favor of the UN Partition Plan that proposed the division of British Mandate Palestine into Jewish and Arab states. However, India did not immediately recognize Israel as a sovereign state due to its concerns over the plight of the Palestinian people.

India's recognition of Israel came in 1950, two years after the establishment of the Jewish state. The decision was made by Prime Minister Jawaharlal Nehru, who was instrumental in shaping India's foreign policy. Nehru's decision to recognize Israel was based on several factors, including India's desire to expand its ties with non-aligned countries and to strengthen its position in the Middle East.

The recognition of Israel by India was not without controversy. It was met with protests from within the country, particularly from the Muslim community, which felt that India was betraying its solidarity with the Palestinian cause. However, Nehru defended his decision by stating that India's recognition of Israel did not imply support for Israel's policies towards the Palestinians.

India's decision in January 1992 to start diplomatic relations with the Jewish State fixed a strange situation that had been going on for more than 40 years. Several things and calculations could have caused the unusual delay. In a way, the decision was the end of a process that began when India recognised Israel in September 1950. Two in-depth studies, by K. P. Misra and B. N. Mehrish, have been done on India's policy on recognition, and most of the time, their conclusions are different. Some of their conclusions about Israel are questionable now that new information and events have come to light. Because of this, it's important to look closely at different parts of recognition.

Within hours of being declared, the State of Israel should be recognised by the rest of the world. Indian Prime Minister Jawaharlal Nehru had given two different dates as to when such a request was made Speaking in the Constituent Assembly in August 1948 he declared:

> *A telegram was received in the middle of June 1948 from Monsieur Moshe Shertok [later Sharett] Foreign Minister of the Provisional Government of the State of Israel, containing a request for recognition of the Jewish State.*

Up until recently, this was thought to be true. But Nehru's Letters to Chief Ministers, which came out in 1985, show that this was asked for even earlier. In his twice-a-month letter from May 20, 1948, Nehru said that his government had received a request for recognition from Israel. Documents from Israel show that on May 17, 1948, Shertok sent a cable to Nehru, who was also India's Foreign Minister. There's no sign that a reminder was sent to India, so the date of mid-June must be a mistake.

It took India as long as 28 months to do what Israel asked. Between May 1948 and September 1950, there were clear signs that India was ready to accept Israel as a full member of the international community.

> *We propose to take no action in this matter [i. e. recognition] at present. India can play no effective part in this conflict at the present stage either diplomatically or otherwise. We can only watch events for the time being, hoping that an opportunity may come when we might use our influence in the interest of peace and mediation.*

So, while Nehru acknowledged that Israel had asked, he put off making a decision until later.

Three months later, he said, "We had to wait because a new state had been made." In the same way, he said in February 1949 that the question of recognition would be decided by "both idealistic and realistic assessments of the situation." A month later, he said again that Israel was definitely a state that was acting like one, and that H. V. Kamath's opinion that it was here to stay might be right. India did not want Israel to join the United Nations, but it did anyway. On June 3, 1949, he wrote, "We shall have to think about our future policy in regard to it [i.e., Israel joining the UN]."

India was careful about what it said in its own country, but it took a stronger stance abroad. By September 1948, it was clear that a positive decision would be made about recognition. The only thing that was still unclear was the exact date. While Nehru was trying to get his country to recognise him, it made sense abroad, especially in the United States, for him to be more friendly and understanding towards Israel. When he met his Israeli counterpart on September 28, 1948, India's Ambassador to the United States, B. N. Rau, talked about normalisation. Mid-May, Nehru's sister, Mrs. Vijayalakshmi Pandit, who had taken Rau's place in Washington, said that India planned to recognise Israel at the right time and that it might happen soon after the Kashmir dispute was settled. In June 1949, Rau, who had moved to the United Nations by then, talked at length about the political issues that brought India and Israel closer together. He also said that there was no conflict of interest between the two countries. On September 30, 1949, when Mrs. Pandit met with Elath, she said that India was steadily moving towards recognising the Jewish state and that the decision could not be put off any longer. Soon after, Elath met with Nehru for a long time when the Indian Prime Minister came to the United States in October 1949. Summing up this meeting the Israeli ambassador cabled:

> *. . Nehru listened attentively, obviously disturbed by mention [of] Turkey's recognition. In reply after announcing complete frankness he explained India's attitude [towards] Israel. People never anti- Semitic, Hitler made them friends of Jews. Many Indians admired in past Zionist and now most sympathetic [to] Israel. . . He had to choose slow, long, way towards recognition [in] order [to] justify it objectively and minimize internal opposition . . . He arrived (at the) conclusion recognition cannot be postponed much longer . . . To my question whether he could mention possible date [of] recognition he replied [he] would deal matter immediately on return India early November and we could expect recognition before January (1950) . .*

When Nehru got back to India, he said, "It is clear that the recognition of Israel cannot be put off indefinitely." Even though he wasn't recognised right away, Ambassador Aubrey S. Eban (later Abba Eban) was invited to the official opening of the Indian Republic by Rau.

The delay in recognition did not stop India from asking Israel for technical help in a formal way. O n 15 November 1947- even before the UN vote on Palestine - acting on the suggestions of K. M. Panikkar and Shiva Rao, Chaim Weizmann offered technical assistance to India which Nehru accepted in principle. As a result of a number of talks and offers, India asked Israel for help with farming in March 1949. "There was no real hostility," an Israeli diplomat said, "because India asked us for a loan of agricultural experts." The most promising statement on recognition came in February 1950 when Nehru declared in the Provisional Parliament:

> *The fact that the State of Israel exists is of course recognized by the Government of India. But formal recognition involving an exchange of diplomatic mission has to be considered in connection with a number of factors*

These meetings and statements made it clear what the Indian government thought and that it was ready to recognise Israel. They also showed how carefully it dealt with the problem.

This delay, however, was not favourably viewed in Israel and Walter Eytan, Director General of the Ministry of Foreign Affairs, summed up its feelings:

> *Two years after the establishment of the State of Israel, India remains one of the few non-Arab, non-Muslim countries which have not recognized her. Israel had always attributed a special value to India's recognition, due to her prestigious status in Asia. During the past two years, considerable efforts have been invested in making contacts with high-ranking Indian personalities but despite many promises and demonstration so f friendship, Indian as not yet taken this step.*
>
> *Now that 60 countries have recognized Israel, recognition by additional one is no longer a burning issue and Israel has ceased trying to persuade vacillating countries, including India. Moreover belated recognition is of lesser political and moral weight than that accorded close to the state's establishment . .*

On September 17, 1950, a clear official message said, "The Government of India has decided to give recognition to the Government of Israel." This was officially told through the Israeli embassy in Washington the day before. The usual statement about wanting to get back to normal diplomatic relations was missing. By tradition, countries recognise the newly formed state and its government. Given the circumstances surrounding Israel's creation, it would have been better to refer to it as the State of Israel.

Indian scholars did not all agree on what the law said about recognition. India did not say in September 1950 if its recognition of Israel was de facto or de jure. Misra said that India had usually given recognition without saying anything about what its de facto or de jure status was. On the other hand, Mehrish came to the conclusion that "if India has only given de facto recognition, that has not been followed by full diplomatic conversations or giving their representatives diplomatic immunity." He used Israel as an example. A careful look, on the other hand, would show that India's recognition of Israel was both de facto and de jure, even though it was not clear.

First, Nehru's statement from February 1950 made it clear that India accepted Israel's de facto status even before it was officially recognised. Second, in the years that followed, several official statements said that recognition was legal. In Parliament in July 1971, when diplomatic ties were not close, the government said, "India gave legal recognition to Israel in September 1950." And thirdly, in his official report following his visit to India, Walter Eytan provides new insights into the controversy when he wrote:

> *Miss Naidu [who was dealing with West Asia in the Ministry of External Affairs when Eytan visited India] also told me of the argument they had had in the Ministry at the time they recognized Israel - whether it should be de jure or de facto. The Secretary General, on being appraised of this problem, had consulted all their legal authorities and had come to the conclusion that he couldn't see what difference there was between de facto and de jure recognition; so they recognized us pure and simple . .*

The state that recognises a state or government has the right to do so, so nations have a policy of "wait and see" until they are sure that the newly formed state or government has met the requirements and is ready to be recognised. India has been very careful about getting recognised, as the examples of East Germany, Algeria, and Bangladesh show. But this doesn't explain why India didn't recognise Israel right away, and there are two other reasons for this.

First, after the communal vivisection of the subcontinent and the riots that followed, the way Muslims felt about Israel became even more important. Early in August 1948, not long after Israel was made, Jhunjhunwala brought the cable sent to Truman and Molotov to the attention of the Constituent Assembly. In this message, the President of the Jamait-ul ulemai-Hind said that Indian Muslims were angry that the superpowers had recognised Israel. A fortnight later Begum Aizaz Rasul raised the following question in the same Assembly:

> *Will the Hon'ble Prime Minister keep in mind the fact that there are a large number of people living in the Indian Dominion whose wishes and sentiments in this regard should be kept in view regarding the recognition of the State of Israel and they are definitely opposed to it?*

In their talks with the Israelis, Indian diplomats and the Prime Minister brought up the feelings of Muslims as a problem, even though they were not allowed inside the country.

For example, on his meeting with Nehru in October 1949, Elath cabled:

> *Turning to recognition he [Nehru] said Indian partition was most painful operation . . . Pakistan however became a theocratic state preventing national assimilation [of] Muslims of India. Hence Indian government must treat its thirty million Muslims most carefully. Palestine was source [of] constant agitation and made deep impression [on] Muslims everywhere . .*

When Walter Eytan met Nehru in March 1952, he said a lot of the same things. If you look at the documents from Israel, there are many times when Indian diplomats talked about how India's Muslim population felt about Israel.

Second, India didn't want to upset the Arabs by moving too quickly. Since Arabs don't like Israel and Indian nationalists have helped the Arabs in the past with the Palestine question, India didn't want to make things worse. In October 1949, Elath said, "Nehru recently talked about Israel with Arab and Muslim envoys in New Delhi. He stressed the need for peace with reality and got them ready for India's inevitable recognition of Israel." As a quick response, the Iraqi delegate to the United Nations "put strong pressure on the Chief delegate of India to take action against Indian recognition of Israel" in November.

Similarly the official note prepared by the Indian Ministry of External Affairs in February 1950 remarked:

> *The consensus of opinion expressed by our Missions in Arab countries, as a result of their conversations with knowledgeable persons in these countries and as a result of their own study of the question, is that the recognition of Israel by India would displease the Arabs and be treated as an unfriendly act and would certainly aggravate our relations with Pakistan. It has been brought to our notice that Saudi Arabia would be particularly concerned at our recognition of Israel. Our Missions have, therefore, emphatically advised us against our recognition of Israel till the outstanding question of (i) settlement of Arab refugees; (ii) boundary between Israel and the Arab world; and (iii) Holy places of Jerusalem are satisfactorily settled. The view has also been expressed that any premature recognition of Israel might affect the position of Indians in Bahrain, Kuwait and other places in the Persian Gulf and the Middle East. The displeasure of Saudi Arabia may also have serious repercussions on Hajj pilgrimage by Indian Muslims and thus give rise to domestic difficulties.*

Also, Nehru's biographer, S. Gopal, said that Nehru's first reaction to the question of Israel joining the United Nations was to not vote. Later, as part of his plan to work with the Islamic States, he told the Indian delegation to vote against because he wanted to work with them.

After he admitted that Israel was a country, Nehru said that the Arabs were to blame for the delay. On 1 October 1950 he wrote: 'We would have done this [recognition of Israel] long ago, because Israel is a fact. We refrained because of our desire not to offend the sentiments of our friends in the Arab countries. Speaking soon after the decision, India's Ambassador in Cairo remarked:

> *For some time now announcements were being made that India did intend to recognize Israel and that it was only a question of time. India's intentions were made known well in advance to the Arab diplomats in New Delhi and to the Governments in the Middle East through Cairo. Some of these Governments requested India to postpone her decision but India felt that any further postponement would not serve any useful purpose.*

Also, by the time India recognised Israel, all of the Arab states that were fighting with Israel had signed an official peace treaty with Israel, which was a way of saying that the Arab states recognised the Jewish State.

It is important to look at why Indians should be recognised. Based on what we know now, there are seven possible explanations. First, India has agreed to the Declaratory theory of recognition, and Mehrish said that from India's point of view, "recognition registers but does not create a situation." In general, India has recognised a state when it has met the basic requirements of a state and shown that it can and is willing to follow international law and commitments. So, it made sense to recognise Israel as a country.

Second, Israel had become a done deal, and a lot of countries had to accept it. Iran and Yugoslavia had already recognised Israel. They had backed the Federal Plan with India in the United Nations Special Committee on Palestine (UNSCOP). Turkey, Iran, and Indonesia, three Islamic countries, had also recognised the Jewish state before India did. And most importantly, Israel had joined the United Nations. Nehru said, "Our policy is to recognise any country that was an independent country that was represented at the United Nations." He was talking about this link. Also, his close friend V. K. Krishna Menon said, "I have always thought that we should recognise any country that is recognised by the UN." Also, while the membership of some countries, like Albania and Jordan, was blocked, the request of Israel was one of the few times that the two sides of the Cold War agreed on something. So, it made sense to give the Indians their rights.

A third thing to think about was India's policy of recognition towards Communist China. India thought that not recognising a country couldn't be based on the kind of government in Beijing. In the Indian Constituent Assembly, there were questions about the "various criteria" that India used to accept new states. Misra said that if India had taken a different view of Israel, it "would have put India in a paradoxical situation."

Fourth, India really wanted to help settle the conflict between the Arabs and Israel. The official spokesman said that continuing to not recognise Israel is not only bad for relations in general, but it also makes it harder for the Indian government to act as a mediator between Israel and the Arab states. This is why India decided to recognise Israel. Even though he didn't want Israel to join the UN, Nehru knew he had to treat Israel with more fairness. In May 1949, he wrote, "It is time to show some of these Arab countries that we are not going to do everything they do."

Fifth, a big and loud part of the Indian public wanted Israel to be recognised quickly. The problem was talked about a lot in the Constituent Assembly, and the government could not have ignored the pressure. In August 1948, a socialist member of Parliament named H. V. Kamath questioned the government's policy towards Israel. Since then, the issue has been brought up at every meeting of the Constituent Assembly. Aside from this happening inside India, a number of well-known Indians living abroad were also working hard to get Israel recognised.

Sixth, both Israel and its supporters in the West worked hard to get things done. Israel never stopped trying to get close to and have an effect on India, and most of these efforts were made in the United States. Asaf Ali, B. N. Rau, Shiva Rao, Mrs. Pandit, and Krishna Menon were among the top Indian diplomats and UN delegates with whom they kept in touch on a regular basis. The US Congressman Emanuel Celler played a key role in this campaign and took part in the Nehru-Elath meeting in October 1949 and, according to Elath,

He [Nehru] arrived [at the] conclusion recognition cannot be postponed much longer. Here he turned [to] Celler saying it would be unwise to grant Israel recognition during his [Nehru's]s tay[int he US] because this [is] liable [to be] interpreted as American pressure

People like Chaim Weizmann, who are well-known in Israel, worked hard to get India's recognition. 5In the same way, Emanuel Olsvanger, who was sent to India as the first official Zionist envoy in the middle of the 1930s, also worked in this direction.Albert Einstein, a famous scientist, tried to get Nehru to help the Jews even before Israel was made. Given this tar-studded lobbying from all over the world, India could only delay and not refuse to recognise.

And finally, K. R. Singh said that India's recognition of the Jewish State was also due to the growing friendship between Pakistan and Arab countries. Gopal, who wrote a biography about Nehru, says that the fact that Farouk's Egypt voted against India in the UN over the Hyderabad issue made him more likely to accept Israel as a fact and recognise it. The fact that India doesn't recognise the All Palestine Government in Gaza should also be seen in this light.

India was upset about the difference between recognising the country and starting diplomatic relations with it. Since there had been no formal ties for a long time, some people said that recognition was a legal act and the exchange of diplomatic relations was a political act. K. P. Misra explained this link by saying, "Recognition cannot be considered a political act just because the executive branch of a government decides on it." But the evidence we have does not support this claim.

In its policy pronouncement on the Chinese question,the US government argued:

In the view of the United States diplomatic recognition is a privilege and not a right. Moreover, the United States considers that diplomatic recognition is an instrument Of national policy which is both its right and duty to use in the enlightened self-interest of the nation.

Shelton Appleton said the same thing: "It is not likely that the government will not use it [recognition] if they are convinced that they can gain significant benefits by giving it or not giving it at their own discretion." As shown by how the West treated Communist China and how the Arabs felt about Israel, recognition was withheld for political reasons, not because of the law. In the same way, there have been times when the entity in question was "recognised" by others, even though it didn't have all of the characteristics of a state. A number of Arab states recognised the self-proclaimed All Palestine Government in Gaza, even though it didn't have the most important thing a State needs: land. Von Glahn said that recognition is more of a political act with legal repercussions.

It is common, if not required, for diplomatic relations to be set up after a country is recognised. Still, a state doesn't have to or have to be able to have relationships with all the states it has recognised. If this was true, the fact that India and Israel haven't had diplomatic ties for more than 40 years shouldn't get too much attention, since India doesn't have ties with other small, faraway countries either. India wanted to keep normal relations with Israel at first, but then couldn't or didn't want to. This makes the case unique. In India, people did not pay enough attention to what India was trying to do, and being recognised was often not seen as a big deal.

In 1956, when the Indian Prime Minister was talking about Spain, he agreed that "a logical consequence of that [recognition] was to exchange diplomatic missions, as long as we had the personnel." 7T2: His point of view can also be used to explain the situation in Israel. An official note written on April 4, 1951, showed that normalisation was seen in a positive light. It said, "In order to get a clear picture of the Middle East, we need to open a mission in Israel as soon as possible." At the time India got its independence, it only had permanent missions in Cairo, Tehran, and Istanbul. In other words, Cairo was the only place in the Arab world where India had permanent missions. At first, the Ministry's main goal was to cut its budget by taking different administrative steps. In its Annual Report for 1949–50, the Ministry said, "In view of the urgent need to cut costs as much as possible, plans to set up consular offices in Mehshed and Koramshahr (Iran), Basra, Bahrain, and Muscat have been put on hold."

In a note written by a government official in December 1950, it was said that the case of Israel would have to wait for better financial times. The following year, the Ministry said that "to save money, the Heads of Mission in some countries were accredited at the same time." So, even in the middle of the 1950s, K. M. Pannikkar, the Indian ambassador in Cairo, was also accredited to Lebanon, Syria, and Jordan. Taking this trend into account, Israel was thinking about having the Indian envoy in Turkey be accredited to Israel at the same time. Soon after recognition, Nehru said that diplomatic exchanges couldn't happen for "financial and other reasons." He also said that the government wanted to avoid making any new commitments abroad at the moment. Two years later, India said, "It has not been possible to set up missions in these countries [Israel, Saudi Arabia, and Yemen] so far, mostly because of the tight financial situation."

This establishes beyond doubt that India had intended to establish a resident mission in Israel. In the words of Gopal:

> *In March 1952 Nehru informed the Israeli government [i. e. when Israeli Foreign Ministry Director General Walter Eytan met him in New Delhi] that there was no major objection to the exchange of diplomatic representatives, but it might be better to wait for the formation of a new government after the elections*

Also, in the early days of India's independence, it was more common than not for there to be no diplomatic ties.

During the 1956 Suez crisis, it was clear that the government had a formal and official negative view of normalising ties with Israel. By that time, India's policy towards Israel was strongly affected by three different things: the anti-colonialist solidarity of Afro-Asians, Israel's growing ties to the imperial powers, and the growing friendship between Nehru and Nasser. After the Israeli invasion, Nehru said that diplomatic talks were impossible because of how angry people were. Since then, the Indian position has been that "the time is not yet right." Later, Nehru himself said that diplomatic ties should have been set up as soon as the country was recognised. 85. Other people, like Krishna Menon and Morarj Diesai, agreed with him. In September 1963, the government said that it didn't want to open a Consulate in Israel because "there isn't enough consular work to justify a post." After the June war, two more "reasons" were given for why India didn't have formal ties with Israel: first, Israel had the "wrong" policies towards the Arabs and the Palestinians, and second, India couldn't accept the idea that religion could be a basis for nationality. However, neither of the premises made sense. Later, as events and needs changed, the reasons were changed to include a call for Israel to go back to where it was before 1967, the right of the Palestinians to decide for themselves, and support for a "just and honourable settlement" within an international framework.

In the end, it must be said that India's recognition of the Jewish State in September 1950 was a big change in the way it dealt with the Middle East, even though it happened slowly and wasn't clear at first. Even more so because it used to side with the Arabs on the Palestine issue and was against the partition plan and Israel joining the UN. In the beginning, the lack of formal diplomatic ties was mostly due to India's financial problems and the fact that Israel wasn't very important to India's interests in the Middle East. However, as time went on, the issue became political. It took India more than 40 years and a lot of changes in the world for the process of recognition to be finished. But it was clear that, at least during Jawahar Lal Nehru's time in office (1947–64), the basic idea of diplomatic ties was not called into question. Following Eytan's visit, K. P. S. Menon (Sr), the then Ambassador in Moscow wrote:

> *I am very sorry that the exchange of Missions between India and Israel has not yet taken place. I hope and trust that it is now only a matter of few weeks. I shall do all I can from this end, as I am really keen that we should establish a Mission in Israel without further delay*

Taking into account the then prevailing political climate, this letter does not appear to be a mere act of diplomatic courtesy.

Israel and India

India was more against Jewish goals than other big countries like Japan or China. India voted against letting Israel join the UN in June 1949. India did not officially recognise Israel until the fall of 1950, after China, the Philippines, and Burma had already done so (Japan was under American occupation until 1952). Turkey and Iran both gave de facto recognition, which made it easier for India to do the same. In 1953, India let Israel open a consulate in Bombay, which is now called Mumbai. This continued until the embassy opened in 1992. For many years, the Indian government put a lot of limits on the consulate's diplomatic work. Most of the talks between the two countries took place in Washington, at the United Nations in New York, and in London.

India didn't want to have full diplomatic relations with Israel because there were so many Arab states, but Israel was only a small country. Arab opposition stopped Israel from joining the Afro-Asian bloc at the UN and then the Non-Aligned Movement (NAM). India was one of the people in charge of these international groups, but it didn't care that Israel is in the Middle East. Also, India's disagreement with Pakistan over Kashmir was a big reason why it didn't become more open to Israeli overtures. India needed the Arab states' help at the UN, and it was afraid that getting along better with Israel could hurt its chances of getting that help.

The Suez Campaign of 1956, in which Israel joined forces with France and Great Britain, two colonial powers that were losing power, to attack Egypt, which was the leader of NAM, made it clear that Israel was a tool of Western power. At the same time, the campaign made Israel look like a strong country, which is helpful in a world where realpolitik is the norm. Also, one of its military-diplomatic successes was getting the naval blockade at the Tiran Straits lifted. This made it possible for Israel to trade with Asia by sea.

After 1956, Israel's diplomatic efforts in Africa were successful, but they were not as successful in Asia. Israel, though, kept going. Israel's Foreign Minister from 1948 to 1956, Moshe Sharett, was sure that Israel should try harder in Asia. He was even willing to become the Ambassador in Delhi, if India would let an embassy be set up there. He thought that Israel and Asia were bound together by fate. In the same way, Ben Gurion gave Asia a lot of importance and thought that China and India, the two countries with the most people, were destined for greatness on a global scale. He also thought that Asian countries could learn from Israel's ways of building nations, farming, and managing water, all of which were problems that tiny Israel was dealing with well. As long as Nehru was in charge, he didn't think that relations between India and the United States could get better. The mood between the countries hadn't gotten any better either. India, for example, started things at the UN that were against Israel.

Even though Israel sent India military equipment (mostly mortars and ammunition) when asked (during India's wars with China in 1962 and Pakistan in 1965 and 1971) and the intelligence services of the two countries worked together in a low-key way over the years, the two countries remained at odds. India's top leaders generally liked that Israel was willing to help and treated their Israeli colleagues with professional respect. However, India's politicians and diplomats remained sceptical of any possible reconciliation with Israel. In the 1960s, Israel became known as an American ally. This made it harder for India to have good relations with Israel, since India was already very suspicious of American foreign policy.

The 1973 oil crisis made India more dependent on Arab oil-producing countries. This made India's policy of staying away from Israel even stronger. India kept supporting sanctions and other ways to punish Israel at the UN, but it also gave the Palestine Liberation Organization (PLO) observer status. After working with the PLO for years, India gave it diplomatic recognition in January 1975. This was despite the fact that the PLO's Covenant called for the destruction of the Jewish state. It backed the infamous UNGA Resolution 3379 in November 1975, which compared Zionism to racism.

The Congress Party lost power in early 1977 to a coalition of parties led by the Janata Party and the Jan Sangh. This did not change India's policy towards Israel in a big way. Even though the coalition had said it was in favour of normalising relations with Egypt and the peace process that led to the 1979 Egyptian–Israeli peace treaty, this happened. (Israel did notice a change in tone, though.

When Indira Gandhi became prime minister again in January 1980, she kept the same policy towards Israel that Nehru had. The Israeli invasion of Lebanon in 1982 and the start of the Palestinian intifada in December 1987 made it very hard for things to get back to normal.

From Israel's point of view, Asia remained a secondary place for diplomatic activism, even though it wanted to end its isolation in the region and get worldwide legitimacy. Israel was consumed by its war with the Arab states and the need to get political and military support from a big power. This meant that Israel's diplomatic focus was on Paris and then Washington for most of the 20th century.

Making Diplomatic Connections

The end of the Cold War made it possible for India to change its out-of-date policy towards Israel. The point of no return was in 1991. India's main diplomatic and strategic ally during the Cold War was the Soviet Union. When it fell apart, India was "forced to reorient its foreign policy to fit the changing international environment."

Relations with the Jewish state were also talked about. The diplomatic benefits of cutting ties with Israel and voting consistently in favour of Arabs at the UN were weighed against the role of Israel in West Asia and the possible benefits of getting closer to Jerusalem.

The decision to improve relations with Israel was also made because several things that were holding them back no longer existed. First, a shift in the political economy of energy sources made the Arab bloc, and oil-producing states in particular, less powerful. Fears of energy crises had gone down a lot by the end of the 1980s. The oil market turned into a buyers' market, which made Arab objections to getting along better with Israel less important. India also realised that it was not possible to stop Arab countries from helping Pakistan with the Kashmir issue.

Also, the Arab-Israeli peace process, which the US brought back to life after the 1991 Gulf War, made it even less likely that Israel's enemies in the area would object to third parties having ties with Jerusalem. The October 1991 peace conference in Madrid, which was a formal meeting with Israel where almost all Arab countries sent their top diplomats, gave states that had been reluctant to get closer to Israel a good reason to do so. After the PLO helped Saddam Hussein, Arab states and other countries gave less support to the PLO and the Palestinian cause it stood for. This affected India's traditional support for the Palestinian cause, which made it harder to reevaluate relations with the Jewish state.

In fact, India told Israel that it was ready to slowly improve its relationship. But Israel didn't want to take small steps. Instead, it insisted on full diplomatic relations, especially before India could join the multilateral framework started at the Madrid Peace Conference. New Delhi was very interested in the multilateral track of the Madrid Conference, especially the Arms Control and Regional Security Committee. It had many interests in the Middle East, such as oil, foreign workers, and radical Islam. China decided to improve its relationship with Israel in order to be a part of the process started by American diplomacy, and India didn't want to fall behind.

India and Israel's relationship has gotten better in part because of how their domestic politics have changed. The rise of the Bharatiya Janata Party (BJP) and the fall of the Congress Party in Indian politics helped get rid of any doubts about Israel. The Hindu and nationalist views of the BJP made Israel less of a diplomatic burden and more of a possible ally against Pakistan and radical Islam. In fact, a clause calling for full relations with Israel was added for the first time at the BJP convention in October 1991. Normalization was also a result of the economic liberalisation started by then-Prime Minister Narasimha Rao of the Congress Party, which relied heavily on trade and technology with the West. India wanted to join the new globalised economy, and Israel was seen as a part of that economy that worked well.

India was also made aware of how much political power Jewish groups had. Isi Liebler, who was Vice President of the World Jewish Congress at the time, met with high-level government officials several times. At the same time, many Jewish groups in the United States talked in depth with Indian representatives.

Washington became even more important as India tried to get a $2–5 billion loan from the World Bank and the International Monetary Fund. In fact, some Indian diplomats who wanted better relations with Israel asked the US to put pressure on them to improve relations with Israel so that they could get their country out of its diplomatic rut. On January 29, 1992, it was announced that all diplomatic ties were now open. It had to do with the fact that Prime Minister Rao was going to the US soon. New Delhi thought that announcing full diplomatic relations with Israel would make things better in the US because Washington and Jerusalem are so close. In the early 1990s, when Russia, China, Turkey, Nigeria, and other Afro-Asian states took similar steps, Israel's relative isolation on the international stage came to an end. This trend after the Cold War made it possible to gradually put more emphasis on building good relationships with Asia, which is becoming more important.

A New Age

Soon, New Delhi saw that establishing full diplomatic ties with Jerusalem didn't cost much, either at home or abroad. Also, the two countries found out that they had the same view on their regional conflicts and a similar strategic plan. Both India and Israel are very aware of how dangerous things are. Low-level violence and terror are always a problem for both countries. The two countries have been fighting for a long time in their own regions, with complicated ethnic and religious factors that aren't always easy for outsiders to understand. They have also fought several large conventional wars against their neighbours.

For India and Israel, the conflict over Kashmir and the one between Israelis and Palestinians are seen as having major destabilising effects, mostly in the immediate area of each country, which makes it more likely that other countries will step in. This kind of help from outside the region is not always welcome. In fact, the two countries have similar attitudes towards the rest of the world, which doesn't seem to be able to understand why they are fighting with their neighbours. Both have enemies who have weapons that can kill a lot of people. Both countries feel like they are being pushed around in their own region. In general, the two countries' strategic cultures are similar, and they have similar ideas about how to act during a conflict.

Even though Israel's strategic situation has improved a lot since the end of the Cold War because of the evolving Arab–Israeli peace process and positive changes in the international system, existential fears have not gone away. The Arab world still hates Israel very much, and some parts of it still want it to die. This means that Israel is still looking for legitimacy and powerful friends like India.

The radical branches of Islam in the Middle East are a threat to both countries right now, and this is something that the two countries have in common. When it came to radical Islam, India and Israel had very similar ideas about how dangerous it was. India thought that some parts of the Arab world were centres of extremism in Islam. The threat was felt closer to home because of the relationship between Saudi Arabia and Pakistan, which India did not trust. Israel was always worried about the radical Islamic groups in the Arab world and in the Islamic Republic of Iran. Also, religious extremism made Arabs hate the Jewish state even more than they did before. Iran's fanatical hatred and its ability to make nuclear weapons made it a clear existential threat. In the same way, people in New Delhi worry that Islamic extremists could get their hands on Pakistan's nuclear weapons.

Their views on the rest of the world, however, are different. After the Cold War ended, India became more vulnerable because its main ally, the Soviet Union, fell apart. This took away a major source of diplomatic support and military technology. Even though relations with Washington have recently gotten better, India still has doubts about American foreign policy and prefers a multi-polar world where it can have more freedom and maybe play a bigger role in international affairs. For Israel, on the other hand, the fall of the Soviet Union, which was a friend of Israel's Arab enemies, was a clear plus.

Israel wants the United States to be in charge for strategic reasons. The US's Middle East policies are also more sensitive to Israeli concerns because of the way its government works at home. Jerusalem was very worried about the loss of American power, especially when Obama was in office. Also, Israel's existential threats haven't gone away since the end of the Cold War, and any rising competitor to the United States is likely to side with the Arabs.

The common strategic agenda is a key part of the two countries' strong relationship in the defence field. India's military has always been less hostile to Israel than the country's political leaders. It was interesting to see what Israel did on the battlefield and in making weapons, and it helped professionals understand Israel's strategic situation and military performance. India eventually got over its fears and started working with Israel on security. In March 1995, the head of Israel's air force went on an official trip to India. In July 1996, the head of India's air force did the same. In June 1996, the scientist A. P. J. Abdul Kalam came to see us. At the time, he was the head of the Indian Defence Research and Development Organisation (DRDO). In April 1997, New Delhi also sent the first military attaché, an air force officer. This was the start of a new time in the relationship between the two countries.

After the Kargil War in 1999, relations between India and Israel became more strategic. Israel quickly sent laser-guided bombs for India's Mirages, Unmanned Air Vehicles (UAVs) to gather timely intelligence, and a variety of ammunition. In fact, the powerful Home Minister at the time, Lal Krishna Advani, called for stronger cooperation in all fields during a well-known trip to Israel in June 2000. The new cooperation between India and Israel began with Ariel Sharon's historic trip to India in September 2003. It was the first time that an Israeli Prime Minister had ever been there. The visit was a chance for the two countries' top leaders to learn more about each other and strengthen their defence and trade ties.

Some of the important strategic interests that overlap are listed below:

Arms Deals and Technology Swaps

India wants the newest military technologies, and Israel wants to sell more of its military goods to more people. The fact that Russia didn't send the promised weapons at the expected price or on time also made New Delhi look for other suppliers. India has bought Israeli products because it had trouble making its own weapons systems. This showed that it needed help with technology from elsewhere. The success of American forces against Russian-made Iraqi weapons showed Indian military planners that they shouldn't rely too much on Russian arms. Instead, they are looking for equipment made in the West, including equipment made by Israel.

By the start of the 21st century, Israel had become New Delhi's preferred source for military technology. It is now the second largest defence supplier, after Russia, with France coming in third. India became a very important market for arms for Israel and a partner in making more advanced weapons. Israeli defence industries need to export most of their products to stay in business, and they are happy to work with other countries to make weapons.

During the first few years of working together, India mostly hired Israeli companies to upgrade some of its old Soviet platforms. This was because the Israelis had a great track record of improving all kinds of old military equipment. Israeli companies, for example, gave India's Mig-21 fighters high-tech avionics, as well as modern fire control systems and thermal imagers for India's T-72 tank fleet and upgrades for Soviet 133mm artillery.

The Israeli defence industries were able to make more money by selling more. Most people know that the Indian military bought UAVs27 and the naval Barak point-defense system from Israel. New Delhi also bought high-tech radar and communication equipment from Israel. Reports say that Indian military planners asked their government to only buy electronic warfare equipment from companies that don't sell to Muslim countries.

India has been trying to get good air defences, especially after Pakistan's nuclear tests in 1998. It talked to Israel about the Phalcon radar, which would be mounted on the Russian-made IL-76 transport aircraft, and the Green Pine radar, which would have a long range. The sale of the Phalcon needed permission from the United States. In May 2003, Israel was finally able to get that permission. During the visit of Israeli President Reuven Rivlin to India in November 2016, India signed a $1 billion contract to buy two more Phalcon/IL-76 Airborne Warning and Control Systems (AWACS).

Co-production, which uses the strengths of Israeli firms in research and design and Indian firms in manufacturing, is an important part of defence cooperation. It also agrees with India's requests to transfer technology and put more emphasis on domestic production. India makes a long list of Israeli military goods, including ammunition, parts for UAVs, and even missiles (the Spike anti-armor, the Python-4 air-to-air, and the Barak-8 surface-to-air).

Terror and Infiltrating

In February 1992, the Indian Defence Minister at the time, Sharad Pawar, said that India and Israel worked together to fight terrorism (CT). Both states have been involved in CT activities for a long time. Their work together in this area is done out of sight of the public. It involves sharing information about terrorist groups' finances, how they recruit people, how they train, and what they do. It also involves comparing the policies and practises of each country. After September 11, 2001, many countries put counterterrorism (CT) higher on their strategic agendas, and the need for international cooperation grew. The terrorist attacks in Mumbai in November 2008 showed that India needed to be better prepared for CT and got Indian and Israeli agencies to work together more.

Low-level conflict at their borders is also a big problem for both Israel and India. They talk about each other's past and compare notes on their equipment and how they do things. Faced with the problem of Muslim fundamentalist terrorism coming from camps inside Pakistan, the Indian military wants to be able to send troops quickly behind enemy lines to do specific jobs. India wants to stop terrorists from sneaking in through its borders. To do this, it needs good border monitoring equipment like what Israel has made over the years to deal with its own infiltration problems. Israel has also given India portable battlefield radars and a wide range of sensors for detecting human movement, hand-held thermals, equipment for night warfare, and electronic fences.

Radicalisation of Islam

India and Israel both have to deal with radical Islam at home and in the area around them. For India, the 1979 Shiite Revolution in Iran gave legitimacy to General Zia Ul Haq's efforts to make Pakistan more Islamic after he took over in 1977. His government and what was going on in Afghanistan gave radical Muslims in the area around India new energy. Pakistan has supported the actions of extremists in Afghanistan and India when it helped it reach its foreign policy goals. Even though Pakistan's "secular" military is still in charge, the country is becoming more radical and could be taken over by radical Islamists.

Even though Pakistan is pretty far away, Israel is worried about what is happening there. It is wary of radical Muslim movements that are against the Jewish state from a religious point of view. Pakistan is also a country with nuclear weapons. So, Jerusalem is worried about two things: the spread of nuclear technology from Pakistan (with government permission or by accident) to the Arab world and Iran, and an Islamic government in Islamabad that has nuclear weapons.

Both countries know that the rise of radical Islamist forces in the Middle East will have political effects on their own strategic environments. The recent rise of the Islamic State in Iraq and Syria (ISIS) has effects that go beyond the war zones in Iraq and Syria. Its offshoots threaten the stability of Egypt and Jordan, which are Israel's neighbours, and are becoming a growing source of worry in South and South-East Asia.

India and Israel both worry that Saudi Arabia is helping Islamic fundamentalism spread to many parts of the world. Even though Riyadh and Jerusalem are getting along better behind the scenes because of Iran's growing influence in the Middle East, Israel knows that Saudi Arabia hasn't stopped supporting radical Islamists. Since the 1990s, Israel's worst enemy has been the Islamic Republic of Iran. It is now more feared than it used to be because of its radical Islamic speech, its support for terrorist groups, and its missile and nuclear programmes. The 2015 nuclear deal with Iran didn't have anything to do with Iran's behaviour abroad or its missile programme, which didn't do much to calm Israel's fears. India does not agree with Israel on this issue, but it does understand Israel's concerns.

India and Israel both have Muslim minorities, and even if only a small number of them become radicalised, this could have big effects on their national security. India has 170 million Muslims, which makes it the second largest Muslim population in the world (after Indonesia). A big part of this group, though, fits in well with Indian society. Arabs make up about 20% of the people who live in Israel. Even though most of them follow the law, Israel is worried about how popular Muslim groups are becoming among them and how close they are to Palestinian groups. In recent years, there has been a big rise in the number of Israeli Arabs who are involved in terrorism, but this is still a small-scale problem.

A Link through Indian Ocean

The link between India and Israel has different effects on the Indian Ocean. India is an important player on the international stage in the Indian Ocean. But Israel is becoming more and more interested in the Indian Ocean because it is worried about Iran and Pakistan and its relationship with India is getting stronger. India also increased its military presence in the Indian Ocean as a response to China's "string of pearls" strategy, which is a way to show its power.

Israel has always thought of the Indian Ocean as a way to get to countries in the East. This is because its land routes were blocked by its hostile Arab neighbours, who did not want Israel to get there. Jerusalem was especially interested in the Bab El Mandeb Straits, which is a choke point in the Indian Ocean and where all of its exports to South and East Asia go. When Israel reached out to Ethiopia and then to Eritrea, it did so with these Straits in mind. Israel's strategy has also paid attention to Kenya and South Africa, which are both on the coast of the Indian Ocean.

After Iraq stopped being a threat in 2003, the Islamic Republic of Iran on the edge of the Indian Ocean became Israel's biggest strategic worry. Iran poses an existential threat, so Israel has increased its strategic reach by air and sea. Since the beginning of the 1990s, Israel has been able to send its air and naval power more than 1,500 km away. Israel also added more ways to refuel planes so that its military could reach farther. Along with its air force, Israel built a navy that can go to sea. This was done with Iran in mind. Israeli Saar-5 corvettes can stay at sea for a long time. They have been seen in the Indian Ocean, and Germany has ordered even bigger ships.

The Israeli submarines were made to be able to fire long-range cruise missiles. One of these missiles was tested in the Indian Ocean, which led to news stories about cooperation between the Indian and Israeli naval forces. India doesn't mind if Israel has a bigger presence in the Indian Ocean. In general, the Israeli strategic community is becoming more interested in the sea as a much-needed strategic depth and for the deployment of a nuclear second-strike force based on submarines. Israel makes these kinds of plans in case Pakistan does more to hurt the Jewish state. Israel needs a bigger navy to protect its gas fields in the Mediterranean.

A Link through Central Asia

Central Asia, which is full of energy and is now easier to get to, is seen as India's "extended strategic neighbourhood." There, India competes for power with China and Pakistan, which are also in the region. Israel also cares about this area, which is now part of the Greater Middle East. Like India, Israel has a small diplomatic and business presence in Central Asian countries and sells them military equipment.

Israel and India both want to stop Iran and Saudi Arabia from having too much power, since they help spread radical Islam. In the same way, they are worried about how Islamic Turkey's foreign policy has become since 2002 and about its presence in the region.

Both countries also want the area to be stable so that oil and gas can flow freely. India and Israel both want energy prices to be low, but they may have different ideas about where the planned pipelines should go. India needs it for its economy, while Israel's view is more political. India is worried that China's "One Belt, One Road" plan along the old Silk Road, which will increase Beijing's power, will hurt India. Israel has become more aware of Chinese projects in the Middle East and in its own country in the past few years. It is suspicious of anything the Chinese do because it is pro-American.

The Washington Dimension

Even though the relationship between the U.S. and India is getting stronger, especially after September 11, it won't bring India into the U.S. Even though New Delhi is a big player in the international system and is able to have a good relationship with Washington on its own, having ties with Jerusalem could help smooth over some of the problems it has with the US. As was already said, people in New Delhi thought that improving relations with Israel would make the U.S. treat India better.

People in America often exaggerate how powerful the Jewish lobby is, but in general, it does work. In the 1990s, American Jewish groups were politically savvy enough to know how important India was to the US and to Israel, as well as how important it could be to keep good relations with the growing Indian community in the US, whose power in Congress is growing. Cooperation between the two diasporas could make the voices of two small groups louder. About 5 million Jews and 2 million Indians live in the diaspora, but they are well educated, wealthy, and attached to democratic countries. They are also facing what they see as a common enemy.

The America-Israel Political Affairs Committee (AIPAC), which is the official Israeli lobby, and Jewish groups like the American Jewish Committee and the Jewish Institute on National Security Affairs (JINSA) keep ties with India and the Indian lobby in Washington. Many members of the Indian lobby US-India Political Action Committee (USINPAC), which was only formed in September 2002, said they wanted to be like American Jewish groups and were interested in building a long-term relationship. "The two communities work closely together on domestic and international issues like hate crimes, immigration, and anti-terrorism laws. They also support candidates who are pro-Israel and pro-India. The Bush administration gave Israel permission to sell Phalcon AWACS to India after Jews and Indians worked together. Also, in July 2003, they were able to add an amendment to a bill that gave money to Pakistan that told Islamabad to stop Islamic militants from entering India and stop the spread of weapons of mass destruction. In the fall of 2008, the Indo-US nuclear deal, which gave India access to nuclear technology for civilian uses even though it wasn't a party to the Non-Proliferation Treaty, was passed with the help of Jewish votes in the US Congress (NPT). This made it easier for New Delhi and Washington to work together.

The US-backed international arms control regimes are another area where India and Israel agree. Both countries did not give in to American pressure to join the NPT, which is seen as flawed and ineffective in both capitals. The two states are working together to stop American plans in that area that were brought back to life during the Obama administration.

What lies Ahead

There is a good chance that the major strategic concerns that overlap and are discussed above will continue. Even though India and Israel's relationship has grown stronger and closer over the years, it is not a military alliance. Neither side wants to get involved in the other's regional conflict. Both countries say that their defence ties are only meant to improve their own self-defense capabilities and stability, not to hurt anyone else. Israel doesn't want Pakistan to think of it as an enemy, so it is very careful with how it deals with China. In the same way, India has many political and economic interests in the Arab world, as well as emotional support for the Palestinians and a growing Indian diaspora in the Gulf. It has different ideas about Pakistan's neighbour Iran than Israel does.

The fall of the US and the rise of China seem to have strengthened the strategic ties between India and Israel in the 21st century. In the Middle East, the Obama administration has given the impression of weakness and helped Iran try to become the most powerful country. This weakness of the US has to affect other parts of the world in some way. In fact, Asian countries are worried about the United States' declining role. Even though the Obama administration talked a lot about "pivoting to Asia," it didn't do much to make its allies feel safe. In fact, many of them now worry about the rise of China, which is going after big goals with a lot of force. People in East Asia think that the United States isn't doing enough to deal with China's growing power and the growing nuclear threat from North Korea. The U.S.'s credibility is now in question, and allies in other places may decide it's best to spread their bets. Under the strange leadership of President Rodrigo Duterte, the Philippines seems to want to change its focus from the United States to China.

India and Israel are worried about these kinds of things. Israel's good luck has been tied to the United States being the most powerful country in the world. China is a very big problem for India's national security. China's growing influence in the Indian Ocean and growing assertiveness in its own region are problems for India. These problems are made worse by China's growing trade and defence ties with India's South Asian neighbours. It's not clear if Donald Trump, the new president of the United States, will have a more assertive foreign policy than his predecessor. It's also not clear how he will deal with China, since he showed isolationist tendencies during his campaign.

The military and defence industries in Israel are very happy with how things are going between the two countries. They know about the common strategic goals, how big India's military needs are, and how willing India is to spend money on defence. In 2016, a senior officer in the Israeli Air Force said that military cooperation with India was very important and added, "India is a very important country, its air force is large, and it operates a variety of western and eastern platforms." Itzhak Gat, who was Chairman of Rafael (Israel's Weapon Development Authority) at the time, said the following on behalf of Israeli industries at the opening of the Israeli pavilion in 2015:

> *India is a superpower that offers a technological opportunity for the (Israeli) defense industry. We must be attentive to their needs. Unless we adapt, we will not be able to develop over here*

Officials in the defence industry hope that less red tape in the Indian bureaucracy will shorten the processes and timelines for tenders, which can take years, and speed up big deals. Space cooperation can be made better. Israel is interested in how India sends things into space, and India is interested in its small satellites. Over the years, Israel has made its diplomatic presence in India stronger by sending more diplomats and opening a consulate in Bengaluru. As India became more important to Israel, the job of Ambassador to India became a prestigious one in the Foreign Service.

Israel is aware that Europe is becoming less important in world affairs, while Asian states are becoming more important at the same time. India is a rising power in Asia and around the world. Shimon Peres, who was the Israeli Foreign Minister at the time, said in New Delhi in January 2002, "We think India is one of the most important countries in the world." During President Pranab Mukherjee's visit in October 2015, Prime Minister Benjamin Netanyahu said, "We are very much a part of the West in many, many ways, but we look to the East... We appreciate Europe, but we admire Asia. ' Also, anti-Semitism is a big problem in Europe, while Asians are much less affected by this social disease in their culture. Jews have been treated very well in India. Israel hopes that India will change the way it votes in international groups that haven't been good to Israel in the past. There are already some signs of change. For example, India has recently chosen to not vote instead of automatically voting with the Arab bloc.

Since 1992, economic ties have moved forward quickly. In 1992, the civilian trade was mostly made up of diamonds and was worth $200 million. In 2015, it was worth nearly $5 billion and was made up of many different things. India has been buying Israeli technology in a number of fields, such as agriculture, water treatment, waste management, and recycling. This has led a number of Israeli companies that work in these fields to expand into India. India is a huge, mostly untapped civilian market for Israel. The two countries are talking about making a trade deal, which is expected to increase trade by a lot.

The Zionists' early interest in India has stayed with the people of Israel. It is mostly shown by the fact that after their military service, tens of thousands of young Israelis spend some time in India. When they go back to Israel, many of them become "ambassadors" for India. This increases interest in India, its people, and its culture. Since normalisation, there have been more Indian cultural shows and academic visits to Israel. However, there is still a lot more that can be done.

India, on the other hand, still has a long way to go before it can trust Israel. Anti-Americanism is still common among intellectual elites, the Indian media, and some political circles. This is because Israel is seen as a good friend of the United States. Many people also feel bad about Israel because they are pro-Palestinian. Israel was happy when Narendra Modi and his BJP party won elections in May 2014. He and his party have wanted to get along better with the Jewish state. In September 2014, Netanyahu and Modi met in New York. The meeting was friendly and showed that both sides were ready to move forward. Israel is ready for him to come.

Conclusion

India and Israel are both very old cultures. They were both British colonies and were the first countries to gain independence after World War II, in 1947 and 1948, respectively. Both countries were born out of messy divisions, and since then, they have kept democratic governments even though things have been hard. Even though the two countries have a lot in common, it took over 40 years for them to build a warm relationship with full diplomatic ties, a thriving trade relationship, and a growing strategic partnership. India and Israel are getting along better, which is an important part of a new strategic landscape that is taking shape in the Greater Middle East, which includes Central Asia and parts of the Indian Ocean littoral.

Good relations between Israel and India show that Israel is aware of how the international system is changing. The centre of gravity is moving to Asia and the Pacific Rim. India is a very important main character who needs Israel's full attention. Also, it looks like Israel is able to use its strengths, especially in technology, to further its national interests. On March 28, 2016, when he met the head of the

Indian Air Force, Prime Minister Netanyahu said, "We're very excited about the possibility of getting closer to India." We think anything is possible. When the interests of the two countries are taken into account, this optimistic assessment is not a stretch.

References

Moshe Yegar, The Long Journey to Asia. A Chapter in the Diplomatic History of Israel, Haifa University Press, Haifa, 2004 [Hebrew], pp. 24-31.

David Ben Gurion, Memoirs, Vol. 1, Am Oved, Tel Aviv, 1971 [Hebrew], p. 431.

For Gandhi's views, see Gideon Shimoni, Gandhi, Satyagraha, and the Jews: A Formative Factor in India's Policy towards Israel, Leonard Davis Institute for International Relations, Hebrew University, Jerusalem, 1977.

For the Indian attitudes and policies towards Zionism and the State of Israel, see P. R. Kumaraswamy, India's Israel Policy, Columbia University Press, New York, 2010.

For the Zionist diplomatic efforts towards India before the UN partition vote, see Moshe Yegar, No. 1, pp. 45-56.

Ibid., p. 142.

Ibid., p. 102.

Moshe Sharett, Travelling in Asia, Davar, Tel Aviv, 1964 [Hebrew], p. 125.

For Israel's aid programmes, see Shimon Amir, Israel's Development Cooperation with Africa, Asia and Latin America, Praeger, New York, 1974. The extensive Israeli involvement in aid programmes did not prevent the beneficiary states from severing diplomatic relations follow¬ing the 1973 war, indicating the limitations of such a diplomatic tool.

Moshe Yegar, No. 1, pp. 66-67.

The PLO committed to annul the articles in the Covenant calling for the destruction of the state of Israel at the 1993 Oslo Accords. Whether it did so, is still debated among various scholars.

P. R. Kumaraswamy, No. 4, pp. 217-21; Moshe Yegar, No. 1, p. 160.

P. R. Kumaraswamy, No. 4, pp. 222, 233.

Efraim Inbar, 'The Indian-Israeli Entente', Orbis, 48, Winter 2004.

H. V. Pant, 'India-Israel Partnership: Convergence and Constraints', MERIA Middle East Review of International Affairs, 8(4), 2004, p. 2.

For the upgrading of Indo-Israeli relations, see Moshe Yager, 'How Was Normalization Achieved in Indo-Israeli Relations?', Nativ, No. 90, January 2003 [Hebrew], pp. 1-11; Giora Bachar, 'The Normalization in Indian-Israel Relations', in Moshe Yegar, Yoseph Govrin and Aryeh Oded (eds), The First Fifty Years, Keter, Jerusalem, 2002 [Hebrew], pp. 543-49.

P. R. Kumaraswamy, No. 4, p. 240.

P. R. Kumaraswamy, 'India-Israel: Emerging Partnership', Journal of Strategic Studies, 25(4), December 2002, p. 198.

Interview with Isi Liebler, Jerusalem.

Moshe Yegar, No. 1, p. 165.

This part relies on Efraim Inbar, No. 14.

See Efraim Inbar, 'Israel's Strategic Environment in the 1990s', Journal of Strategic Studies,

25, March 2002; Efraim Inbar, 'Israel's National Security Amidst Unrest in the Arab World', Washington Quarterly, 35, Summer 2012.

For this dominant threat perception that has been shared by all Israeli governments since Yitzhak Rabin's (1992-95), see Efraim Inbar, Rabin and Israel's National Security, Wilson Center Press and Johns Hopkins University Press, Washington and Baltimore, 1999, p. 138.

Efraim Inbar, 'US Mideast Retreat a Boon for Moscow and Tehran', Middle East Quarterly, Summer 2016, at http://www.meforum.org/6042/us-mideast-retreat (Accessed February 10, 2017).

For the strategic engagement between the two states, see Efraim Inbar, No. 14; Efraim Inbar and Alvite Singh Ningthoujam, 'Indo-Israeli Defence Cooperation in the Twenty-First Century', MERIA Journal, 15, December 2011; S. Samuel C. Rajiv, Indian Responses to Israel's Gaza Operations, Mideast Security and Policy Studies No. 119, Begin-Sadat Center for Strategic Studies, Ramat Gan, May 2016, pp. 11-24.

Defence News, May 12, 2003, p. 10.

The latest deal for 10 Heron TP UAVs was in November 2016. See 'Israel Signs $1.4

Billion Contracts with India', Israel Defence, November 25, 2016, at http://www. israeldefense.co.il/ en/node/27690 (Accessed February 10, 2017).

Defence News, May 12, 2003, p. 10.

'Israel Signs $1.4 Billion Contracts with India', Note 27.

Statesman (New Delhi), February 28, 1992, quoted in P. R. Kumaraswamy, Israel and India. Evolving Strategic Partnership, Mideast Security and Policy Studies No. 40, Begin-Sadat Center for Strategic Studies, Ramat Gan, September 1998.

See the remarks of Maj. Gen. Uzi Dayan, National Security Advisor, in Amit Navon, 'The Indian Knot', Maariv, Weekend Magazine, September 20, 2002, p. 22.

'India, Israel Defence Ties to Get a Boost', Hindustan Times, May 22, 2003.

For an exposition of Saudi mischief, see Dore Gold, Hatred's Kingdom: How Saudi Arabia Supports the New Global Terrorism, Regnery Publishing, New York, 2003; for concerns regarding the rise of Wahhabism in India, see Sunil Raman, 'The New Threat to Islam in India', February 4, 2016, at http://thediplomat.com/2016/02/ the-new-threat-to-islam-in-india/ (Accessed April 26, 2017); see also Abhinandan Mishra, 'Saudi Cash Floods India to Promote Wahhabism', June 27, 2015, at http:// www.sunday-guardian.com/news/saudi-cash-floods-india -to-promote-wahhabism (Accessed April 26, 2017).

Defence News, May 12, 2003, p. 25.

See The Times of India [online version], June 17, 2002.

Olga Oliker, 'Conflict in Central Asia and South Caucasus', in Olga Oliker and Thomas S. Szayna (eds), Faultlines of Conflict in Central Asia and the South Caucacus: Implications for the US Army, RAND, Santa Monica, 2003, pp. 225-6.

For a recent analysis of the relations between the two states, see C. Uday Bhaskar, 'India's perspective of US political leadership', in Efraim Inbar and Jonathan Rynhold (eds), US Foreign Policy and Global Standing in the 21st Century: Realities and Perceptions, Routledge, London, 2016, pp. 139-58.

See Larry Ramer, 'Pro-Israel Activists Seeking Allies Among Immigrants from India', Forward, October 11, 2002; Alan Cooperman, 'India, Israel Interests Team Up', The Washington Post, July 19, 2003, p. A5.

See P. R. Kumaraswamy, Beyond the Veil: Israel-Pakistan Relations, JCSS Memorandum, 55, Jaffee Center for Strategic Studies, Tel Aviv, 2000.

Talya Yariv and Shachar Zorani, 'Indian Air Force Commander Visited Israel', trans. Ofri Aharon, Events Log, Israeli Air Force, March 31, 2016, at http://www.iaf.org.il/4445-46314- en/IAF.aspx (Accessed February 10, 2017).

Amir Rapaport, 'The Israeli-Indian Alliance is Warming Up', Israel Defence, March 18, 2015, at http://www.israeldefense.co.il/en/content/"-israeli-indian-alliance-warming-up (Accessed February 15, 2017).

'India and Israel Vow to Fight Terrorism', BBC, September 9, 2003, at http://news.bbc.co.uk/ 2/hi/south_asia/3089466.stm (Accessed February 15, 2017).

Ben Sales, 'With Israeli-EU Relations Strained, Netanyahu Looks toward India, China', The Jerusalem Post, December 2, 2015, at http://www.jpost.com/Israel-News/Politics-And- Diplomacy/With-Israeli-EU-relations-strained-Netanyahu-looks-toward-India-China-436029 (Accessed February 10, 2017).

'Indian Air Force Chief Marshal in Israel for Official Visit', United with Israel, March 18, 2016, at https://unitedwithisrael.org/indian-air-force-chief-marshal-in-israel-for-official-visit/ (Accessed February 10, 2017).

Chapter 2
India–Israel Growing Partnership

Introduction

India and Israel work together in the areas of defence, trade, strategy, intelligence, and security. Over time, the relationship is likely to become broader and more comprehensive, including research, development, and co-production in the defence sector, water resource management, science and technology, bilateral trade, and the non-defense sector. Based on a wide range of security, geopolitical, and economic interests coming together, this growing partnership shows how Delhi has changed its attitude towards the Jewish state from one of hostility to one that is more pragmatic and realistic.

During the Cold War, India and Israel were not able to build a strong relationship with each other, even though they had a lot in common. For example, they are both ancient civilizations that won their independence by fighting against the British Empire and creating the only working democracies in places that were not democratic. With the end of this global conflict and the fall of the Soviet Union and the Communist bloc, Delhi gave up on the Cold War ideology set by Jawaharlal Nehru, its first prime minister and a long-time leading politician. Instead, it took a realistic approach based on a pragmatic assessment of its national interests. Because of this, relations with Israel went from being completely hostile to being a close, multifaceted partnership.

Historical background

India became its own country on August 15, 1947, and Israel did the same on May 14, 1948. Still, it was hard for Delhi's ruling Congress Party to get used to the idea of a Jewish state. India, along with Iran and Yugoslavia, was part of a small minority at the United Nations' Special Commission on Palestine (UNSCOP), which was set up to find ways to end the Arab–Jewish conflict in Mandatory Palestine. This group opposed dividing Palestine into Jewish and Arab states and instead favoured a single Arab–Jewish state. As the committee went with what the majority wanted, Delhi voted against the 29 November partition resolution, just like it did in 1949 when it voted against letting Israel join the UN. The next year, though, it recognised the Jewish state, and at a meeting of South-East Asian prime ministers in Colombo in April 1954, Nehru refused to sign a resolution that said the creation of Israel was against international law. But he didn't make diplomatic ties with Jerusalem. It seems he didn't do this because he was afraid that if he did, the Arab states would back Pakistan's plan to move the Kashmir dispute from the Security Council to the General Assembly. Nehru privately liked Israel, but as a founder of the Non-Aligned Movement (NAM), he was on the other side of the issue and strongly supported the Palestine Liberation Organization (PLO), which was founded in 1964. After that, India was one of the first non-Arab countries to recognise Palestinian independence, and it was also one of the first countries to let the PLO open an embassy in its capital. Delhi's decision not to make diplomatic ties with Israel was a result of its activism in the Third World, its desire to limit Pakistan's influence in the mostly Muslim Arab world, and its desire to keep getting oil from the Gulf states without interruption.

But at the beginning of the 1970s, there was some small, secret military and intelligence cooperation between the two countries. This was because India's wars with Pakistan had shown Delhi how important Israel was to its national security.

But it wasn't until the Soviet Union fell apart that India had to rethink and change its foreign policy to fit into the new international order, which was moving radically towards a US-led unipolar world. India put itself in a new place in the world by opening its economy and making diplomatic efforts with many countries. India's most important strategic ally and defence supplier, the Soviet Union, was losing power and influence, so New Delhi tried to work with the United States, which was the only superpower at the time. At the same time, India reached out to the strategically important and powerful countries with which it had not been able to build strong bilateral ties during the Cold War, either because of the way the world worked or because of pressures at home.

Most of India's political leaders knew right after the Cold War ended that it was important for India to have good relations with the United States, which was the only hegemonic power in the new world order. Indian leaders came to believe that normalising relations with Israel would help India get closer to the U.S. They thought this because they thought the American Jewish lobby had a lot of power over Washington's foreign policy decisions. In particular, Indian Prime Minister Rao was sure that normalising relations with Israel was needed to improve India's standing with the American Jewish community and the US political establishment.

In light of these international events and ideas, India decided to change how it felt about Israel and start talking to it diplomatically. India was ready to fix its messed up and inconsistent West Asian policy. Because of this, India gave Israel full diplomatic recognition on January 29, 1992, and both countries set up embassies in each other's countries. India and Israel made a 10-year deal to work together in a strategic way. Israeli officials went to New Delhi to check out the diplomatic and political climate. In 1992, Moshe Yaeger, who was the deputy director of the Israeli Foreign Ministry, was the last person to go there. 6 Before 1992, India's diplomatic relationship with Israel was not official until the Palestinian problem was solved. But in 1992, the minority government led by Congress Prime Minister Narsimha Rao changed its position on the Cold War. This was a shift from Nehruvian anathema to a more practical and realistic view. No longer did the relationship with Israel depend on Palestinian independence, This was in line with what many countries around the world were doing towards Israel.

By this time, Islamic militancy in Kashmir was making itself known. With the fall of the Soviet Union, the Cold War restrictions on the relationship between India and Israel ended, and India had begun to change its relationship with the United States, the only remaining superpower and a strong and reliable strategic and defence partner of Israel. Since then, the relationship between India and Israel has changed and is going in a very positive direction. But even though the exchanges in different areas have grown, the overall links have been kept quiet on purpose. It was thought that this was the only way to keep India's other interests in West Asia from being hurt by the Arabian countries' dislike of Israel.

After diplomatic ties were established in 1992, the relationship between India and Israel began to grow, but it could not be turned into a full-fledged defence relationship. But economic, diplomatic, and cultural ties were made, and things were going in a good direction. Two years after diplomatic relations were established, in 1994, the then-director general of the Defence Ministry, Major General (ret.) David Ivry, signed an agreement with the Indian Defence Ministry for security cooperation between the two countries. But because of political instability and a mix of socialist, left-wing, and Congress party governments in power, this budding goodwill could not translate into strategic and defence cooperation. But things started to change when there was a big change in India's government. The Hindu nationalist right-of-center Bharatiya Janata Party (BJP) came to power in 1996 for 13 months and then for a full term in 1998. The two most important leaders of the BJP, Prime Minister Atal Bihari Bajpayee and Deputy Prime Minister and Home Minister L. K. Advani, admired Israel for being able to stay alive in a hostile area, and they shared Israel's view that global Islamist terrorism was a threat. In 1998, India did a nuclear test, and Pakistan did one two weeks later. India got a lot of flak for starting a nuclear arms race on the subcontinent, and the US, Japan, Britain, and China all put India under strict rules. But France, Russia, and Israel understood what India was worried about when it came to security threats.

A number of Indian politicians with a lot of influence went to Israel. During the time that the BJP was in power, two important ministers visited Israel quickly after each other. This showed how important Israel had become to India's strategic and security goals. The first was the visit of L. K. Advani, the Indian Home Minister, who is known for being very strict about Islamist terrorism. The international media paid a lot of attention to his trip because he was accompanied by a group of delegates, including the heads of India's intelligence agencies Research Analysis Wing (RAW), Intelligence Bureau (IB), and the central police organisation fighting terrorism. His interactions with Israelis outside of what was required by protocol also drew attention, as did his hardline stance against Islamist terrorism.

This Indian group, led by Advani, met with the head of the Mossad and Israeli security ministers to talk about working together on managing internal security and to formalise an agreement to share intelligence and work together. Israel helped India fight terrorism, and Israeli intelligence agencies agreed to open offices in New Delhi, similar to what the FBI does in the United States (FBI). Israel agreed to work more closely with India on defence technology.

In July 2000, Jaswant Singh, the first Indian foreign minister and a member of the BJP-led government, made the first high-profile trip to Israel. The visit led to good conversations, and a joint commission to fight terrorism was set up. Singh and his Israeli counterpart, David Levy, agreed to meet every six months to talk about strategy and strengthen their partnership in counter-terrorism, IT, and science and technology. During the visit, Singh said that "India's Israel policy became a captive of domestic policy that came to be unwillingly as an unstated veto to India's larger West Asian policy." He also called the growing ties between India and Israel a "tectonic shift of consciousness." Since then, many top officials and ministers have made frequent trips to Israel and signed many bilateral agreements on diplomatic, economic, strategic, and defence issues. This is a clear sign that India has moved from Nehruvian hostility to a realpolitik based on a shared strategic vision. Also, the 9/11 terrorist attacks, the spread of Islamist terrorism, and the exclusion of India and Israel from the US-led War on Terror in Afghanistan while making Pakistan an ally in this effort brought security, defence, intelligence, and counter-terrorism issues to the forefront of the growing Indo-Israeli strategic partnership.

During this time, top civil and military officials and high-profile politicians and ministers met and talked with each other often. An Israeli parliamentary delegation went to the Indian parliament for the first time since diplomatic ties were set up in 1992. This happened at the end of November 2001. In the beginning of that month, a group of defence officials led by Ministry of Defence Director General Amos Yaron met in New Delhi for a strategic dialogue. In December 2001, three official Israeli delegations met in New Delhi for the biannual political dialogue between the two countries. In January 2002, a group of people from India went to Israel to talk about the fight against terrorism. In this situation, Sharon's trip to India in September 2003 was a big deal because it showed the rest of the world that India was no longer shy about its growing relationship with Israel.

There were worries that the rise of the United Progressive Alliance (UPA) would hurt the relationship between India and Israel, but this did not happen. In fact, the UPA government not only kept the relationship going, but also made it stronger by sending many ministers to Israel and making agreements in all areas of life. So, for example, Minister of Science and Technology Kapil Sibal went to Israel in July 2005 and signed a bilateral agreement to work together on technological projects, such as setting up a joint industrial research and development fund. In September 2005, Minister of State for Rural Development Kumari Selja also went to Israel. In November 2005, Kamal Nath, the Minister of Commerce and Industry, went to Israel. While there, a Joint Study Group (JSG) was set up to increase trade between the two countries from $2 billion to $5 billion by 2008. In the same month, Sharad Pawar, the Union Minister for Agriculture, Consumer Affairs, Food, and Public Distribution, went to Israel to represent India at the official memorial ceremony marking the tenth anniversary of Prime Minister Rabin's death. During his visit, the two countries talked about how to expand and deepen their cooperation in agriculture, including micro-irrigation and dairy farming. In February 2010, Jyotiraditya Scindia, India's Commerce Minister, went to Israel to talk about a free trade agreement. He met with President Shimon Peres, Industry, Trade, and Labor Minister Benjamin Ben-Eliezer, and people from Israel's water technology and high-tech industries.

Growing Cooperation against Terrorism

India and Israel both have to deal with and work hard to stop terrorism. Both countries are democratic and have a lot of different kinds of people living in them. There are also a lot of Muslims living in both countries, and their neighbours support Islamist terrorism. Because they are both in the same situation, they have learned more about each other's strategic and security concerns.

Both countries see non-proliferation systems like the Nuclear Non-Proliferation Treaty the same way (NPT). Even though they talk about it in terms of principles, India's main problem with the NPT has to do with regional security, just like Israel. But while Israel still has the status of a threshold nuclear power, India has given up its long-held nuclear ambiguity by doing nuclear tests in May 1998. Since the fall of the Soviet Union and the end of the Cold War, the US has paid more attention to some of China and Russia's strategic moves.

Also, as was said above, neither country was included in the War on Terror led by the US after 9/11. Washington didn't want Israel in the coalition so that it could include the Arab states. It also needed Pakistan, which used to support the Taliban, so it kept India at a distance, even though New Delhi supported the War on Terror in every way. So, it's not surprising that India, despite being so big, thinks like Israel that it needs to make its own tools to protect its people and borders from terrorism.

Since Israel has been dealing with cross-border terrorism for a long time, New Delhi has found it more and more helpful to learn from Israel's experience. India and Israel both have to deal with terrorism, which comes from both disgruntled groups inside their own countries and from neighbouring states, most of which are not democratic and are getting better at giving terrorist groups access to weapons of mass destruction. Terrorism has been used as a tool of foreign policy for a long time by countries like Pakistan and some of the countries near Israel. So, there are clear structural similarities between the kinds of terrorist threats that India and Israel face. It is also important to remember that when radical mullahs tell their followers to take up arms in support of jihad, their main goals have always been the "liberation of all of mandatory Palestine and Kashmir" and the destruction of the United States.

India has the second-largest Muslim population in the world, and close ties between Israel and New Delhi can help Jerusalem on the diplomatic and political fronts and make the Arab-Israeli conflict less about religion. A group of Indian Muslims went to Israel in August 2007. This is something to talk about. This delegation of the All India Organization of Imams and Mosques, led by Mawlana Jamil Ilyas, was put together by the American Jewish Council. They helped show that the Israeli claim that the Palestine question is mainly a political issue, not a religious one, and that an interfaith dialogue between democratic countries is possible (indeed, the Israel visit followed a trip to India by Jewish rabbis for an interfaith meeting). Because of this, India and Israel have come to a basic agreement that there can be no compromise with terrorists, no matter how different the circumstances are in each case. India sees Israel as a source of training and professional/material help in its fight against terrorism, and Israel is more than happy to let India learn from its vast experience.

Defence Cooperation

Defence cooperation between India and Israel is the main thing that keeps the two countries close. Since the fall of the Soviet Union, Israel has become India's most important source of arms. India was Moscow's biggest customer for arms and had licences to make some weapons platforms. When the Soviet Union broke up, India was left with a lot of old, useless military equipment. The Israeli defence industry has been specialising in developing electronic subsystems for planes, ships, and tanks for a long time. These technologies, which include ammunition, night vision equipment, navigation equipment, target acquisition systems, and sensors, make old platforms much more powerful. This was a big help for the Indian military, especially its air force, and Jerusalem took advantage of the fact that other big arms makers, like the U.S., were reluctant to fill the void left by the Soviets and enter the Indian defence market strongly.

Since it was founded, Israel has been in many major wars and faced major threats to its national security, citizens, and borders. As a result, it has built one of the best defence industries in the world, and its products are the best in many fields. Israel's defence industries are a big part of its economy. They make a wide range of things, from small arms and artillery to sophisticated electronic systems, unmanned aerial vehicles (UAVs), satellite systems, and the world's most advanced tank.

Israel's arms export policy has shown a lot of flexibility and creativity in order to compete with countries that are much bigger than it is. In the case of India, Israel was willing to go around the P5 embargo on the transfer of sensitive high-tech defence technology to New Delhi because it refused to sign the NPT. This allowed it to make significant inroads into the Indian defence market by providing anti-missile systems, high-tech radars, sky drones, night vision equipment, satellite systems, and other sophisticated equipment.

India's decision to modernise and diversify its weapons systems is likely to increase the chances of working together in the defence industry. In fact, Israel's strong R&D defence industry is a great match for India's defence industry. This could be good for both countries' future economic and strategic interests.India and Israel's defence cooperation has grown, especially in the area of missile defence. This is because India has put more effort into its missile defence programme in response to possible threats from Pakistan and China. India wants to work with countries whose missile defence systems are the best in the world. India started working with the US on missile defence after supporting a Bush administration plan for a missile defence system in 2000. At the same time, India was working with Russia. But India's partnership with Israel on missile defence is better than any other bilateral partnership in this field. Israel has made great progress in missile defence and is now a world leader in technologies that can stop missiles. In some ways, it's even better than European and American products, which India knows.

The first big arms deal was for two Green Pine early warning systems to protect against Pakistani missiles that hit the ground. The Arrow II system is the most wanted Israeli technology for stopping missiles. The Arrow Weapon System (AWS) is supposed to be a much more reliable defence shield than the Patriot system, which the US used during the Gulf War in 1991. The Arrow II can find up to 14 incoming missiles and keep track of their movements. It is useful because it is put up along the Line of Control (LoC) to protect the people and military bases in Kashmir. Israel has also made a number of improved air and ground defence systems, like the Barak anti-ship missile, the Spyder, the Hawk, and the Nimrod. The short-range interceptor is called "Iron Dome," and the medium-range one is called "Magic Wand."

India wanted to buy the Israeli Arrow-2 system from Israel, which needed US approval. However, Washington was against the deal, citing commitments to the Missile Technology Control Regime (MTCR) and offering the PAC-3 instead.Israel sold India the Arrow II Anti-Tactical Ballistic Missile (ATBM) and the Phalcon Airborne Warning and Control System (AWACS). India also bought the Green Pine early warning and fire-control radar that goes with the Arrow II ATBM. The Indian Navy bought the Barak anti-ship system, which will be co-produced in India. For air defence, the Indian Air Force (IAF) is looking at the Spyder system from Israel. Even though Israel Aircraft Industries is in charge of most of the sales of weapons systems to India, there are also other companies involved. There are a lot of state and private companies in the Indian defence industry market. Israel Aircraft Industries and Rafael, which are owned by the government, make things like the Barak Naval Missile System, Searcher Drones, and the Gil anti-tank missile. Private companies like Soltam, Elbit Systems, and Tadiran Communications convert Russian 133mm cannons into 155mm howitzers and improve T-72 tanks.

Economic and Business Ties

India and Israel are getting closer because they work together on defence and fighting terrorism. However, the two countries are also working together to broaden their relationship, and the fact that they are now industrialised and technologically advanced has opened up many areas for them to work together.

Since the early 1990s, Israel's high-tech industry has grown at a rate that has never been seen before. This has made Israel a "start-up nation," as many applications made in Israel are now used by the biggest multinational companies in the communications, computers, information systems, medicines, optics, consumer goods, and software industries. India's trade with Israel has grown by six times in the last ten years, making New Delhi Jerusalem's second largest trading partner in Asia for non-military goods and services. And while the relationship between the two countries has mostly been about defence and security products, it is quickly moving into other areas. India sends almost all of its exports to Israel in the form of diamonds, medicines, and plastics. On the other hand, Israel sends almost all of its exports to the subcontinent in the form of fertilisers, polished diamonds and gems, and electronic equipment. There is a chance that the number of products could grow. India has been thinking about signing a Free Trade Agreement (FTA) with Israel since 2007. In February 2015, an Israeli delegation went to New Delhi to continue talks on the subject after Modi and Netanyahu talked about it during a meeting in September 2014 on the sidelines of the annual session of the UN General Assembly.

Israel has made great strides in managing water harvesting, and areas like water technology, biotechnology, and nanotechnology offer new ways for the U.S. and Israel to work together. Israel is also a world leader in water management and high-tech agriculture, such as breeding "advanced" seeds and using fertiliser and irrigation. India, on the other hand, has a huge labour force and a huge market, which are two skills that go well together. Same thing with alternative energy: Israel has worked on solar power, and India has worked on wind power.

In the future, trade and economic ties between India and Israel are likely to be based on high technology. In June 2011, the two countries signed an agreement to encourage innovation and entrepreneurship across borders. With a deal between the Confederation of Indian Industry (CII) and the Israel High Tech Industries Association, they have added high technology to their trade. There is a chance that Israel's ability to be creative and India's large number of talented people could work together. The software industry works well together because Indian companies are all about the process and Israeli companies are much more about the products.

Challenges and Limitations

Even though India and Israel are getting along better on a number of issues, there are still problems that both countries need to solve. First of all, India's politics are based on the Muslim vote bank, and their feelings continue to be a problem in the relationship between the two countries. India is home to about 150 million Muslims, which is the second largest Muslim population in the world. These Muslims tend to be moderate and are not very hostile to Israel. Indian policymakers and political parties are all aware that they need to be careful when dealing with Israel. This doesn't matter much when the BJP is in charge, but it does when the Congress Party is in charge. Indian Muslims have always voted for the Congress party up until now. Any decision the Congress Party makes about Israel has to take this into account, which means it can't be too friendly towards Israel.

The large number of Muslims and their support for the creation of a Palestinian state, as well as India's consistent support for this move, are two things that make it hard to do. New Delhi has given a lot of humanitarian aid to the Palestinians and criticised many Israeli policies and actions in this area. It has also stopped actively supporting the Arab world's anti-Israel policies and laws, but it still votes for UN resolutions that criticise Israeli policies, such as during the Mavi Marmara incident in 2010.

Even as it welcomed Sheron in 2003, the Indian government made it clear that it would not change its long-standing support for the Palestinian cause or give up on Yasser Arafat as the leader of the Palestinians. India thought of Arafat as a symbol of Palestinian nationalism and a key part of any peace process until he died in November 2004. This was in complete contrast to the Sharon government, which wanted Arafat kicked out of the territories and a new Palestinian leadership to take over. Even though there was a disagreement about Arafat's role, this does not mean that India was not quietly rethinking its policy in the Middle East.

New Delhi has to be careful with Israel so that it doesn't look like it agrees with the "Clash of Civilizations" argument or with claims that Hindus and Jews are against Islam. Israel's policy towards the Palestinians will also be a big issue, since it would be hard for India to explain why it has a good relationship with and supports Israel if Israel's policy became very harsh.

In a broader sense, the two countries' relationship depends on India's policy towards the Middle East, its interests in the Gulf region, and the Muslim factor. From the outside, the Muslim constraint is related to how dependent New Delhi is on the Middle East. India trades with countries in the Gulf, and about 3 million Indians work in the Gulf, which has the most hydrocarbon energy sources. India's policy towards Israel is based on a fear of hurting its strategic and close ties with the Muslim and Arab worlds, not on a real interest in or concern about the Arab–Israeli conflict. This makes it hard for diplomatic and political ties to get closer, and it makes India try to keep its relationship with Israel out of the public eye.

India's closer ties with Iran can also be a factor that slows things down. Tehran is still one of Israel's biggest existential threats, if not the biggest, and Israel is worried about India's growing ties with Iran, especially in the military and defence fields (e. g. sharing some of the technologies derived from Israel). Israel wants India to recognise that a nuclear Iran is a threat, and it also wants India's help in trying to make West Asian security less unstable. India and Israel's relationship doesn't have to depend on a third country, but India will have to be very careful and subtle when dealing with the Middle East.

Lastly, the US does not stay out of the relationship between India and Israel. Washington has been a bit of a mixed bag, acting as both a limit and a boost. Since the late 1960s, the US has been Israel's main source of weapons and advanced military technology. Because of this, the US has a lot of power over Israel's defence sales. In 2003, Washington didn't want Israel to sell India the Arrow anti-ballistic missile defence system, which was a joint project between the US and Israel. This caused the deal to fall through. The US factor has hurt the Indo-Israeli defence partnership less than it has hurt the military ties between China and Israel. In 2000, Washington stopped Israel from selling the Falcon to China. However, in 2004,

Israel signed a defence deal with India to sell three Falcon systems. One reason for the more positive attitude is that Washington was worried that Israeli military sales to China would directly hurt its strategic interests, but the sales to India were not seen as such a threat. The defence ties between India and Israel are important to the US from a geostrategic point of view. In this way, a strong, progressive India that is helped by Israeli technology seems to be the most likely and practical option.

An Opinion

The fact that these problems haven't hurt the relationship between India and Israel shows that both sides respect each other's limits. Both sides have come to realise and understand the limits imposed by their domestic politics, international interests, and security environment. Before 1992, India made the normalisation of its relationship with Israel depend on the resolution of the Palestinian problem. However, in 1992, it broke the link between the two issues and made it clear that it was not willing to hold its relationship with Israel hostage to a problem that hadn't been solved.

Over the years, the Indian government has also softened its response to Israel's policy towards the Palestinians, which now gets little more than mild disapproval. At the same time, it has become more vocal in its condemnation of Palestinian suicide bombings and other acts of terrorism in Israel, which were once seen as justified because of how the Palestinians were thought to be treated. In the same way, both India and Israel have kept quiet in international forums about issues that could hurt their relationship. Even though Israel doesn't like that India still supports the Palestinian cause, it still respects New Delhi's position.

So, for example, when Israel got a lot of criticism in May 2010 for its violent detention of a Turkish-led flotilla trying to break the naval blockade of the Hamas-controlled Gaza Strip, during which some alleged Islamist militants were killed in clashes with Israeli soldiers, Foreign Minister Avigdor Lieberman "reminded" UN Secretary-General Ban Kimoon that while "the international community remained silent and passive" in the face of Israel's actions, the international community 31 As India complained about being included on the list of states with deadly violence, the Israeli Foreign Ministry said that New Delhi's name was included by mistake. This made the controversy go away.

Since diplomatic ties were established more than 20 years ago, the two countries have become very close partners. They work together on all strategic, defence, and security issues. India has become more practical and realistic about the way the world has changed, and its relationship with Israel shows this shift. But the Indian government will have to walk a very thin line between its relationship with Israel and its wider Middle Eastern policy in order to deal with problems like the Israel-

Palestine conflict, New Delhi's growing relationship with Iran, and the demands of the country's Muslim population. Still, given the current security threats and new geopolitical and geoeconomic dynamics, it seems likely that the relationship between India and Israel will grow deeper and wider.

Emerging Partnership

India's relationship with a single country shouldn't cause too many problems, especially if the country in question isn't a great power. Bilateral relationships are based on shared political, economic, cultural, or strategic interests. If two sovereign countries don't have any relations with each other, it shows how important each country thinks the other is. But India's foreign policy has never been the same when it comes to Israel. One of the most controversial parts of India's foreign policy was its long-term reluctance and refusal to set up normal diplomatic relations with the Jewish State. People have talked about and even criticised the four decades when the two countries didn't talk to each other and the last ten years when they did.

The new friendship between India and Israel is not just another example of two countries getting along. India's foreign policy moved into a new phase of assertive independence when it ditched old rhetoric and ideological baggage in favour of realism based on its own interests. Its policy towards Israel had been held back for a long time by different regional pressures and domestic concerns. Normalization is a change from the past.

Its hesitant recognition in 1950 did not come with the setting up of permanent missions. India's initial desire to set up normal diplomatic relations was not followed through on, and it soon became a hostage to different domestic pressures and fears in the region. So, for the next 40 years, India's Middle East policy was based on not having any ties with Israel. When Prime Minister Narasimha Rao fixed this problem and finished the work started by Jawaharlal Nehru on January 29, 1992, India became the last major country that wasn't Arab or Islamic to make diplomatic ties with Israel.

The importance of the changed international climate after the end of the Cold War was a big reason why Rao was able to change India's long-standing dislike or even hatred of Israel. The end of the bipolar world order gave regional powers more room to define their own interests and improve their own security. At the same time, you could say that by breaking with the past, Rao also showed that India wanted to become a great power. Even though there was political instability at home and changes in coalitions, different governments still worked to get closer to Israel on both the political and security fronts. Even parties like the Communists, who have been known to be against Israel in the past, have quietly come around and seen how useful the new situation is.

Consequences of the Past

You can't understand how important India's new relationship with a small state in the always-unstable Middle East is without knowing a little bit about India's traditional relationship with Israel. This policy goes back to the beginning of the 20th century, when Indian nationalists and Arabs of Palestine joined forces to fight against British imperialism. Even before independence, the Judeo-Christian heritage of the West made people sympathetic to the political goals of Jews in Palestine. However, Indian nationalists looked at the whole situation through an Islamic lens.

Even though they felt sorry for the Jews' centuries of suffering and oppression, they couldn't understand and support the Zionists' hopes for a Jewish national home in Palestine. Mahatma Gandhi said it best when he said, "Palestine belongs to the Arabs in the same way that England and France belong to the English and French."

Jawaharlal Nehru, for his part, saw the conflict between Arabs and Jews as a part of the larger anti-imperialism that was sweeping the colonies. He said that there were no historical Jewish claims to Palestine and that "Palestine is basically an Arab country, and no decision can be made without the Arabs' consent." So, even though they tried half-heartedly in the 1930s, the Zionists were not able to win over the Indian nationalists.Gandhi's moral arguments and Nehru's anti-imperialist rhetoric are both important, but neither of them can explain why India doesn't care about Jewish goals. Arab–Jewish conflict in Palestine got worse at the same time that the Indian National Congress and the Muslim League were fighting with each other. This conflict spread to the Middle East when the Palestine question was presented as an Islamic agenda. Indian leaders started to look at Jewish claims through the lens of Islam. The fact that the Zionists didn't care about India only made Indian nationalists more pro-Arab and pro-Islamic.

When the issue of Palestine came up at the United Nations in 1947, India had the chance to explain its independent position to the world and change the way things were going in Palestine. India, which was one of the 11 members of the United Nations Special Committee on Palestine (UNSCOP), stood up for the Arab cause in Palestine and shared the views of Indian nationalists.

Partly because the Congress party was against the "two-nation theory" of the Muslim League, India tried to ignore the Zionist demands and, with the help of Iran and what was then Yugoslavia, proposed a minority plan. The seven-member majority wanted Palestine to be split up, but the minority wanted Palestine to be a federal country with enough freedom for the Jewish population. On November 29, 1947, when the UN General Assembly approved the majority plan, India joined the Arab and Islamic countries in opposing the splitting of Palestine.

At the same time, the creation of Israel and the international community's acceptance of it forced India to deal with new political realities in the Middle East. On September 18, 1950, after a lot of thought, persuasion from Israel, and pressure from its pro-Arab past, India officially recognised the Jewish state. Shortly after that, Israel opened a trade office in Bombay, which is now called Mumbai. Over time, this office turned into a consular mission, and in June 1953, the first Israeli Consul took office. India wanted to open a resident mission in Israel, but it couldn't afford to and didn't have enough diplomats, so it put off any moves towards Israel.

Non-Relation

What started out as a normal problem quickly turned into a question about foreign policy that is very controversial. When Nehru promised normalisation to Israel in early 1952, he ran into trouble at home, especially from his senior cabinet colleague Abul Kalam Azad. Aside from the fact that Indian Muslims were thought to be against the Arabs, fears about the Arabs' position on the Kashmir question also helped to solidify pro-Arab policy. Most of all, New Delhi was worried about Pakistan's diplomatic efforts in the Middle East, especially its push for an Islamic bloc.

Even though it was never officially said, India's policy towards Israel became a hostage of its diplomatic competition with Pakistan in the Middle East. In the years before India got its independence, the Congress party did not like the Zionists because it was in competition with the Muslim League. After 1947, India's policy towards Israel was shaped by its competition with Pakistan.

Over time, a number of regional and international changes made it harder for India and Israel to communicate and understand each other. People in India and around the world criticised the lack of ties. The growing friendship between Nehru and Egyptian President Gamal Abdul Nasser changed the way India felt about Israel. Nehru thought of the Egyptian leader as a leader of Arab nationalism and the fight against colonialism in the Middle East. Nehru liked and supported Nasser because he stood for secularism and socialism and was against military alliances backed by the US. It was only natural that Israel's invasion of Sinai in 1956 and its cooperation with the colonial powers would anger Nehru. For the first time, he ruled out diplomatic ties with Israel, saying that "the time is not yet right." Since then, this has become a common way for the Indian government to say why it doesn't have diplomatic ties with the Jewish State.

After that, things got worse, and India became more friendly with the Arabs and less friendly with Israel. Even when Israel helped India with its military during its wars with China in 1962 and Pakistan in 1965, this downward trend did not stop. During the war in June 1967, it was clear that India would side with the Arabs.

India found the newly formed Palestine Liberation Organization (PLO) to be a useful ally in the Middle East. In January 1975, Mrs. Indira Gandhi recognised the PLO as the sole and legitimate representative of the Palestinian people.

Even the non-Congress government led by Janata, which came to power in 1977, thought it was smart to keep the Middle East policy that Nehru and his daughter had set up. So, Israel's Foreign Minister Moshe Dayan's secret trip to India during Morarji Desai's time in office was more controversial and didn't lead to many good results.

On the international stage, there was also more and more opposition to and hostility towards Israel. Countries that were neutral or even friendly to the Palestinians before Israel was created began to see the political benefits of helping the Palestinians and took advantage of them. People who got economic and security help from Israel in the past thought it would be smart to act against Israel in public.

Since Israel was kicked out of the Bandung conference in 1955, the Afro-Asian community and the countries that don't belong to any group have been very critical of it. With the Soviet Union and its allies providing a strong ideological base, it became popular and politically correct to say bad things about Israel. India wanted to be a leader in the Afro-Asian world, the non-aligned movement, and among the Third World countries. It thought it would be smart and prudent to take an unfriendly stance towards Israel and use every chance to criticise Israel and prove itself to the Arabs. India's policy of not being friendly to Israel hasn't changed much, even after Nasser's defeat in the June 1967 war and the rise of Islamic revivalism and religious extremism, or after the major powers of the Middle East took a stand in favour of Pakistan.

When Indira Gandhi came back to power in 1980, she changed the Palestinian mission in New Delhi from a consulate to a full-fledged embassy and gave it all diplomatic rights and protections. At the same time, the Israeli consul in Bombay was stuck there. Even this small amount of representation was cut after the Israeli consul at the time, Yossef Hasseen, gave a controversial interview to the media in June 1982 in which he said that India was competing with Pakistan to win over the Arabs. Even though he was right, his comments angered the government, and in a move that had never been done before, Hasseen was told he was no longer welcome. India stopped giving Israelis visas to attend international conferences and sports events that were held in India. In 1983, Israel was officially kicked out of the Olympic Council of Asia (OCA), the top sports organisation on the continent.

A steps towards Normalization

When Indira's son Rajiv moved to Israel in 1984, it was the start of a new trend in relations between India and Israel. The old ideologies didn't appeal to the young leader, who wanted to lead the country into the next century as a modern, technologically advanced country. He got rid of the Congress Party's socialist roots and started a policy of economic liberalisation. He also took a less ideological approach to foreign policy. India's policy towards Israel was also affected by his desire for change and a break with the past.

Rajiv was also helped by a change in the world that made things better for Israel. Before the Palestinian intifada started in 1987, things were getting better and less bad for Israel in the 1980s. After the war in June 1967, many countries in the Communist bloc cut ties with Israel. After that, some countries in the Third World looked at their relationship with Israel again.

Despite its peace with Israel, Egypt was gradually readmitted into the Arab and Islamic blocs. Putting aside their different ideologies, both the Soviet Union and China have regular, low-level contacts with Israel. Strangely, India and Israel got along better at the same time that Israel and the Soviet Union started to get along better.

Rajiv Gandhi's policy towards Israel was improved by these events. During his five years in office, he made a few small but important steps towards making things better with Israel. Unlike some of his immediate predecessors, he met with Israeli officials and people in the US who supported Israel. Without saying anything for sure about the hard-to-answer question of normalisation, he showed that India's view of Israel was changing. In some ways, his incremental measures towards Israel became an integral part of his policy vis-à-vis Washington. Among other things, he put back a full consul in Bombay, expanded the consular area to include the southern state of Kerala, made it easier for Israeli passport holders to get visas, and ended a ban on sports with Israel by hosting the Davis Cup tennis tournament in 1987. 10

But there were things that made it hard for Rajiv Gandhi to fully normalise relations with Israel. The start of the intifada took away a lot of the progress Israel made in the early 1980s. Even places in the US that have always supported Israel found it hard to agree with how Israel handled the Palestinian uprising. Under these conditions, getting back to normal was out of the question. Rajiv Gandhi also had a lot of problems at home, especially after accusations of bribery in arms deals, which made it harder for him to get things done.

But the progress made during Rajiv Gandhi's time in office (1984–1989) helped Narasimha Rao when he became Prime Minister in 1991. After Rajiv Gandhi was killed and during the election campaign, there was a lot of political uncertainty. Rao started to take advantage of this. Rao had to continue the policies of his Congress predecessors, especially those of Indira Gandhi and her son Rajiv, because it was good for politics. At the same time, the economic crisis, which forced Rao to ask for help from other countries and open up the economy, made him realise that foreign policy needed to be updated and made better.

On December 16, 1991, India voted with the majority to get rid of the 1975 UN General Assembly resolution that said Zionism was the same as racism. This was a big change from the past. India was one of the first countries to back the infamous resolution, so Rao's decision showed a change in how India would treat Israel. Even though the opposition said that Rao had "abandoned" the traditional support for the Arabs, he kept moving towards normalisation and set up formal diplomatic contacts with Israel. Following this path to its logical end, India announced on January 29, 1992, that it would have normal diplomatic relations with Israel.

Post Normalization

Rao was able to change the long-held dislike of Israel because of both international and domestic factors. When the Madrid conference started in October 1991, a lot of the bad effects of opening up to Israel were lessened. The Middle East peace process showed that both sides of the long-running Arab-Israeli conflict wanted to find a political solution through direct talks. In some ways, the Palestinians' willingness to live together with Israel proved that India was right to want a peaceful end to the conflict.

When the PLO was willing to accept Israel's existence and negotiate with the Zionist state, there was no good reason for India to be more Catholic than the Pope. In the 1970s, the peace between Egypt and Israel did give India a chance to change its policy towards Israel, but Arab opposition to President Anwar Sadat's separate peace with Israel cut off any wiggle room. Things were a bit different in 1992, when even "confrontationist" states like Syria knew they had to make peace with Israel and try to reach an agreement based on mutual recognition and living together.

The end of the Cold War, along with the fall of the Soviet Union and its eventual disappearance, was also a big blow to the ideological opposition to Israel. Even though India's policy against Israel didn't start during the Cold War, the divide between East and West gave it a strong ideological foundation. Israel was left out of the Third World, the nonaligned movement, the Group of 77, and many other groups because it was thought that Israel was too close to the West. This was also due to the ideological opposition of the East.

On the home front, the Communists, whose support was crucial for Indira Gandhi, especially during her first term in office (1966–1977), gave the anti-Israeli policy a strong ideological base. The end of the Cold War weakened this ideological link within the Indian Left, and anti-Israel rhetoric was no longer the same as being pro-Arab.

On another level, Rao saw that India's policy towards Israel didn't make sense when he was forced to open up the economy. The West, especially the US, contributed a lot to the success of the market economy by giving money and sharing technology. Since the end of the 1940s, Washington has been putting pressure on India to change how it treats Israel. As Rajiv Gandhi's Foreign Minister, Rao had to deal with repeated American pressures about Israel. At the same time, some of Rajiv's moves towards Israel at the time were friendly gestures towards the US. Even the decision to improve relations with Israel was made public the day before Rao went to New York for the Security Council summit and to meet with President George H. W. Bush.

Pakistan is still a big part of India's foreign policy calculations and moves, but by the 1990s, it seemed like Pakistan was losing power in deciding India's policy towards Israel. India has reluctantly come to accept some facts about the Middle East. India's long-term and consistent support for the Palestinian cause did not make it popular in the area, especially after Nasser died. Even the Indian bureaucracy knew that a number of Arab and Islamic countries sided with Pakistan when things were important. The Palestinian factor is becoming less important because the Arab world is divided and the Palestinians are not liked because they supported Iraq during the Kuwait crisis. In short, Rao didn't need anti-Israeli rhetoric nearly as much as Indira Gandhi did.

More to the point, there was a lot of sympathy and understanding for Israel around the world, especially because it didn't fight back when Iraq fired Scud missiles at it. Several countries started to renew their ties with Israel or look for new ones. Before the Madrid conference started, the Soviet Union put back in place diplomatic ties that had been broken in June 1967. China also got closer to Israel, recognised it, and made ties with it, putting aside ideological differences and a long history of hostility. India couldn't just ignore what was going on.

Lastly, as time went on, it became clear that worries about how Muslims felt about Israel were unfounded. K. M. Panikkar, a well-known historian, diplomat, and close friend of Nehru, said that the role of the Muslim community in India was the reason why Indians didn't understand or care about the political goals of Jews as early as April 1947. Since Nehru's time, every important Indian leader has talked about how the country's large Muslim population is a big part of India's policy towards Israel, even though they don't want to talk about it in public.Narasimha Rao did have some tactical advantages, though. Since the mid-1980s, the Congress party has been steadily losing its traditional support among Muslim voters. In the 1991 election, the so-called Muslim leadership did not back the party and told its followers to vote for V. P. Singh's Janata Dal. This made them much less powerful in their dealings with the Congress party.

At the same time, Rao's action also made people feel bad. A move that took more than 40 years to figure out was called "hurried and without principles." They thought that India should have waited until there was a full peace in the Middle East. Conservatives said that normalising ties was a mistake and a betrayal of India's traditional commitment to the Palestinian cause as long as Israel kept occupying Arab territories.

One scholar went as far as to call the move towards normalisation a "anti-Muslim" alliance. But such a charge is kind of funny. Normalization was always pushed by the Jana Sangh and its successor, the Bharatiya Janata Party (BJP), for many years. The final choice was made by a Congress government that was officially committed to secularism.

There were rumours that some of Rao's senior colleagues had doubts about this matter. India's repeated statements of support for the Palestinians and frequent denials of any military or security cooperation with the Jewish State showed that there were pressures and disagreements within the country over this issue. Also, the Palestinian leader Yasser Arafat went to Israel before or after every major event that happened there.

With the exception of a short visit by Foreign Minister Shimon Peres in May 1993, there were no major contracts or visits between the two countries in the beginning. India's problems with the destruction of the controversial but historically important mosque in Ayodhya and Israel's deportation of more than 400 suspected Hamas activists in December 1992 kept bilateral relations from being very visible right away.

But nearly a decade after Rao's decision, relations between India and Israel are now strong. Even though there were disagreements about some parts of the Middle East peace process, bilateral relations no longer caused problems for India's foreign policy. With the help of economic liberalisation, which led to the decentralisation of power, state governments run by different political parties have looked for and pushed for strong economic ties with Israel.

Even parties, like the Janata Dal, that were against Rao's decision in 1992 have come to see the benefits of economic cooperation with Israel. In the summer of 2000, when veteran communist leader and then-West Bengal Chief Minister Jyoti Basu came to visit, it was a good reminder that most people in India support normalisation.

From Expression to Reality

If the Congress party was in charge of setting up the administrative framework needed to promote bilateral ties, the BJP has given those ties more weight. The

BJP's foreign policy towards Israel is unapologetic, which is in line with its history of being pro-Israel. Both India and the Middle East were surprised when Home Minister L. K. Advani and Foreign Minister Jaswant Singh went there in the middle of 2000.

Even when the second intifada broke out later that year and got a lot of bad press, India's position did not change much. The way Israel dealt with the Palestinian uprising brought back the hostility and anti-Israeli rhetoric from before 1992. However, the Indian government was happy with general platitudes and didn't join the rest of the world in criticising the way Israel handled the violence. One expert said, "There isn't much reason for India to go back to the way it used to do diplomatic business in the region."

On the contrary, the regular meeting of Indian envoys in the Middle East was held in Israel in December 2000, right in the middle of the crisis. Even bad news about the Indian soldiers in the United Nations Interim Force in Lebanon (UNIFIL), which is based in Lebanon, did not stop India from making defence deals with Israel.

There were rumours and suggestions in the news that a number of Arab and Islamic countries were worried about and unhappy with how things were going between India and Israel. Official trips to the area were sometimes moved because the host country didn't like India's policy towards Israel. One Arab diplomat who didn't want to be named even said that Hindutava and Zionism have similar ideas.

The government's history of foreign policy, on the other hand, shows that the Israel policy did not make the Middle East angry. Instead, it led key players like Iran and Saudi Arabia to work closely with India. If the first country wants to send oil to India through pipelines, the second country wants to strengthen ties with New Delhi. The Arab and Islamic countries don't seem to let the Arab-Israeli conflict affect their relationships with India. Even Iraq wanted to get along better with India.

The political leaders of both countries created an environment that was good for business. In 2000, trade between the two countries went over $1 billion, and Israel became India's main trading partner in the area. Even though the diamond trade is still a big part of the overall trade, its share is going down. Israel is also one of the biggest investors from outside of India. A lot of agreements have been made between state governments, public-sector businesses, and private and individual businesses with their Israeli counterparts. Direct air links have made it easier for the two countries to work together on business, and they have also brought more Israeli tourists to India. There are also more cultural contacts and exchanges.

But the real progress in bilateral relations seems to be happening in an area that neither country wants to talk about: working together on defence. One could say that the idea of working together on defence was one of the things that helped normalisation happen. India didn't have any ties with Israel, but that didn't stop it from asking for and getting small arms and ammunition from Israel.

After being hesitant at first, both countries are now working together on a wide range of defense-related projects. On the day that terrorists attacked the World Trade Center and the Pentagon, Israeli National Security Adviser Major General Uzi Dayan was in New Delhi talking about terrorism with top Indian officials. In December of the next year, a high-level Indian delegation went to Israel to talk about how to fight terrorism.

Fighting against Islamic fundamentalism, which is often brought up as a possible common enemy, doesn't seem like a good idea. Even though some terrorist groups that work against India and Israel use religion as a tool, both countries have been careful not to make it look like they are working together against militant Islam. India has become a top target for international and cross-border terrorism in recent years, so it makes sense that counterterrorism is a big part of their talks, especially during Advani's visit.

Some of the most important defence deals include remotely controlled vehicles (RPVs), Barak anti-missile systems for the navy, ammunition for the Bofors guns during the Kargil operations, upgrading MiG jets, and the supply of Phalcon airborne early warning systems. After months of talks, India signed a series of defence contracts worth about $2 billion in August 2001. These contracts were for the supply of long-range surveillance equipment, night-vision equipment, and ammunition.

If these ties are built and maintained well, they can grow beyond the cash-and-carry model. Israeli technology can meet most of India's needs in areas like avionics, updating aircraft, and making weapons and missile systems more up-to-date. Both countries need to be better and have their own technology because they are in a hostile region. This is important for their long-term security.

India can't make technological progress and become self-sufficient without help and participation from other countries. For its part, Israel's ability to stay ahead of its Arab enemies in terms of quality depends on how well its defence industries can make money. Israel has some unique advantages over other arms suppliers, such as its experience with weapons and systems from both former blocs, its no-questions-asked policy for its arms trade, and its reputation as a reliable supplier and expert in technological innovation and skill upgrading.

In short, India's need for technology and Israel's need to save money on defence research go hand in hand. Both countries have a number of strategic programmes that work well together. These include the Lavi (India's unnamed LCA) aircraft, Merkava (Arjun) tanks, Jericho-I (Prithvi), Jericho-II (Agni), and RPVs. With the exception of the US, major defence frames are no longer built by one country alone, so there is no reason why India and Israel can't work together to save money on their defence production. Space and satellite programmes are another area where countries could work together for a long time.

Aside from this possibility, Washington's "yellow light" approach to the issue also helps possible defence cooperation. Except for a short time after India did nuclear tests in May 1998, the US hasn't cared much about defence ties between India and Israel. This is different from how the US treats defence ties between Israel and China. In the past, China was thought of as using Israel to get access to Western technology. The Reagan administration did not say anything about reports that Israel might give military technology from the United States to China.

After the end of the Cold War, things started to change when high-level American officials started to do something about what they thought was wrong with Israel's defence ties with China. Early in 1992, Israel was accused of illegally giving China Patriot anti-missile technology. This was a very serious and controversial move. 37 The dispute happened at a time when there was already a lot of tension between the Bush administration and the right-wing Israeli government led by Yitzhak Shamir. This caused each side to question not only the truth of the other's claims but also their motivations.

Unlike in the past, mainstream American media actively looked into the claim, and the Bush administration did something that had never been done before: they sent an investigation team to Israel to check out the claim. Even though the inspection did not confirm the allegation in a formal way, the controversy had done a lot of damage to US-Israeli relations and led to tighter export rules and less military aid from the US to Israel. In short, the US is no longer willing to ignore military ties between Israel and China because of technological and strategic worries.

This is different from what Washington thinks about defence ties between India and Israel. Even the United States' anger and the sanctions that followed India's nuclear tests did not hurt the relationship. Even though the US has been more worried about rumours of cooperation in the nuclear field, the general American attitude has been one of indifference and pretending to be worried. The long-term talks about the nuclear issue and the gradual improvement of Indo-US relations will only help and strengthen the defence ties between India and Israel.

In short, India is seen as a possible friend and ally in Asia's strategic calculations, but there is no reason for Washington to be worried about this. As long as India and Israel keep their policies and statements in line with American concerns about not spreading weapons of mass destruction, the United States is unlikely to notice when the two countries work together on defence.

In terms of foreign policy, the normalisation was also a sign that India was determined to reduce Pakistan's role in its Middle East policy. India's obsession with Pakistan is clear in the way it deals with Israel in the Middle East. India let its rivalry with Pakistan cloud the way it thought about and treated Israel. Pakistan has become India's "centre of gravity" in the Middle East because of how often it talks about being secular and how strongly it supports Arabs.Because of this preoccupation, India did a lot of things towards Israel that were not very nice.

At the same time, this policy hasn't paid off much, especially during times of trouble. Also, India has made it harder for the world to see it as a great power by giving Pakistan a strong position in its foreign policy. The Pakistani factor was also weakened by the fact that the Palestinian card was losing its value. In fact, when Foreign Minister Jaswant Singh went to Saudi Arabia in early 2001, India went out of its way to say that the relationship between the two countries was not meant to hurt Pakistan. In response to Pakistani worries about his visit, Singh said that such worries "would be a misunderstanding of India's intentions and an insult to the Saudi leadership's wisdom." India's growing political and economic ties with countries like Iran, Saudi Arabia, and Turkey show that it is trying to keep its Middle East policy from being held hostage by its relationship with Pakistan.

Conclusion

Since normalisation, the political, economic, cultural, and, most importantly, security ties between India and Israel have grown a lot. Long-term neglect and apathy have not slowed down the pace of ties. After some initial doubts and worries, the relationship is now solid. Even though the pace could be changed by things like the Middle East peace process or a change of government in India, the overall direction is good.

Even though some Arab countries, especially Egypt, put pressure on India, it has set its priorities and moved towards a policy that is less talk and more action. Because of this, nearly a decade later, normalisation is not a controversial topic in India. Instead, it has a lot of support. Even if a government that doesn't like Israel took over in New Delhi, it wouldn't be able to undo what has been done since 1992. India and Israel are getting along better now that their relations with the US are getting better. This is in addition to the fact that they haven't had any fights or disagreements with each other in a long time.

References

P.R. Kumaraswamy, "India and Israel: Emerging Partnership," Journal of Strategic Studies 25, no. 4 (2002): 193-200.

A.G. Noorani, "Dissent in Israel," Frontline (May 2003): 10-23.

Harsh Pant, "India-Israel Partnership: Convergence and Constraints," Middle East Review of International Affairs 8, no. 4 (2004): 60-73.

Dan Raviv and Yossi Melman, Every Spy a Prince (Boston: Houghton Mifflin, 1990), 157, 436-7.

Arielle Kandel, "Indo-Israeli Relations in the Post-Cold War Period," Blitz, February 21, 2010, http://www.weeklyblitz.net/535/indo-israeli-relations-in-the-post-cold-war-period. The Indian realization that lobbying played a significant role in US foreign policy making drove it to imitate the Israel American lobby's practices. The Indian Americans, the India caucus and the lobbying firms hired by India have lobbied for US-India ties, often supported and assisted by the Jewish American lobbying groups. The US-India nuclear deal is an example of how these two lobbies groups worked together to clear its passage in the US Congress. See Ashok Sharma, "Indian Americans: Migrational Pattern, Professional Success, Cultural Emergence and their Political Activism," in Indian Diaspora: Contributions to their New Home, ed. Ajay Dubey (New Delhi: MD Publications, 2011), 49-82; Ashok Sharma, "Growing Influence of Indian American Lobbying on Indo-US Relations," World Focus (July 2008): 261-264.

R.K. Jasbir Singh, ed., India Defence Year Book 1998-1999 (Dehradun: Natraj Publication, 2000), 119-20.

"India Works with Israeli Intelligence," Far Eastern Economic Review, June 29, 2000: 10.

"India-Israel Growing Ties," Asiaweek, June 30, 2000.

BBC, "India and Israel join forces," July 3, 2000.

Noorani, "Dissent in Israel," 10-23.

Amnon Barzilai, "Looking Out for Number One," Haaretz., December 27, 2001.

"Bilateral Relations: Historical Overview," Embassy of Israel, New Delhi, http://delhi.mfa.gov.il/mfm/web/main/document.asp?SubjectID= 2010&MissionID = 93&LanguageID = 0&StatusID = 0&DocumentID = -1 (accessed July 19, 2010).

Ora Coren, "India-Israel to Hold Free Trade Talks," Haaretz, February 25, 2010.

P.R. Kumaraswamy, "India and Israel: Evolving Strategic Partnership," Mideast Security and Policy Studies, no. 40 (September 1998, BESA Centre, Bar-Ilan University).

Tufail Ahmad, "Dialogue of Democracy: Indian Muslims Visit Israel," Yale Global Online, November 7, 2007, http://yaleglobal.yale.edu/content/dialogue-democracy-indian-muslims-visit-israel.

Paul Watson, "Arms at the Heart of India-Israel Embrace," Los Angeles Times, September 9, 2003.

Kumaraswamy, "India and Israel: Evolving Strategic Partnership."

Watson, "Arms at the Heart."

Ashok Sharma, "India's Missile Defence Programme: Threat Perceptions and Technological Evolution," CLAWS Manekshaw Paper (New Delhi: Knowledge World Publishers, 2009).

Barzilai, "Looking out for Number One."

Dan Senor and Saul Singer, Start-Up Nation: the Story of Israel's Economic Miracle (New York: Twelve, 2009).

Sachin Parashar, "India, Israel to Restart Free Trade Agreement Talks," India Times, February 1, 2015.

Coren, "India-Israel to Hold Free-Trade Talks."

David Rosenberg, "Israel, India Look to Hi-tech as Trade Ties Expand," Jerusalem Post, June 3, 2011.

"India Condemns Israeli Attack on Aid Flotilla," Times of India, June 1, 2010.

Harsh Pant, "India and the Middle East," in Indian Foreign Policy in a Uni-polar World, ed. Harsh Pant (New Delhi: Routledge, 2009), 251-76. See also Parmit Pal Choudhary, "It's Time to Look Beyond Arafat: Israel to India," Hindustan Times, September 8, 2003 and Pranay Sharma, "Terror and Truce Mix for Sharon," Telegraph, September 9, 2003.

Pant, "India and the Middle East."

Arielle Kandel, "Despite Closer Ties, 'Muslim Factor' Still Undermines India-Israel Relationship," Yne, December 26, 2010.

"Tel Aviv Worried about New Delhi's Ties with Iran," Times of India, September 11, 2003.

Arielle Kandel, "The Significant Warming of Indo-Israeli Relations in the Post-Cold War Era," Middle East Review of International Affairs 13, no. 4 (2009): 69-77.

"Flotilla Attack: Israel Cries Foul, Drags India into Row," Indian Express, June 2, 2010.

Among others see, India, Ministry of External Affairs, India and Palestine: The Evolution of Policy (New Delhi, nd), M.S. Agwani, 'The Palestine conflict in Asian perspective', in Ibrahim Abu-Laghod (ed.), The Transformation of Palestine (Evanston, IL: Northwestern University Press 1971) pp.443-62; and Leonard Gordon, 'Indian nationalist ideas about Palestine and Israel', Jewish Social Studies (New York) 37/34 (Summer-Fall 1975) pp.22-134.

Harijan, 26 Nov. 1938, in The Collected Works of Mahatma Gandhi (New Delhi: Publications Divisions, Government of India, 1958 ff.) Vol.68, p.137.

Nehru's speech to the Asian Relations Conference in March 1947, Asian Relations: Report of the proceedings and documentation of the first Asian Relations Conference, New Delhi, March-April 1947 (New Delhi, Asian Relations Organization 1948) p.70.

For discussions on Gandhi's position see, Gideon Shimoni, Gandhi, Satyagraha and the Jews: A Formative Factor in India's Policy toward Israel (Jerusalem: Leonard Davis Inst. for Int. Relations 1977), PR. Kumaraswamy, 'Mahatma Gandhi and the Jewish national home', Asian and African Studies (Haifa) 26/1 (March 1992) pp.1-13; and Margaret Chatterjee, Gandhi and His Jewish Friends (Basingstoke: Macmillan 1992).

Indeed, consistent with this position, in May 1949 India voted against the majority when the Assembly approved Israeli application for UN membership. It is essential to remember that India was advocating a plan that it found unsuitable for the subcontinent where the Hindu-Muslim relation was less inimical than the Arab-Jewish ties in Palestine.

P.R. Kumaraswamy, 'India's recognition of Israel, September 1950', Middle Eastern Studies (London) 31/1 (Jan. 1995) pp.124-38.

Michael Brecher, Nehru: A Political Biography (London: Oxford 1959) pp.571-2; and The New States of Asia: A Political Analysis (London: Oxford, 1968 reprint) p.130.

It is often overlooked that at the UN the Kashmir question was discussed at the Security Council where the Arab states did not have a major say.

This move permanently excluded Israel from Asian Games even though Israel had participated in a few Games in the past.

P.R. Kumaraswamy, 'India and Israel: Prelude to normalization', Journal of South-Asian and Middle Eastern Studies (Villanova, PA) 19/2 (Winter 1995) pp. 53-66; and 'India, Israel and the Davis Cup tie 1987', Journal of Indo-Judaic Studies (forthcoming).

Even at the height of anti-Israeli sentiments, India never endorsed the extremist aspirations of the Palestinians against the existence of Israel.

Indeed, at one time being a Leftist meant taking an anti-Israeli posture. Reeling under that influence one scholar described Israel as 'the illegitimate offspring of retreating imperialism'. There are suggestions that in 1982 only American pressure prevented the closure of the Israeli consulate.

The return of a consul to Bombay and the extension of consular jurisdiction to Kerala were preceded by meetings between Indian leaders and American friends of Israel.

For example see Foreign Secretary J.N. Dixit's outspoken interview in The Week, 9 Feb. 1992, p.37.

Within days after the Chinese move, India followed suit. For a discussion on this linkage see, P.R. Kumaraswamy, 'South Asia and People's Republic of China-Israel diplomatic relations', in Jonathan Goldstein (ed.), China and Israel, 1948—1998: A Fifty Year Retrospective (Westport, CO: Praeger 1999) pp.131-52.

On the eve of India's independence Panikkar told the Jewish delegation from Palestine: '... once Pakistan is established, Hindu leaders and politicians may well take a pro-Zionist line'. Panikkar quoted in S.H. Bergmann and Yaacov Shimoni, Report on the Inter-Asia Conference, d.17 April 1947, Central Zionist Archives, Jerusalem, S25/7485. On 4 April 1947, Panikkar handed over a confidential note titled 'A memorandum on Hindu-Zionist relations' to the visiting delegation. For a discussion on this see, P.R. Kumaraswamy, 'Sardar K.M. Panikkar and India-Israel Relations', International Studies (New Delhi) 32/3 (July 1995) pp.327-37.

Foreign Minister Jaswant Singh's reference to Indian Muslims shaping India's Israel policy at a lecture in Jerusalem in June 2000 evoked strong criticisms and rebuke.

Eliahu Elath to Moshe Sharett on his meeting with Nehru d. 14 Oct. 1949, Documents on the Foreign Policy of the State of Israel (Jerusalem: Israel State Archives) Vol.4, pp. 547-8. Declassified Israeli documents frequently mention Indian diplomats referring to the feelings of the Indian Muslim population as a factor.

Among other see, Mani Shankar Aiyar, 'Chutzpah' Sunday, 6 June 1993, pp. 14-17.

Punyapriya Dasgupta, 'Betrayal of India's Israel policy', Economic and Political Weekly 27/1516, 11-18 April 1992, pp.767-72; and Bansidhar Pradhan, 'India's policy toward the PLO', in Riyaz Punjabi and A.K. Pasha (ed.), India and the Islamic World (New Delhi: Radiant 1998) p.73.

According to a former foreign secretary, 'Arjun Singh felt that this decision might affect Muslim support for the Congress and went on to imply that establishing relations with Israel would be a departure from the Nehruvian framework of our foreign policy'. J.N. Dixit, My South Block Years: Memoirs of a Foreign Secretary (New Delhi: UBSPD 1996) p.311.

Congress leader Natwar Singh highlighted this dilemma of the opposition. While India should maintain good relations with Israel, 'it could not be at the expense of our relations with Palestine people'. The Hindu, 22 Oct. 2000.

For example see, Sukumar Muralidharan, 'Peace, and war', Frontline (Chennai/Madras), 10 Nov. 2000, pp.15-18.

K.K. Katyal, 'West Asia crisis tells on foreign policy consensus', The Hindu, 18 Oct. 2000.

C. Raja Mohan, 'India's West Asian stakes', The Hindu, 16 Oct. 2000.

The Hindu, 4 Dec. 2000.

Michael Jansen, 'Indian summer', Middle East International, 27 July 2001, pp.10-11.

John Cherian, 'India's changing stand', Frontline, 10 Nov. 2000, p.14.

There were no high-level contacts between the two countries since Indira Gandhi's visit to the kingdom in 1982.

Right in the middle of the intifada, Iraqi vice-president Taha Yassin Ramadan paid an official

Chapter 3

India-Israel Defence Cooperation and Security Ties

Introduction

India's defence and security ties with West Asia have been going on for more than a hundred years. In what may have been the last cavalry charge in history, Indian cavalry soldiers wrote a brave story about courage and sacrifice. The Jodhpur, Mysore, and Hyderabad Lancers, who were part of the 15th Imperial Service Cavalry Brigade, took part in this unique cavalry action on September 23, 1918. Their goal was to take the port city of Haifa in what is now Israel. The goal of the Brigade, which was part of the Fifth Cavalry Division of the Desert Mounted Corps, was to bring the Turkish Seventh and Eighth Armies together (Ottoman Empire).

Since 1516, Haifa was thought to be the last stronghold of the Ottoman Army that was fortified. In the next battle, the Jodhpur and Mysore Lancers led a cavalry charge while being heavily shot at by machine guns. As a result, the Regiment took over 700 prisoners and a lot of heavy weapons from Haifa. Major Thakur Dalpat Singh, who was the CO of the Jodhpur Lancers, died in the operations, though. For this action, he was given the Military Cross, and Captain Aman Singh Bahadur was given the Indian Order of Merit (IOM). One officer and seven other ranks were killed, and 60 horses were lost. Six officers and 28 other ranks were hurt.

After Independence, the three Lancer Regiments were combined to make the 61st Cavalry, which is the only mounted horse cavalry in the world. The day it was built, September 23, is still known as "Haifa Day" or "Rising Day." Since the victory and liberation of Haifa helped Israel grow into what it is today, the sacrifices of Indian officers and soldiers are still remembered with love by the people of Haifa. The Teen Murti Memorial, which was built in 1924 near South Avenue in New Delhi, is a tribute to the brave Indian Regiments and cavalry troops who died while doing their jobs.

India and Israel didn't talk to each other for about 40 years. But changes in the geostrategic situation in the rest of the world forced India to make full diplomatic relations with Israel in 1992. The main things that made India think twice about establishing diplomatic ties with Israel were the Gulf War, which broke up the Arab world, the end of the cold war, which made it easier to find peaceful solutions to many international problems, like Arab-Israeli peace talks, the urgent need for better relations with the US, and Pakistan's propaganda against India in the West Asian and North African states in order to gain influence. India also knew about Israel's advances in agricultural technologies and better industrial know-how, which could open up a lot of opportunities for working together.

After things got back to normal, both countries were free to look into as many areas as they could. India and Israel's relationship grew quickly in the areas of trade and agriculture, and both countries kept looking for ways to work together in as many areas as possible. One area that both countries are looking into is "military."

The former Soviet Union has always been a strong friend and partner of India in the military field. Even though the fall of the Soviet Union had an effect on Russia's military-industrial complex, and their production capacity isn't as high as it was during the Soviet era, their goods are cheap and geared towards export. Israel, on the other hand, didn't start diplomatic ties with India until much later, but it has become an important partner in many fields, including the military. India's willingness to work together is based on its realistic view of the global and regional security situation as well as its technological needs. More importantly, 2017 was not only the 100th anniversary of the Battle of Haifa, but it is also the 25th anniversary of diplomatic ties between India and Israel.

Since full diplomatic ties were made between India and Israel in January 1992, defence and security cooperation has been getting better and better. Even when full diplomatic relations were not yet in place, India asked Israel for help with security and got it. This was most noticeable during the wars between India and Pakistan in 1965 and 1971. Some of the things Israel gave to these wars, like 160 mm mortars, were used again 20 years later in the Kargil War. Since 1992, defence and security cooperation has been the most important part of the strategic partnership between India and Israel. India bought high-tech equipment from Israel to meet important security needs and help modernise its military. Because the Indian defence industry wasn't able to meet these needs, India had to buy this equipment from other countries.

Israel, on its part, exhibited political will to provide niche equipment to India, unencumbered by restrictions on such transfers by Israel's close ally, the United States (US). The US, for instance, prevented Israel from going ahead with the 1998 contract with China for airborne early warning and control aircraft (AWACS). Due to US pressure, the contract was terminated in 2000, with Israel even having to pay damages for not fulfilling the terms of the contract. The US put pressure on Israel over fears that such niche capabilities could aid Beijing's efforts to forcefully take over Taiwan.

During Narendra Modi's visit to Israel in July 2017 – the first time an Indian prime minister had been there in 25 years – the two countries formally recognised their "strategic partnership." This chapter gives a historical and modern look at the defence parts of the India-Israel strategic partnership.

Shapes of Cooperation

Since establishing diplomatic ties in 1992, India has slowly increased the number of defence products it buys from Israel. In 1996-1997, India bought Searcher unmanned aerial vehicles (UAVs) and Super Dvora patrol boats, with the first contract going back to 1996. As a result of the Kargil war, India and Israel became closer in terms of defence. India got important things like artillery gun ammunition. Since then, India has bought a lot of different kinds of equipment, including assault rifles, Phalcon airborne warning and control systems (AWACS), fire-control radars, missiles, and a lot more. In the sections that follow, we'll talk about some of the most important parts of the two countries' defence cooperation. The main focus will be on procurement and joint development programmes related to surveillance capabilities, missiles, and niche equipment like assault weapons and aircraft parts.

Initial Hiccups in Policy Building

Over the past seven decades, India and Israel have had a lot of interactions. Some of these interactions have been mutually beneficial because both countries have similar interests. This was most clear in the first few years they were their own countries. Both India and Israel got rid of British rule in a short period of nine months. India became independent on August 15, 1947, and Israel did the same on May 14, 1948. In a way, India and Israel's coming together and becoming functional democracies in the wake of different security threats from their immediate neighbours can be seen as "miracle stories" in the world after World War II. Even so, it wasn't until September 1950 that India legally recognised Israel by opening a consular office in what was then Bombay to make it easier for Indian Jews to move to Israel.

Some of India's policy needs can be traced back to its need for energy and economic security with the Gulf Arab states, its dependence on the Soviet Union during the Cold War, its perceived leading role in the Non-Aligned Movement (NAM), and its policymakers' sensitivity to the needs of its large Muslim population and their long-standing support for the Palestinian cause. Even though this was the policy, after the US, UK, and France put an arms embargo in place, Israel sent the Indian Army a small number of heavy 160 mm mortars through other channels during the 1965 and 1971 Indo-Pak wars. These were used by two Artillery Regiments. Their steep trajectory and heavy calibre charge made them very effective in mountainous areas. It's important to remember that eight of these heavy mortar guns were also used in the Kargil Conflict in 1999.

What happened after the Cold War?

The fall of the Soviet Union and the pro-Soviet regimes in Eastern Europe in 1989, which together had been the source of 70% of India's military equipment, and the decline in rupee trade led to a new, unstable international order with major fault lines in the balance of power. All of these things went wrong for India. This was also when the insurgency in Jammu and Kashmir, which was supported by Pakistan, really got going. So, a two-pronged strategy was made: the first was to give India access to Western technologies that could be used in military equipment, and the second was to look for new ways and partners to start joint research and development (R&D) projects in key areas. Israel was a good choice to meet both of these criteria, but a careful shift was needed for the policy goals to be met in all of their parts.

The real people to thank for this major "policy change" in West Asia and the reevaluation of India's foreign policy are former Prime Minister Narasimha Rao and his very professional and smart Foreign Secretary at the time, J. N. Dixit. Due to changes in geopolitical conditions, these two people worked together to give India's foreign policy interactions a new direction. This was most clear when New Delhi and Tel Aviv got back to having full diplomatic relations. Because of the direct Israeli–Palestinian peace process talks in Madrid in October 1991, the policy decision was made easier from a political point of view.

Another thing that had to be taken into account was that China was seriously thinking about establishing full diplomatic relations with Israel, which it did on January 24, 1992, five days before India did. Given the power of the 326 N. A. K. Browne Jewish lobby in Washington, this move could also help improve relations between India and the US. Together, and because of this, India and Israel started full diplomatic relations on January 29, 1992, and India's embassy opened in May of the same year. But it would take another five years to put together a defence wing. The significance of these events was truly historic, and they need to be seen in the context of not only changes in the international order but also domestic pressures. This was clear from what J. N. Dixit himself said: "I think establishing relations with South Africa and then with Israel were the most important changes to India's foreign policy during my time as Foreign Secretary."

Establishment of Defence Wing in Tel Aviv

In order to move the process forward, the then-Prime Minister Rao and then-Foreign Secretary Dixit met with the then-Air Chief Marshal (ACM) S. K. Kaul in early 1994 to talk about formal ways to work with the Israeli defence establishment. In April 1994, it was suggested that the Air Chief lead a four-person delegation from the Indian Air Force (IAF) to Israel (other members of the delegation included an Air Vice Marshal, a Group Captain and, the junior-most, a Wing Commander). Maj. Gen. Herzle Bodinger, the head of the Israeli Air Force (IsAF), was the official host, and both sides were told to keep the visit a secret. More importantly, the delegation took a letter from Rao to Yitzhak Rabin, who was Prime Minister and Defence Minister of Israel at the time.

The first impressions were very good, as Rabin himself greeted the delegation warmly and led them to his Hakirya office in the Ministry of Defence (MoD). He then read the letter from the prime minister out loud in his usual deep baritone voice. The delegation was promised all possible help, and it was a good chance to talk about the IAF's immediate and long-term needs, as well as the possibility of working together on defence modernization, joint research, and production. So, the first official talks with the Israelis about defence and security issues started in April 1994.

The following year, Rabin was tragically killed. Back in New Delhi, Rao approved "in principle" in 1995 that a Defence Wing should be set up for our mission. But the date would be decided at a later time. After Israeli President Ezer Weizman went to India in December 1996, the creation of the Wing was finally given the green light. I had the honour of opening the Defence Attaché's office in Tel Aviv on April 7, 1997, as the most junior member of ACM Kaul's group. After the Israeli Defence Attaché (IsAF Col.) moved to New Delhi, a similar arrangement was made.

Swapping Strategic and Defence Tech

One interesting part of this two-way relationship was that Israel's well-developed research and development (R&D) industry and engineering and technology support from their different institutions made it easier for India to do business there. The Israeli government agency MAFAT (which stands for Administration for the Development of Weapons and Technological Infrastructure in Hebrew) and its close partnership with India's Defence Research and Development Organisation kept an eye on everything (DRDO). Given the lack of access to technology in the early 1990s, and especially after the nuclear tests in May 1998, which led to the sanctions regime, this newfound access to strategic technologies gave the Indian defence scientific community a unique chance. During his time as the Scientific

Advisor to the Defence Minister, Dr. A. P. J. Abdul Kalam led this effort as part of an agreement between governments called the Indo–Israeli Management Committee (I2MC).

With joint funding and a long-term goal of having domestic defence industries make these niche technologies, the project had a broad mandate for research into common projects related to sensors and weapons systems. The results of these efforts have been good. The Green Pine multi-functional radar and the development of air defence missile systems, such as the Indian Navy's Long Range Surface-to-Air Missile (LRSAM) and the Indian Air Force's Medium Range Surface-to-Air Missile (MRSAM), have shown that this approach makes sense.

So, India's need for technology and Israel's need to save money on defence research now go hand in hand. Dr. Kalam was still very well known and respected in the Israeli defence research community. He once said, after going to the famous Al Aqsa mosque in the middle of Jerusalem, "I have come to pray for peace in the Holy Land." People admired him a lot for how smart he was, but they also thought he was a very simple person. The last time Dr. Kalam went to Israel was in February 2008, when he spoke at the 48th Israel Annual Conference on Aerospace Sciences.

AWACS and the US factor

The US has had a big impact on defence relations between India and Israel, but not in a direct way. As part of an annual package of defence and economic aid worth about $3 billion (of which about $1.6 billion is set aside for defence), the US helps Israel get access to important dual-use technologies that need end-user clearances. It also has a close relationship with the US because both countries want strong political and economic support at multilateral forums. These conditions mean that the US can successfully stop a new programme or stop a project that is already going on, no matter how much it costs the customer or the supplier. So, we were very interested when the US put pressure on Israel to stop the sale of the Phalcon Airborne Early Warning and Control (AEW&C) project to China in 2000. This project was made by Israel Aircraft Industries (IAI). This phased-array radar system was already being tested at the Ben Gurion airport on a modified Russian IL-76 platform when the project was scrapped. The Chinese plans to improve the Harpy anti-radiation attack drone were also said to have been scrapped.

In those early years, it was clear that the strategic part of the relationship would have to be carefully managed at "different levels" to avoid what happened between China and India. To the credit of our contacts and actors in New Delhi and Tel Aviv, a similar situation did not come up, except for a short time after the nuclear tests in May 1998. For the record, a trilateral memorandum of understanding (MoU) between India, Israel, and Russia made sure that the IAF's strategic Airborne

Warning and Control Systems (AWACS) project on three similar IL-76 modified platforms was finished and delivered successfully between 2009 and 2011. It also showed that only a small number of Israeli defence experts and companies still worked closely with their Jewish counterparts in Eastern Europe and the former Soviet Union. After the dramatic events of the late 1990s, these experts and contacts were now available for the Israeli defence establishment to use. The AWACS project showed that India was able to meet a long-term operational need for a "eye in the sky" long before the DRDO could build similar systems on its own.

Israel's response to Pokhran II

As things went on after the Pokhran tests in May 1998, it was important to note that Israel was one of the few countries that did not condemn the tests. Gen. Amnon Lipkin Shahak, who was in charge of the Israel Defence Forces (IDF) at the time, was set to go to India a week after the tests. We knew that the visit would have to be rescheduled because of the "changed circumstances." Still, a small event that is worth telling shows how pragmatic and real-world Israeli interests and policy are. Back in New Delhi, one of the effects of the May tests was that most foreign countries cancelled the National Defence College's (NDC) study tour abroad.

So, it was asked of the Director General (DG) of the Israeli Ministry of Defence (MoD) if they could accept the trip with more students. Not only was the response positive, but they went out of their way to make sure two busloads of visitors felt welcome. On the last day, before the meeting with the DG was over, one of the senior students asked why the hosts had agreed to the visit. DG Ilan Biran avoided the embarrassing question in a diplomatic way. But as soon as the guests left the room, he pulled me aside and told me in his simple, country way:

> *"Our experience is that when two elephants fight, only small animals get hurt. Within two years when you people make up with each other, then where does that leave tiny Israel? We have worked so hard to reach this point in our relationship and if we also turn our back on India now, then you will never forgive us."*

In a way, these simple words summed up Israel's response because they showed that they had a good grasp of geopolitics and their own best interests. Building strong ties between the two countries was a clear strategic goal. From a diplomatic point of view, it all turned out to be a sign of the hard times that were to come.

Kargil Conflict

From a different point of view, it has also been thought that the long-term talks about the nuclear issue and the gradual improvement of relations between India and the US would only help and strengthen the relationship between India and Israel. India's "temporary isolation" after the nuclear tests, which was forced on it by some countries, only helped Israel, and this was most clear during the Kargil War in 1999. Israel gave the Indian Army "around 40,000 rounds of 155 mm and 30,000 rounds of 160 mm mortar ammunition," according to reports. It also gave them "laser-guided bombs and unmanned aerial vehicles," or UAVs. Israel's reputation as a reliable arms supplier, even in a crisis, was boosted by how quickly it responded to India's request for military help. This helped to strengthen the relationship between the two countries.

One interesting thing about the Kargil War that hasn't gotten enough attention is the key role played by a piece of IAF equipment that was put to use for the first time as the war went on. On the icy mountain tops of the Saltoro ridge, where Pakistani defences were, it turned the tables on them. But first, some background: In the 1980s, the IAF's ability to strike precisely with Laser Guided Bombs (LGBs) and their Laser Designator Pods was limited to the Mirage fleet, and only during the day. The IAF chose the Israeli Litening Pod in 1997 to equip the Mirage and Jaguar fleets with a weapon system that could be used both during the day and at night. The targeting pod was still being made, and the process of putting it on the Mirage 2000 at Gwalior and at the Aircraft and Systems Testing Establishment in Bangalore took a long time and was hard work in 1998.

But when fighting broke out in the Kargil sector at the end of May 1999, things changed almost overnight. Due to the strict rules of engagement that say you can't cross the Line of Control (LoC), the Indian Air Force (IAF) had to change its plan for hitting high altitude targets between 15,000 and 17,000 feet that were protected by Pakistani Man Portable Air Defence (MANPAD). This meant that the LGB weapons had to be released closer to 30,000 feet, which was not something they had done before. Also, the pod designers at Rafael Industries (north of Haifa) hadn't thought about how hard it would be to operate in, so they had to make big changes to the software and hardware as the war went on.

The problem was made worse by the fact that the Mirages were sent to their forward operating base with prototype pods. The Litening test benches were in the factory in Haifa and Bangalore, while the original Mirage test benches were in Gwalior. The whole cyclical process had to be coordinated between Air Headquarters, the Defence Attaché's office in Tel Aviv, and other agencies, while software changes were "tweaked" every day. Even though the locations were far apart, the results showed that time was very tight during actual operations and that there was a time zone difference of 02:30 hrs.

The airstrikes on Muntho Dalo (16,500 feet), Tiger Hill (17,000 feet), and Point 4388 in the Drass sector stood out among the 240 attack missions flown by Mirages. On June 16, a Mirage on the Litening pod saw a large supply and logistics depot at Muntho Dalo in the Batalik sector. The next day, four Mirages hit this target and blew it up. Also on June 24, a Mirage LGB hit the Battalion Headquarters on top of Tiger Hill. Soon after, four more LGBs hit Tiger Hill during the day and night. The Indian Army took back Tiger Hill on July 4 with the help of these airstrikes. A veteran Pakistan Air Force (PAF) pilot named Group Captain Kaiser Tufail wrote in his blog about the Kargil War and the PAF:

> *"By June 16, [the] IAF was able to open up the laser guided bombing campaign with the help of Jaguars and Mirage 2000 [...] The Mirage 2000 scored at least five successful laser guided bomb hits on forward dumping sites and posts."*

Even though the brave young officers, jawans, pilots, and ground crew were the real heroes of this short but difficult campaign, the software engineers and other "backstage boys" who were responsible for making this weapons system work in record time and under very difficult conditions should also be recognised for their important work. A senior IsAF test pilot told me this was true, and he thanked the IAF because the IsAF had also bought the same Litening pod and was testing its performance. In this case, though, the IAF just skipped the whole process and put a key piece of equipment to use right away.

Cooperation in Space Technologies

Israel was interested in working with the Indian Space Research Organisation (ISRO) on joint programmes as a way to strengthen its relationships with other countries and work closely with scientists. In January 2002, Shimon Peres, who was at the time Deputy Prime Minister and Foreign Minister, went to ISRO. In November 2002, the head of Israel's Space Research Program at the time, Col. Aby Har-Even, and the head of ISRO at the time, Dr. K. Kasturiarangan, signed a deal to work together in space. With strong political will on both sides, these protocols became the real tools that made it possible to push the envelope even further. So, in January 2008, ISRO launched TecSAR, an Israeli surveillance satellite with SAR technology. Then, from the Sriharikota Space Centre, India launched the SAR imaging satellite RISAT-2, which was made in Israel, on a rocket called the Polar Satellite Launch Vehicle (PSLV), which was made in India. Space cooperation continues to show off the technological skills of both countries because of how well their technologies work together and how well they do in certain niches. In the next 10 years, cooperation is likely to get better in programmes related to other space applications, such as the cyber domain.

Counter-Terror Cooperation

On a different note, Judaism was one of the first religions from outside India that was written about (AD 68). On the other side, the Sufi saint Baba Farid went to the Holy Land in the 13th century and meditated in the Holy city of Jerusalem, where the Indian Hospice is now. More importantly, Indian Jews are a religious minority, but unlike in many other parts of the world, they have never been treated badly or hated because they are Jewish. Most Indian Jews moved to Israel after 1948, but new Jewish communities were started in Mumbai, New Delhi, and Bangalore at the start of the 21st century. The Chabad-Lubavitch movement set up these communities and sent Rabbis to meet the religious and social needs of Jewish business people, tourists, and Israeli backpackers (about 40,000 of whom visit India every year). The Nariman House in Mumbai is the centre with the most people.

On November 26, 2011, terrorists attacked this very Nariman House in Colaba. Ten Lashkar-e-Taiba (LeT) terrorists took over the building, and several people who lived there were taken hostage. Both terrorists were killed in the security action that followed, but not before they killed Rabbi Gavriel Holzberg, his wife Rivka, who was six months pregnant, and four other hostages. Pakistani jihadi groups had a clear plan to go after Indian and Israeli interests when they attacked Chabad House and other places in Mumbai, killing 166 civilians in horrible ways. In this situation, it's important to remember what National Security Advisor (NSA) Brijesh Mishra said in 2003 at the American Jewish Committee (AJC) about how India, Israel, and the US could work together to fight extremism. Mishra pointed out that "such an alliance would have the political will and moral authority to make bold decisions in extreme cases of terrorist provocation."

Israel offered help with Homeland Security (HLS) in 2009, and the Maharashtra government sent a delegation to get hands-on experience. This was in addition to forming a Joint Working Group (JWG) on counterterrorism, which got a big boost after 26/11. From a bigger picture point of view, both India and Israel face major threats to their national security. Given that both India and Israel see Islamist terrorism as a threat (though from different angles) and that managing borders to stop infiltration is hard, intelligence sharing, HLS cooperation, training, and the development of counter-terrorism strategies are likely to be important parts of future security ties between India and Israel.

Progress in Strategic Exchanges

Over the past 20 years, there has been a slow but steady change in the level, scope, and nature of defence ties between the two countries. The defence departments of both countries have taken a practical approach that is backed by strong political support and has no extreme positions. After the fall of the Soviet Union, it was important for India to make technological progress and become self-sufficient. However, India was not able to do this on its own. It needed help and participation from outside sources right away. Israel, on the other hand, had some advantages that no other arms supplier had. Among these were its experience with weapons and systems from both sides of the Cold War, its no-questions-asked policy in the arms trade, its reputation as a reliable supplier, and its knowledge of how to improve and create new technologies.

Also, Israel needed new defence markets to keep its defence industries financially stable. This need has led Israeli defence companies to form joint ventures with Indian firms and other public sector organisations (PSUs) that want to increase their market share by forming "production and manufacturing partnerships" and take advantage of domestic market opportunities. At the same time, the Israeli government has actively supported the commercialization of technologies that can be used for both civilian and military purposes by giving money to these businesses.

With growing confidence and a shared goal to find workable solutions, the processes have been formalised through a Joint Working Group (JWG) between the respective Ministries of Defence and a Sub-Working Group (SWG) on Defence Procurement, Production, and Development between DG, Acquisition, MoD, and his Israeli counterpart, Director SIBAT (Hebrew acronym for International Defence Cooperation Directorate). Functional engagement between the Service Headquarters in the form of Staff Talks is also a good way to share domain knowledge and expertise in areas like training, safety, and working together.

It is interesting to note that the IAF's increased use of US-made platforms (C-130J Special Operations aircraft, C-17 strategic airlift aircraft, Apache attack helicopters, Chinook heavy lift helicopters, and their associated weapon systems and communication protocols) gives them some things in common with IsAF platforms. It is thought that in the not-too-distant future, joint bilateral exercises and training between the two services could help boost the potential power of aerospace even more. Also, recent political events have shown how important the Indian Ocean Region (IOR) is to India's security. This means that any move towards cooperation between the two navies needs to be looked at more closely.

Israel's strategic community has been pushing for expanding the range and power of its navy, in addition to developing its highly effective and powerful air power. In general, the Israeli strategic community is becoming more and more interested in the sea, both to gain depth and to set up a 332 N. A. K. Browne nuclear second-strike force based on submarines. Saar-5 Corvettes from the Israeli Navy, which can stay at sea for a long time, have been seen in the Indian Ocean. In fact, Israel wants to triple the number of submarines it has and build more Saar-5 Corvettes. In this situation, it is important for both countries to have access to the energy corridors that go through the IOR and to be able to deal with the fact that some of the coasts around it are becoming more unstable. This calls for more interoperability, cooperation, and access to the region. Overall, these changes would be very interesting to watch, not just in West Asia but also in the Asian subcontinent, especially in India's immediate neighbourhood.

Wide-Ranging Relationship

Still, a number of strategists and policy experts have gone out of their way to say that "the changing relationship is not a military alliance." According to P. R. Kumaraswamy, neither side wants to get involved in the regional conflict of the other. Both countries say that their defence ties are only meant to improve their own defence capabilities and stability, not to hurt anyone else. 16 Within this framework, it's easy to figure out the compulsions, which are also limitations, and why certain activities need to be in sync with their core interests. A trip to Israel as Chairman of the Chiefs of Staff Committee (COSC) and Chief of the Israeli Air Force (IAF) in January 2013 confirmed this. I was lucky enough to not only see the growing ties from a realist point of view, but also see how quickly this relationship has changed over the years, in the context of a changed West Asian landscape. Even though the geopolitical environment had a lot of problems, it also had some good things for both sides. Luckily, the last 20 years have given this important relationship the support it needs and laid the groundwork for a stable, long-lasting, and, most importantly, consistent defence and security policy that will guide it.

But, as shown above, defence ties have not been one-dimensional. The two countries have worked together on things like defence and security, as well as trade and commerce, agriculture, science and technology, education, and cultural ties. Bilateral trade has grown a lot since 1992, when it was only $200 million. It now tops $5 billion. Agriculture may be the field that has benefited the most from these relationships. There is a "plan of action" for 2015–2018 that includes moves into new fields like dairy and water management. Several agricultural centres of excellence have been set up in states like Haryana, Rajasthan, and Gujarat, among others. India has benefited from Israeli know-how in horticulture mechanisation, micro-irrigation, and post-harvest management, as well as from partnerships and joint funding. Also, high-level political contacts have kept the relationship between the two countries moving forward. President Pranab Mukherjee's historic visit to Israel in 2015, where he also spoke to the Knesset, was followed by a reciprocal visit by Israeli President Reuven Rivlin in November 2016, followed by a visit by External Affairs Minister Sushma Swaraj in early 2016, and will be followed by a visit by Prime Minister Narendra Modi in July 2017. These visits show that both countries have similar goals.

Indian Defence Industry

India's modern military industry is very diverse. India has been buying weapons for a number of political, economic, and security reasons. India has been in several armed conflicts with its neighbours in the past. This led the government to try to increase both the production of military equipment in India and the import of arms.

It was thought that India needed a strong military to deal with threats from the outside, to back up its position in world affairs, to strengthen its fight for regional power status, for national prestige, and to fulfil its wish to be known as a technologically advanced country.

India has always had the goal of being able to take care of itself. The two most important parts of becoming self-reliant have been protecting against any disruptions in the supply of spare parts caused by changes in the international political system and putting in place systems that are suited to the unique conditions of the subcontinent, such as the high altitudes of the Himalayan mountains, the heat and dust of the Rajasthan desert, and the high ambient temperature of the Indian ocean. Indian military and industrial leaders have tried to get cutting-edge weapons not only to keep up with technology but also to show that India's capabilities are on par with those of industrialised countries. Local production based on native designs was also meant to help the country's balance of payments and give jobs to people with scientific and technical skills who might have looked for work abroad otherwise. Native designs were also meant to boost India's reputation around the world and save money on foreign exchange.

When its main supplier, the Soviet Union, broke up, India knew it had to make its military manufacturing complex stronger by making weapons on its own. India works hard to be technologically independent, but it still imports a lot of important systems and parts. India's defence officials said that they needed as many as 100,000 spare parts to fix Soviet-made planes, tanks, guns, missiles, naval ships, and other weapons. Light Combat Aircraft (LCA), Main Battle Tank (MBT), Arjun, and Advanced Light Helicopter are all made in India, but a lot of their parts come from other countries.

Each of the three services (Army, Navy, and Air Force) needs new equipment. This includes new fighter planes, frigates, submarines, and missile systems, as well as new transports, helicopters, and electronic warfare systems. It also needs to improve its air defence and communication systems. Also, the military has had a hard time modernising because it hasn't had enough money.

India, on the other hand, is speeding up its plan to become self-sufficient. Since there were problems with buying from Russia, it was important to buy from other places. Many people looked at the Israeli offer in this way, thinking that it would be free of any strings. India could ask Israel for help and technology in both dangerous and non-dangerous areas where Israel has done good work. It included weapons, systems, and support equipment like radar, electronic warfare equipment, and a variety of engineering items used for border fencing. Israelis are very good at making weapons better. The biggest benefit of working with Israel in the military is that most of its technology is made there, which makes it easy to transfer technology without any problems for the end user. India can't buy as much military gear as it would like because it doesn't have enough money. So, the answer is to improve the weapons that are already there and get more powerful weapons.

Industrialisation of Israeli Military

Israel built up its armed industry mainly because of security concerns, its susceptibility to being manipulated by (embargoes), national pride, the need for high-tech jobs, and the chance to replace imports with exports.

Israel has gotten to the point where it can make a lot of its own weapons. Israeli weapons also included small arms, ammunition, and communication devices, as well as force multipliers, remotely controlled vehicles, electronic and anti-electronic warfare systems, night vision devices, and a wide range of naval equipment, such as command and control systems, missiles, and anti-missile systems, and patrol boats. Radar, avionics, and command and control systems are all fields in which Israeli high-tech companies are known to be among the best in the world.

Israel's defence companies have found a technological niche for which they are becoming known around the world. This is helping them upgrade weapons systems. In the beginning, Israel's defence industry was mostly focused on making basic weapons like tanks, fighter planes, artillery, and patrol boats. Now, it is putting more effort into making advanced electronic subsystems instead of making new platforms. By focusing on advanced electronic subsystems, Israel's military industry has made a lot of technologically advanced parts that give 20 or 30 year old weapon systems new life and a quality edge and improve the capabilities of fighter aircraft, helicopters, combat vehicles, and command, control, communication, and intelligence systems.

Earnings from exporting weapons are seen as important for three reasons: first, the health of Israel's defence industries, which are a key part of the country's security; second, the stability of Israel's economy; and third, the funding of R&D, which helps Israel stay on the cutting edge of weapons technology. Also, the costs of building many Israeli projects depend on how much money they make from exports. "If there was no hope of exports, some projects would not have been started. Without exports, some businesses would go out of business and some projects would have to be scrapped ". The Israeli arms industry is able to do well because it can sell weapons to other countries.

When it comes to relations with India, Israel's main policy goal is to get closer and work together more with New Delhi. During Israeli President Ezer Weizman's trip to India, Israeli Aircraft Industries (IAI) Director of Corporate Communications Doron Suslik said that India is one of Israel's most important markets. He said that Israel would meet India's needs for both military and civilian planes, as well as its needs for high technology and computer software. The way Israel did things couldn't be called "in a donor's mode." Businesspeople in Weizman's group made it clear that they wanted to work with Indian companies not just to sell Israeli goods, but also to create and improve new software and technologies that they could sell to other third world countries.

Military Cooperation between India and Israel

India and Israel's goals brought them both to the world stage and made them good partners in the military area.

India's first Prime Minister, Jawahar Lai Nehru, set up the basic structure of the relationship between India and Israel. He kept the relationship low-key because he valued the relationship with the Arab countries more, but the Israeli government still tried from time to time to improve the relationship. All of New Delhi's different governments have been polite to visiting officials without raising the level of their diplomatic representations. They have also asked Israel for help with military issues. Before they had full diplomatic relations, the two countries worked together in secret on military and intelligence matters. Three months after the border fight with China, in January 1963, the Indian government was ready to talk to Israeli military experts about military issues. The Israeli Chief of Army Staff and the Chief of Military Intelligence were then invited to New Delhi to talk with India's top military leaders, including the Chief of Army Staff.

In the years that followed, Israeli dignitaries like Yigal Alon, a member of the Israeli cabinet in 1965, and Moshe Dayan, a general in 1977, made trips to India. "The Indian Research and Analysis Wing (RAW) and its Israeli counterpart, the Mossad, also worked together for a long time (Israeli secret agency). Even when Indira Gandhi was prime minister (1966–1977 and 1980–1984) and Rajiv Gandhi was prime minister (1984–1989), people worked together in this way.

Other sources also showed that India was in touch with Israel behind the scenes. A controversial book called "By Way of Deception" by Victor Ostrovsky, a former Israeli agent and expert on testing weapons who was hired by Mosad, says that in 1984, India sent a group of top nuclear scientists on a secret mission to Israel. He said that the secret Indian mission went to Israel to get information from there.

India and Israel have had diplomatic ties since 1992. Since then, there have been more than 50 military visits, contacts, and consultations between the two countries. When talking about defence ties, Israel was more open, and it even offered to help India with defence issues. Israel was eager to work with India on making weapons and fighting terrorism, but the Indian government was slow to respond. Minister of State for Defence S. Krishna Kumar said, "There was no proposal, initiative, or offer for any kind of defence ties with that country. This topic had not even been formally discussed in the Defence Ministry."

The main reason for this was India's traditional policy towards the Arab world, which was based on two important factors. First, because Arab countries send India the most oil and the most money in hard currency from NRIs (Non Resident Indians), India didn't want to upset them by making diplomatic ties with a country that was against them. Second, Congress did not give up on the idea that having diplomatic ties with Israel would hurt its chances of getting elected at home by making Muslims angry.

Even though at first the Indian government didn't want to talk about military cooperation in public, it couldn't hide its desire to get help from Israel. Defence Minister Sharad Pawar said that the formal establishment of full diplomatic ties between India and Israel made it possible to use Israel's successful experience to stop terrorism. And that India would like to learn more about how Israel has developed technology to help fight terrorism. Krishna Kumar also said, "Technically, no country could be left out of this, and Israel had some defence capabilities that were worth noting." By the middle of 1992, India and Israel had made a lot of progress towards working together on military issues. A six-person Israeli defence team went to India and met with officials from several ministries. The Ministry of Defence (MOD) had asked the team to come, but they didn't say what they talked about. This visit, which happened only five months after India and Israel set up full diplomatic relations, was a big sign of how quickly relations between the two countries were improving.

From both sides, there were sometimes signs of hope. In an interview, Prime Minister of Israel, Yitzhak Rabin talked very positively of defence ties with India. "I think India could join if they want to. We are more than willing to work with India on defence issues whenever and wherever it makes sense for India. Rabin had said that they had been affected by fundamentalism and terrorism for a long time and that this was also India's main concern. After the bombings in Bombay, J. N. Dixit went to Tel Aviv, which added to the idea that the two countries might want to work together to fight terrorism.

In May 1993, Shimon Peres, who was then the Israeli foreign minister, went to India. Peres also talked about terrorism and India's right to be independent. He also agreed with what India said about Kashmir. "We agree with the Shimla Agreement and fully support India's right to keep its territory as it is."

In the first week of April 1995, General Helz Bodinger was in India. During his visit, India was offered a package deal that included Airborne Warning and Control Systems, Remotely Piloted Vehicles, access to an air platform for anti-detection and anti-jamming manoeuvres, and specialised weapons. In July 1995, a high-level

Indian team led by K. A. Nambiar, who was the Defence Secretary, went to Israel. The Defence Secretary had to go because it was important to find the avionics and weapons systems for the MIG-21 Bis, which was being upgraded for India as part of a joint venture between India and Russia. Upgrade talks for the Russian T-72 tank were also on the list of things to talk about. India was also interested in Remotely Piloted Vehicles at that time.

In January 1997, President Ezer Weizman went to India. He pointed out that India could be a partner in the aircraft business. During his trip, the two countries decided to swap military attaches. After the meeting, top Indian officials went to Israel to look at advanced defence systems. Scientists from India's top defence ministry were also said to have gone to Israel in secret to look at satellite and missile programmes. In May 1998, just after India tested its nuclear weapons, a high-level group from the IAI went on a tour of India. The goal was to speed up the sale of Israeli anti-ship missiles that don't need a pilot.

In February 1997, T. K. Banerjee, who was India's Defence Secretary, led a high-level defence group to Israel. From March 8-13, 1998, the Chief of Army Staff, General V. P. Malik, went to Israel. India's military attache, Col. Brown, said that it was a friendly visit. "We hope to build a strong defence relationship that will last for a long time."

IAI made a big deal with India in 1998 to sell Advanced Electronic Equipment (AEEA). The equipment was made in Israel, and there was no American technology in it. Israel and India have been talking about AEE for more than a year, and an Indian delegation went to Israel to check out the equipment. Due to India's nuclear tests in May 1998, the US was against the mis deal. It told Israel that it had to stop these talks. After India did nuclear tests, the US started to put pressure on Israel. Before that, the US didn't object to arms deals between India and Israel. The US says that the deal broke an international treaty on limiting arms. The US tried to get Israel to stop selling AEE to India, but Israel did not agree. Officials from Israel told New Delhi that contracts worked out over the past year would be kept. A later report said that Israel sold India advanced electronic warfare systems even though the US tried to stop the deal after India did nuclear tests in May 1998. The report didn't say much, but it did say that it was for defence. A representative for IAI also wouldn't say anything.

During the recent events in Kashmir, Israel agreed to speed up shipments of arms and military equipment to India after the Indian government asked them to do so. The Indian government had already put in orders for arms before the recent events. The Israeli military establishment gave a good answer.

In recent years, India and Israel have worked together a lot on security issues. Prime Minister Ehud Barak is interested in how relations with India are going, and he has even held a special debate on the subject. There are two ways for the two countries to talk to each other: one is between their foreign ministries, and the other is between their defence ministries. At regular meetings, the two sides talk about how things are going in the Middle East and Asia.

At the heart of the relationship between India and Israel seemed to be the fact that they both had a similar view of how the world's politics worked. Both have strong and hostile neighbours on all sides. A high-level Israeli official said, "We found a common language the day we set up diplomatic relations seven years ago." He said that there was a strong agreement between the two countries to talk in a smooth and clear way.

Some of the ongoing programmes in India aren't all that different from the ones in Israel. Some of them are the Light Combat Aircraft (LCA) (Israel's Lavi), the Arjun (Israel's Merkava), the Prithvi (Israel's Jericho I), and the Agni (Jericho II). The same can be said about a number of other Indian programmes, such as Remotely Piloted Vehicles, the Airborne Early Warning System, and anti-ballistic missile systems. Israel can help India in this way because Israeli weapons are more advanced and have been used in battle.

Areas of Cooperation

Upgrades to Aircraft

MiGs: Since the early 1990s, India has been working to improve its fleet of MiGs. In order to upgrade the old MiG-21s, which would be replaced by the LCA in the early part of the next decade (2005–2020), the Indian Ministry of Defence looked at proposals from several countries, including France, Russia, and Israel, as well as a joint proposal from two state-owned Indian aerospace manufacturers (Hindustan Aeronautics Limited (HAL) and Aeronautical Development Agency) (ADA). During the same year, Israel worked harder to get the lucrative contract to upgrade the MiG-21bis planes used by the IAF. Industry sources say that representatives from IAI and Elta, which is a part of IAI that makes electronic weapons systems, have met with high-level officials from the defence ministry several times. Even though the IAI package was pricey, Israel insisted that it was technically better than the Russian package.

According to Jane's Defence Weekly, India's choice of avionics comes from a number of different companies, and Israel was supposed to improve the layout of the MiG-21 cockpit by adding a head-up display. During the same year, it was said that the IAI had been given the contract to install the electronic warfare equipment in the IAF's MiG upgrade. But according to the most recent news, Russia is in the process of upgrading two Mig-21 planes. After that, the rest of the planes will be upgraded in India.

LCA Programme

India's Comptroller and Auditor General says that the LCA programme, which has been going on for 17 years and has been delayed by more than a decade, still has a lot of technical problems and cost overruns (CAG). The CAG report said that almost every important part of the plane was late, which forced the Indian Air Force (IAF) to upgrade around 125 MiG 21 bis fighters as a stopgap measure to make up for the lack of planes. The LCA was supposed to start replacing the Mig 21s, which are the most important planes in the IAF, by the late 1990s. The LCA's airframe, its multimode radar, and its flight control system are all late.

Also, the first two LCA prototypes were to be powered by US General Electric F404-FJ23 engines, which were bought in 1986 for the prototypes despite objections from the US government after Washington put sanctions on India for its 1998 nuclear tests. The US engines would eventually be replaced by the Kaveri, which was made in Russia and has been tested a lot there. 45 Dr. A. P. J. Abdul Kalam, who is head of the DRDO and the government's scientific adviser, said that each LCA was expected to cost $22 million and that participation from other countries would bring the cost down to $15–$18 million.

Israeli knowledge of avionics, airframes, and putting the engine and weapons inside the airframe can help with the development of the LCA.

Helicopters that are getting better: The 1998 nuclear tests in India caused Washington to put sanctions on India, which hurt the development of Advanced Light Helicopters (ALH). Because the ALH could no longer get its turbo shaft engine from the US because of the US embargo, almost all work on it stopped. It was suggested that the government quickly find a new engine supplier and stop doing business with companies in countries that impose sanctions. Again, Israeli technology and know-how can be used to solve problems in this area.

AWACS stands for Airborne Warning and Control System. India was eager to work with Israel on the project to build its own AWACS. The IAI sent a proposal to the Defence Research and Development Organisation (DRDO) about the chances of working together on the project. Sources from the Ministry of Defence say that Israel offered to sell three AWACS planes to India. But finally, in a recent move, Russia sent two advanced early warning aircraft to the Indian Air Force. They have arrived at the airbase in Chandigarh. One version of the plane is a joint project between Russia and Israel, according to information that has been made public. Even though India's Centre for Airborne Systems is working on an Airborne Early Warning System for the Indian military, the recent Pakistan-backed invasion of Kargil has made the need for AWACS even more urgent. India needed the planes quickly because it had to keep a close eye on anything that moved in Indian and Pakistani airspace, along the Line of Control, and at the international borders. The Kargil war showed how important it is to have the latest surveillance technology.

Surveillance Technologies and UAVs

UAVs are seen more and more as strategic force multipliers because they can send data and pictures from deep inside enemy territory in real time while avoiding enemy radars. It can give information about where the enemy's forces are, what kind of weapons and equipment they are using, and how ready they are to defend their borders.

Israel is one of the top countries in the world when it comes to making UAVs. The Israeli UAVs are a lot smaller and lighter, which makes them easier to move and gives them more strategic value. IAI, a well-known player in the UAV market, has shown that there is a big chance to export. In June 1995, Israel showed off its widest range of UAVs at an air show in Paris.

One of the most important areas of defence cooperation between India and Israel has been surveillance from the air. India and Israel have already made a deal for unmanned aerial vehicles (UAVs) that will help India's air surveillance arm. Both countries are looking into ways to make UAVs together. The talks about a possible joint production of the UAV "Heron" for the Indian Navy are already well along. The "heron" is the most modern UAV made by IAI. It has a longer range and a more advanced payload than the "searcher," which India agreed to buy from Israel in 1996. The latest news says that India is getting ready to buy UAVs from Israel that are more advanced and have a longer range. This will help India keep a closer eye on the high altitude ranges in Jammu and Kashmir that border Pakistan. After what happened in Kargil, getting UAVs has become even more important. The IAF thought that it was one of their most important needs. The head of the Indian Air Force, A. Y. Tipnis, confirmed that the IAF had pushed for the UAVs to be used right away so that humans could get more information about the high altitude ranges along the line of control in the Kargil sector, which are 140 km long and hard to reach. The Indian military already has a few UAVs, which were used during the Kargil War. Unfortunately, the UAVs were not as effective as world-class UAVs, which is mostly because not many international UAV manufacturers make high altitude UAVs.

In terms of the RPVs, the MOD and Israel have reached the last stage of the deal. India planned to buy RPVs all at once, including the transfer of technology, which would not only meet India's operational needs but also help the country's own RPV project grow.

India has bought important tools like UAVs, AWACS, and radars to improve its military's ability to keep an eye on things. India has used unmanned aerial vehicles (UAVs) made in Israel to improve its security operations along its coast and to keep its own people safe. India bought more than 150 UAVs made by Israel Aerospace Industries. These were the Searcher and Heron models (IAI). The second one is a medium-altitude long-endurance (MALE) UAV that can fly nonstop for more than 50 hours. The first one can only fly for up to 18 hours. The Western Naval Command put together its first UAV squadron in January 2011 at Porbandar, Gujarat. The UAVs were bought from Israel. This was five years after the first UAV squadron was put together at Kochi.

The then Chief of Naval Staff, Admiral Arun Prakash, inaugurating the Kochi squadron, stated that the Israeli UAVs were being inducted after three years of flying trials and that the Indian Navy was 'now amongst the pioneers in the esoteric art of UAV operation at sea'. Admiral Prakash emphasized that the Israeli assets would enhance the country's 'maritime domain awareness manifold'. A third UAV squadron made up of Searchers and Herons was set up along the Tamil Nadu coast in 2012. In 2019, India reportedly signed a $500 million contract with the IAI for 50 additional Heron UAVs.

Apart from the Herons and the Searchers, the IAI also has in its stable, the Heron-Turbo Prop (TP) unmanned combat aerial system (UAS). It is described as an advanced multi-role, long range, MALE UAV for 'strategic missions', equipped with satellite communication systems, automatic take-off and landing, an endurance of more than 30 hours and capable of carrying a variety of lethal and surveillance payloads. As against the Heron, which has a payload weight of about 500 kg, the Heron-TP is advertised to carry multiple payloads five times that weight.

The maximum payload weight of the Searcher tactical UAV, meanwhile, is about 100 kg. The Israeli Air Force is the only Air Force currently operating the Heron-TP system.

Reports in mid-2018 noted that India had decided to procure at least ten Heron-TP drones, at a cost of $400 million, to enhance the country's 'cross-border military strike' capability. Pertinently, this alluded to possible usage of the drone across India's western front. Reports in 2021, however, noted that India will lease four Heron-TPs for use in the eastern sector, given the changed security situation along the China border. The leased Heron-TPs are reportedly non-lethal, to be used solely for surveillance purposes. By December 2021, these drones have reportedly been deployed on the border.

The leasing of the Heron-TPs was the second such procurement decision to make use of the leasing provisions of the Defence Acquisition Procedure 2020. Two General Atomic MQ-9B Sea Guardian drones have been leased by the Indian Navy. The IAI on its part is a veteran in leasing arrangements, with its drones leased to countries like Canada, Australia and Spain. India will have one of the few armed forces in the world to use the Heron-TP, apart from Israel. Reports in August 2021 also noted that the Indian armed forces will undertake a massive modernization exercise involving the Israeli UAV's in its arsenal, amounting to over Rs 5000 crores. The programme seeks to even arm previously-procured Herons as well as improve their surveillance capabilities.

Hindustan Aeronautics Limited (HAL), along with Dynamatic Technologies Limited (DTL), signed a strategic partnership agreement with the IAI at the Defence Expo 2020, for marketing, manufacture and sale of UAVs. HAL also signed an MoU with Elbit Systems for exploring the feasibility of joint development and production of 2000 kg vertical take-off and landing (VTOL) UAVs for both maritime and land-based operations for domestic as well as international customers.

The March 2004 deal with Elta for three Phalcon AWACS worth $1. 1 billion, has been one of the largest defence deals that India has concluded with Israel. The first and second AWACS aircraft were delivered in May 2009 and March 2010, while the third was delivered in mid-2011. The Rajya Sabha had been informed in May 2010 that procurement of additional AWACS aircraft was on the anvil.

India, though, is increasingly focusing on indigenous procurement of such assets. India has two indigenous airborne early warning and control (AEW&C) systems mounted on Embraer aircraft – Netra, in its inventory. The first of the aircraft was handed to the IAF in February 2017. The Netra aircraft took part in the Balakot surgical strikes in February 2019.

Meanwhile, reports in December 2020 noted that India intends to spend more than Rs 10,000 crores to equip its Air Force with six additional AWACS aircraft. The DRDO would acquire six Airbus aircraft from the Air India fleet (319/320/321), and equip them with indigenously developed active electronically scanned array (AESA) radars. The original Request for Proposal (RfP) for six AWACS was issued in 2014 but uncertainty over choice of the aircraft to mount the radar, among other issues, delayed the decision. In September 2021, the Cabinet Committee on Security (CCS) finally approved the Acceptance of Necessity (AoN) for the DRDO to issue the Request for Proposal (RfP) to procure the aircraft.

Apart from UAVs and AWACS, India has bought a whole range of radars from Israel for its aircrafts, ships and land forces. One of the earliest radars that India bought was the ground surveillance/battlefield surveillance radar (BFSR) EL/M-2140 in 1998, with the ability to detect tanks/vehicles/troops up to a range of 40 km. The range of the Israeli radars was subsequently expanded to enable beyond line-ofsight (LOS) detection. A large number of Elta's air search radars for use on frontline warships like frigates, destroyers and aircraft carriers have been procured. The EL/M-2221 fire control radar was bought for use along with the Barak-I surface-to-air missile (SAM) system, a point defence system installed on many warships.

Combat aircraft radars for purposes of modernization of aircraft like the Jaguars began to be procured from 1999 onwards. While the initial combat radars were 'mechanically steered array' (MSA) radars, Elta subsequently provided AESA radars (with the first Jaguar fitted with the radar flying in 2018), making the Jaguar the first combat aircraft in India's inventory to be fitted with these advanced radars.

Multi-mode radars, co-developed with Elta, have been integrated into the Light Combat Aircraft (LCA). The EL/M-2052 AESA radars replaced Elta's manual EL/M-2032 radars in the LCA, as indeed in aircraft such as Jaguar (in 2018 as noted above) and on Mirages in India's inventory. The LCA's Helmet-Mounted Display and Sight (HMDS) is also provided by the Israeli company, Elbit.

The contract with Rafael Advanced Defence Systems for two aerostat radars was entered into in 2002, at a cost of around Rs 676 crores ($145 million), to meet the requirements of low-level surveillance. The radars, positioned at a height of around 14,000 feet, can detect lowflying aircraft at a distance of 250 km. These were commissioned in 2007 and 2008, respectively.

The Aerial Delivery Research Development Establishment made the country's first aerostat radar, called Akashdeep. It was launched in 2010. (ADRDE). In October 2015, about 22 months after the project began in January 2014, Nakshatra made its first flight with improvements. But within a year, the project was over because of problems with the laminated fabric that was made in India and was used to make the balloon that held the radar. ADRDE officials, on the other hand, insisted that the Army would not pay for more user trials, so the project was put on hold. In February 2016, news articles said that the IAF wanted to buy at least six aerostat radars to meet its operational needs.

Main Battle Tank (MBT)

Another very important DRDO project is the design, development, and production of the Main Battle Tank, called Arjun, which is meant to replace the older Vijayanta tanks, which were made under licence. The MBT project started in the 1970s, and the first plan called for it to be used in the mid-1980s. But because technology has changed so much over the years, the army's needs for the tank have also changed, which has led to a change in costs. Indian defence industry sources say that the chassis for the Arjun MBT has had technical problems and cost increases. Again, Israeli know-how can be very helpful in this area because Arjun is the same as the Israeli tank Merkava.

Missiles

In 1983, India started its ambitious Integrated Guided Missile Development Program. This programme involved the design, development, and production of five missile systems: the Intermediate Range Ballistic Missile (IRBM) Agni, the surface-to-surface missile Prithvi, the short-range surface-to-air missile Trishul, the medium-range surface-to-air missile Aakash, and the anti-tank missile Nag. Israel has a large number of its own missiles, such as the Gabriel ship-to-ship missile, the Python air-to-air missile, the Popeye air-to-surface missile, the Jericho

I surface-to-surface missile, and the IRBM Jericho II. Before India's guided missile development programme started in the early 1980s, they were made and some were even used. This means they are more advanced and have been used in battle.

Israel is in a good position to help make missile defences work better and cost less. Media reports say that India is negotiating with Israel for missile technology to improve the launch and guidance systems of the Prithvi, a surface-to-surface missile made in India. India is also asking Israel for help with the electronics for its Sagarika missile, which is launched from a submarine.

India has also asked Israel for some technical help in making Akash, the country's own missile system. Pakistan's M-ll missiles are a threat, but these missiles can stop them. India is also getting help from Israel to make cutting-edge air-to-air missiles.

In January 2006, a contract worth Rs 2,600 crore was signed for the joint development of a long-range surface-to-air missile (LRSAM) for the Indian Navy (IN). The system has a range of 70 km and is used to protect points and large areas from threats like aeroplanes and missiles. In 2017, the first batch of five LRSAM missiles was given to the Indian Navy by the DRDO. In December 2015, the first test firing of the missile took place off the coast of Chennai. In January 2019, the LRSAM system was fired successfully from the INS Chennai and the INS Kolkata. This was called the Joint Target Coordination (JTC) firing. The last batch of products was given to the IN in February 2021. The dual-pulse rocket motor is part of the missile's "indigenous content." The Multi-Function Surveillance and Threat Alert Radar is made by the IAI (MF-STAR).

The Rs 10,000 crores contract for the joint development of mediumrange SAM (MRSAM) for the IAF was concluded in 2009. India and Israel signed a MoU worth $1. 6 billion for MRSAMs for use by the Indian Army in April 2017. The first test of the system was done in December 2020. The Indo-Israel joint venture, Kalyani Rafael Advanced Systems (KRAS), produces MRSAM missile kits for integration by the public sector Bharat Dynamics Limited (BDL). The IAF has also procured the Spyder low-level quick reaction surface-toair missile (LLQRM) systems equipped with Python and Derby missiles for protection against aerial targets, including aircraft, cruise missiles and UAVs.

The contract for the procurement of Barak-1 missiles for Indian Navy warships was signed in October 2014 with Rafael Advanced Defence Systems Ltd. , at a cost of Rs. 875. 49 crores. The Barak protects a wide range of ships, including destroyers and frigates. In September 2013, reports flagged shortages of missiles and the efforts to replenish them were facing difficulties, because of an anti-corruption probe by the Central Bureau of Investigation (CBI) against individuals who had allegedly received kickbacks for the October 2000 deal. The IAI was placed on the MoD blacklist in 2006, because of the CBI investigation. This impacted the procurement of missiles for the warships. Due to 'paucity of evidence', the CBI closed the case, paving the way for the Indian Navy to buy the missiles from IAI. While a special court accepted the closure report of the CBI in January 2017, it was not until April 2018, however, that Rafael was taken off the MoD's blacklist.

The orders for Spike anti-tank guided missiles (ATGMs) are a unique example of the dynamics associated with the India-Israel defence partnership. The December 2020 orders – as well as orders for more than 200 Spike missiles in the aftermath of the Balakot strikes in February 2019, signified operational imperatives guiding procurement decisions, amidst lack of viable, domestic alternatives.

These orders came despite the Government announcing in late 2017 – just ahead of Prime Minister Netanyahu's visit in January 2018– that it was not proceeding with importing the systems for the Indian armed forces, ostensibly in favour of inducting indigenous systems like the Nag. Reports in January 2018 flagged that the Army had an ominous shortage of ATGMs in its inventory – to the tune of nearly 70,000 ATGMs. When this report was brought to the attention of the Government in the Lok Sabha, Minister of State for Defence, Subhash Bhamre affirmed that the Government was taking appropriate measures to maintain 'desire(d) level of operational preparedness commensurate to the threat perception in a dynamic strategic scenario'.

In October 2014, India's Defence Acquisition Council (DAC), headed by the Raksha Mantri, gave the go-ahead for procuring 8,000 Spike ATGM, valued at over $500 million. The Acceptance of Necessity (AoN) for the missiles was given earlier in June 2009 for procuring 8356 missiles and 321 launchers under 'Buy and Make' category of the Defence Procurement Procedure with transfer of technology (ToT) to Bharat Dynamics Limited (BDL). The Spike missile was preferred over other competitors like the US-made Javelin ATGM. The Javelin offer by the US was a component of the Defence Trade and Technology Initiative (DTTI) for co-development and manufacture. The Request for Proposal (RfP) for the missiles was issued in April 2010.

The Spike saga unfolded in the backdrop of the huge requirement for third-generation ATGMs in the Indian armed forces, which had in its inventory second-generation ATGMs like the 'wire-guided' Russianmade Konkurs-M and the French Milan systems. The Government's auditor, the CAG, in 2010, also expressed concern over the Army continuing with its procurement of second- generation ATGMs like Milan, despite the availability of third-generation ATGMs globally.

Delays in development of indigenous ATGMs like the Nag, further added to the woes of the armed forces. The testing of the missile began as far back as the 1990s. In user trials specifically in desert conditions, problems with the missile's imaging infra-red (IIR) seeker guidance system were detected. After modifications, orders for over 400 missiles were placed by the Army in 2010.

Even as reports in 2015 indicated that the Spike deal was facing delays due to issues over price negotiations, India did go ahead with finalizing the contract and the stage was set for inducting the Israeli systems. The Spike RfP, issued in 2010, was, however, retracted on December 20, 2017. Defence Minister Nirmala Sitharaman informed Parliament that the decision was taken to encourage 'indigenous' development of the ATGM by the DRDO.

Reports said that the Nag missile was ready for use, and the final user trials were done in October 2020. Meanwhile, Indian start-ups like Tonbo Imaging Private Limited are making new, cheaper technologies for use in man-portable ATGMs. Systems like the Nag and the Spike use more expensive, cooled IIR seekers, but Tonbo made IIR seekers that didn't need to be cooled and were also lighter and better for man-portable ATGMs.

Assault weapons, Ammunition and Aircraft Parts

India and Israel have worked together on important equipment like UAVs, AWACS, radars, and missiles. They have also worked together on assault weapons, ammunition, niche aircraft parts, and other important equipment. The HAL has worked with Israeli companies and their subsidiaries, such as the IAI and Elbit Systems, for a long time. In 2003, HAL's Korwa plant signed a Memorandum of Understanding with Elbit subsidiary Elop Electro-Optics Industries Limited to make Head-Up Displays (HUD) for IAF planes. More than 500 of these screens have been put into IAF platforms like the Su-30MKI, Jaguar, and MiG-27M.

At the Aero India 2021, HAL entered into an agreement for digital overhead HUDs (used widely in transport aircraft) with the same company. IAI and HAL also have an agreement for the supply of main deck cargo doors for Boeing 737 aircraft. In joint development programmes, electronic warfare (EW) suites have been co-developed in association with Elisra, for the Light Combat Aircraft (LCA), Tejas. Elisra was also involved in co-developing the Dual Colour Missile Approach Warning System (DCMAWS) for the Su-30 MKI aircraft.

Artillery ammunition was developed by three ordnance factories (Ambajhari, Kanpur, and Chandrapur) in association with Israel Weapons Industries (IWI). 5. 56 mm Tavor assault rifles, for India's Special Forces, were bought in 2005, at a cost of $18 million. Israeli Smart, Precise Impact, Cost-Effective (SPICE) guided ammunition kits were used in the February 2019 Balakot air strikes by the Indian Air Force (IAF) inside Pakistan-occupied Kashmir (PoK). Reports in December 2020 noted that India ordered additional SPICE kits for $200 million, along with Spike ATGMs.

The Indian Army also uses the Negev NG-7 light machine gun (LMG). In 2020, over 16,000 of these guns were ordered to stop Pakistan from breaking the ceasefire at the Line of Control more often. In November 2021, SSS Defence, a division of Stumpp, Schuele and Somappa Springs Private Limited Ltd, beat out an Israeli company to upgrade a small number of AK-47 rifles for the Southwestern Command, which is based in Jaipur. In fact, SSS Defence is only the second private company to get orders from the MoD. The first was PLR Systems, which is part-owned by the Israel Weapons Industries (IWI).

Navy

IAI's "Super Dvora" Mark II, Fast Attack Craft is a project that India and Israel are working on together. India bought two Super Dvora Mark II attack boats in 1997, and it has the right to build four more. After that, the contract to make the boats was given to IAI's Ramta Division, Beersheba Shipyards limited, and Goa Shipyards limited. If India's efforts to make fast patrol boats work out, the two countries could work together to make up to 80 boats for India's Navy and Coast Guard.

Other reports say that Israeli companies have also updated the electronic warfare equipment on the aircraft carrier INS Viraat, which is part of the Indian Navy.

Maritime surveillance: Israel has offered the Indian Navy its advanced multimode maritime surveillance radar as a way to counter the threat from the Pakistani navy, which has P3C Orion maritime surveillance aircraft made in the US. David Traim, the IAI's Deputy Director of Elta Electronics, said that the Indian Defence Ministry has been given a proposal to give the radar to the Navy. The Israeli radar will meet most of the Navy's immediate needs, and it can be put on patrol helicopters.

Nuclear Issue

After India set off a nuclear bomb in May 1998, both India and Israel have been criticised, and unproven claims have been made that they work together in the nuclear field. The Indian diplomats didn't believe that Israel helped India with the tests in May. They also didn't believe that India and Israel worked together in the nuclear and missile fields. Ranjin Mathai, India's ambassador to Israel, said that his country didn't have any nuclear ties with Israel. The same thing was said by a spokesman for the Ministry of External Affairs. He said, "India and Israel worked together in different areas, but they had nothing to do with its nuclear programme." The same thing happened in Israel. Alon Ben David, a reporter for Israel's Army, said, "It is important to point out that the defence ties between India and Israel did not involve nuclear issues. Instead, they were only about the export of conventional arms."

In terms of how Israel reacted to India's nuclear tests, Israel's Foreign Ministry did not say that India's tests were wrong. Mr. Haim Koren, a spokesman for the Foreign Ministry, didn't say anything special about how Israel felt about India's tests. He also wouldn't say if Israel would put sanctions on India or re-evaluate the close military ties between the two countries. The Foreign Ministry of Israel, on the other hand, said, "Israel has signed the CTBT, which makes it illegal to test nuclear weapons or do any other kind of nuclear explosion. We hope that all states will join this treaty." There is, however, a group in Israel that thinks India's nuclear tests could be a threat to Israel in a roundabout way. Professor Gabriel Ben-Dor is an expert on security at Haifa University. He says that this was bad for Israel in many ways." First, it brings up the idea of punitive US action against India, which could be used as a model for similar action against Israel in the future. Second, the Indian tests are likely to give the Pakistani nuclear programme more momentum and legitimacy. The Pakistani nuclear programme is thought to be where the so-called Islamic bomb comes from." David Bar Illan, a spokesman for Prime Minister Benjamin Netanyahu, shared the same worry: "We are worried that Pakistani tests will make Tehran and Baghdad more likely to get nuclear weapons."

India's nuclear tests did not seem to change the way the two countries' militaries worked together. A report said that Israel was giving India information about Pakistan that it got from its spy satellite. In exchange, India let Israeli military intelligence experts do missions on Indian soil to keep an eye on points of interest. The deal on AEE was also made after the tests in May.

Defence Diplomacy and Military Exercises

Strong interactions between the defence forces are an important part of the strategic relationship between India and Israel. In September 2002, the first meeting of the Joint Committee on Defence Cooperation between India and Israel took place. As part of defence diplomacy, Indian naval ships have been going to Haifa all the time. In the last 25 years, ten heads of defence forces from each country have gone to the other country (See Appendix).

Joint working groups (JWGs) on defence cooperation, helmed by the respective MoDs, as well as consultations by the Foreign Ministries, are an essential feature of such institutionalized cooperation. The 16th round of Foreign Office Consultations, for instance, were held in December 2020, in virtual mode, where the entire gamut of the bilateral relations were reviewed, including issues relating to defence and security, water, counter-terrorism, cyber security, science and technology and innovation cooperation. At the 15th India-Israel Joint Working Group (JWG) on defence, held in Tel Aviv in October 2021, both countries agreed to set up a sub-working group (SWG) on defence industry cooperation. A SWG on Defence Procurement, Development and Production is functional.

Indian and Israeli forces also take part in joint exercises to learn from each other's best practices. The Blue Flag Exercises conducted by the Israeli Air Force (IsAF) are an important facet of Israel's military diplomacy. The first Blue Flag Exercises took place in November 2013 and since then the multilateral Exercises have acquired a quiet momentum. A 45-member Indian Air Force (IAF) contingent, including Garud commandos, along with a C-130J special operations aircraft, participated in these exercises for the first time in 2017. France, Germany, Greece, Italy, Poland and the United States were the other participating countries in the 2017 event.

While participation by other nations involved fighter aircraft at this event, India sent a special operations transport aircraft. Given the presence of Garud commandos, the C-130J was a tactical choice in order to enable them to be exposed to best counter-terrorism practices from the Israeli experience. Another factor that could have precluded participation of a fighter aircraft was the need for over-flight clearance from countries in the Gulf which did not have diplomatic relations with Israel. This factor, in the aftermath of the Abraham Accords of September 2020, has, however, significantly diminished. The Indian C-130J, meanwhile, reportedly had a stop-over in Egypt, on its journey to the Uvda Air Force Base, the base conducting the Blue Flag Exercises. Even prior to India's first ever participation in the Blue Flag Exercises, commentators had opined that the presence of American aircraft like the C-130J in India's inventory creates 'a certain degree of commonality with IsAF platforms'.

India's participation in the 2021 iteration of the Blue Flag Exercises saw the involvement of IAF's Mirage 2000 as well as Rafale aircraft. External Affairs Minster S. Jaishankar, who was also visiting Israel during that time, interacted with the fighter pilots participating in these exercises from other countries. After the event in Israel, the IAF contingent also participated in air exercises in Egypt. In March 2021, the IAF had also participated in air exercises in the United Arab Emirates (UAE) for the first time. The UAE exercises saw the participation of the US, French, Saudi Arabian, South Korean, and Bahraini air forces.

Joint military exercises play an important role in military forces getting familiar with the operating procedures and best practices of each country. While India does not conduct multilateral air exercises on its soil, it is a part of significant numbers of military exercises involving the armies, navies and air forces across the world. For Israel, the United States and countries in Europe continue to be the main training partners.

Commentators have also flagged the promise of naval exercises between India and Israel, given the mutual complementarities and interests of both countries in the waters of the Indian Ocean and the Mediterranean Sea. The Israeli Navy is a potent regional force. Israel, though a 'brown water' navy, is still equipped with significant naval capabilities in the form of the German-sourced Dolphin submarines as well as Saar-5 corvettes. Reports have also flagged that Israel has been testing long- range missiles in the waters of the Indian Ocean.

India and Israel, meanwhile, have had long-standing cooperation in the naval field. Apart from military diplomacy in the form of visits of Indian naval ships at the Haifa port, India secured Israeli patrol boats (Super Dvora Mk-11) in the 1990s. Niche Israeli equipment is an essential part of frontline Indian naval warships, including radars and point defence missiles like the Barak, as flagged in previous sections.

Analysts say that Israel is becoming more interested in the waters of the Indian Ocean, in addition to its main interests in the waters around it, like the Mediterranean Sea and the Red Sea. This is because of its ongoing rivalry with countries like Iran in the world of politics. India and Israel have similar goals when it comes to things like maritime terrorism and worries about the spread of weapons of mass destruction. India could also be a big help to the Israeli Navy if it needed help with logistics for its ships at sea. In the future, India and Israel could also look for ways to work together more on "non-contentious" issues like humanitarian aid, disaster relief, and protecting sea lanes of communication.

Enablers For Defence Cooperation

India bought specialised defence equipment from Israel because it needed to be able to deal with growing regional, cross-border, and internal security problems in a better way. In the last few decades, India's external security environment has become more difficult because of the terrorist threat from Pakistani safe havens, the cooperation between Pakistan and China in the strategic domain, such as sharing nuclear, missile, and defence technology, and China's increasingly aggressive actions along the Line of Actual Control (LAC) and on India's borders. Defence Minister George Fernandes, for example, knew about Chinese work on electronic surveillance equipment on the Coco Islands as early as 1998. This work had been going on since 1994.

The 1999 Kargil conflict highlighted gaps in surveillance and intelligence capabilities of the armed forces. The 26/11 terror strikes in Mumbai highlighted gaps in coastal surveillance. Even successful cross-border strikes as in Balakot in February 2019, as well as India's recent border tensions with China, revealed the need for multiple systems for greater effectiveness. The modernization requirements of India's armed forces, meanwhile, continue to be gargantuan. Israel's niche technological prowess, in supplying key equipment like avionics, radars, missiles, point defence systems, among others, has gelled well with the country's requirements of these niche equipment.

The failure of developmental efforts of indigenous weapons systems has led India to procure similar equipment from Israel. India's indigenous efforts to develop an aerial surveillance platform (ASP), for instance, got a jolt, when an Avro HS-748 test aircraft, crashed in January 1999. The DRDO had initiated the ASP programme in 1985, at a cost of Rs 52. 09 crores. After the crash, Defence Minister Jaswant Singh informed Parliament that the programme was 'short-closed'. Defence Minister George Fernandes in April 2000 admitted that delays in indigenous development of critical technologies as well as sanctions imposed after India conducted the nuclear tests in 1998 had negatively impacted a wide range of programmes. These included the light combat aircraft (LCA), remotely piloted vehicle (RPV) Nishant, anti-tank missile system, Nag and the integrated electronic warfare (EW) system for the Army. Fernandes informed the Rajya Sabha in August 2000 that 'technological problems associated with indigenous developments' were responsible for the delay in the development of Nishant pilotless aircraft. The procurement of the Israeli Barak point defence system was an essential requirement to protect frontline assets of the Indian Navy, given that the indigenous Trishul system failed in user trials. Defence Minister Manohar Parrikar, while touting the indigenous achievements of the DRDO, in response to a query in Parliament in 2016, did note that the import content of the indigenously developed AEW&C system (excluding the Embraer aircraft) was still pegged at 16 per cent.

The CAG in 2018 pointed out that there was 'inordinate delay' in the indigenous development of UAVs by the DRDO. Those that were developed 'failed to meet the requirements of the Indian Army'. The CAG also pointed out that delays in development of MALE UAVs 'adversely affected the aerial surveillance capabilities of the Indian Army'. The MALE UAV project was sanctioned in February 2011 with a total cost of over Rs 1500 crores but the 2018 CAG report noted that there were 'multiple issues' with the development project, including with the airframe, line replaceable units (LRU), engine and payload. Reports highlighting the conclusion of a strategic partnership agreement between the IAI, HAL and Dynamatic Technologies Limited (DTL) in February 2020 pointed out that the Rustom-II MALE UAV being indigenously developed by the DRDO crashed during flight trials in September 2019.

As with the UAVs, India had to procure Israeli radars due to nonavailability of similar domestically developed products for optimum surveillance coverage on its Western borders. The DRDO lab, the Aerial Delivery Research Development Establishment (ADRDE), first tested an indigenous aerostat radar (Aakashdeep) in December 2010. Audit reports have also highlighted delays in execution of projects due to inconsistencies in monitoring of the projects, change of requirements by the user and lack of cohesion among multiple agencies executing the projects. The CAG Report No. 38 in 2015, for instance, highlighted the closure of several radar projects like Rohini, Aslesha, and Revathy by the DRDO.

Even as successive Israeli governments have nurtured strategic ties with India assiduously, the transfer of some of the niche Israeli equipment was not vetoed by the United States, which was involved in developing some of the niche equipment that India procured from Israel. The US, for instance, vetoed the sale of the Phalcon AWACS to China. Israel went back on the 1998 contract to supply AWACS to Beijing in July 2000, on account of American pressure and had to even pay a penalty for its decision.

It is equally true that the US vetoed the sale of sophisticated missile defence systems like the Arrow to India. India's request for Arrow followed its open embrace of President George W. Bush's missile defence plans. The Bush administration championed missile defence as an effective deterrent to face the threats posed by the 'rogue' states like Iran, Iraq and Libya, especially so in the aftermath of the September 2001 terror strikes in New York.

The US Department of State in July 2002 acknowledged that there was an Israeli request for transferring the Arrow system to India but that it gives importance to strategic stability in South Asia and to the Missile Technology Control Regime (MTCR). Analysts noted that India evaluating the Arrow was in the context of plugging gaps in its air defence architecture, and that it preferred the system over comparative systems from Russia like the S-300. India did become a member of the MTCR in June 2016 and has since procured an even more advanced version, the S-400, from the Russian Federation.

This deal continues to be under the sanctions cloud of the US, following the passage of the Comprehensive American Sanctions and Divestment Act (CAATSA) in July 2017, on account of Russia's actions in Ukraine, among other places. Apart from India, Turkey's decision to go in for the S-400 system, has invited American backlash. Ankara had to suffer consequences, including being shut out of the F-35 programme, in which it had a significant part.

Interactions between the foreign policy and national security establishments of both India and the US, meanwhile, are a continuing process to overcome the disadvantages posed by CAATSA. This, even as India-US defence trade has grown by leaps and bounds in recent times. The extent to which US sanctions targeting Russia for its February 2022 invasion of Ukraine would affect India-Russia defence trade, remains to be seen. Reports say that US sanctions could hit deliveries of the S-400 as well as other key procurement programmes like Talwarclass frigates (which are equipped with engines made in Ukraine).

Israel was able to address India's growing defence requirements given its capabilities in such niche technology areas like UAVs and surveillance systems. Elta's AESA radar used in the Phalcon system, for instance, was touted as superior to that of mechanically rotating antennas, then used widely, endowing the system with 'greater operational flexibility ...'

The prowess of the Israeli systems was in contrast to the capabilities of other comparable systems that India tested in trials. Defence Minister George Fernandes informed the Upper House of Parliament in August 2000 that 'the performance of the Russian A-50 AWACS, as observed during the demonstrations, did not meet the requirements of Indian Air Force'. The Defence Minister's comments were after the A-50 was taken on lease for a period of 30 days to test its effectiveness and suitability.

Israeli companies have also been successful in bidding for contracts, given India's procurement policy framework, which privileges awarding the contract to the lowest bidder. The relative price advantage ostensibly helps them win the contract, which favours the lowest bidder. Elta, for instance, in 2007, was the lowest bidder in response to a request for proposals (RfP) for medium-power radars for the Indian Air Force in a contract worth over Rs. 800 crores. It is equally true that India did not go ahead with critical procurements like additional Phalcon AWACS when Israel and Russia quoted higher prices.

More recently, the Israeli firm, Elbit, quoted a cheaper price than a French gun-maker in a Government tender to supply towed artillery guns. Further, the firm also offered to make 70 per cent of the order in India, which was more than 50 per cent of the requirement, and offered to provide faster transfer of technology. Reports, though, noted that the MoD did not finally go ahead with the Israeli offer for artillery guns, and instead focused on the DRDO-designed Advanced Towed Artillery Gun System (ATAGS), as well as procurement of the Larsen and Toubro-made K9 Vajra guns, made in collaboration with a South Korean defence firm, to fill operational gaps in the Eastern sector.

Israeli defence companies, meanwhile, invest substantially in research and development (R&D) to maintain their lead in terms of innovation. The IAI, for instance, lays a premium on innovation and is a corporate partner in domestic as well as global start-up accelerators like Starburst. Its US unit is part of the New Space Consortium, consisting of Lockheed Martin, US Air Force, NASA, MAXAR and SAIC. Seventyfive per cent of IAI's sales ($3 billion in 2019; $4. 2 billion in 2020; $4. 5 billion in 2021) are to export markets. The company's sales in 2021 were the highest in its history. The IAI spent over $1 billion on R&D in 2021, more than the $900 million it had spent in 2019. The company's profits in 2021 were $696 million, an increase on over 15 per cent from the previous year. The IAI is one of Israel's largest industrial exporters and employers, with 16,000 employees.

The IAI's main domestic competitor, Rafael Advanced Defence Systems Limited, had sales of over $3 billion (as against $2. 8 billion in 2020) and an order backlog of over $7 billion. The company makes the Iron Dome point defence system, as well as the Spike and SPICE bombs, among a plethora of cutting-edge equipment.

The company invests close to 10 per cent of its sales on R&D. Israel has continued to maintain its position as one of the biggest arms exporters in the world. During 2016-20, Israel was the eighth-largest arms exporter in the world, behind the US, Russia, France, Germany, China, the United Kingdom and Spain. Cutting-edge, niche equipment like missiles and sensors overwhelmingly make up the quantum of defence exports from Israel.

Israel is also a big exporter of unmanned aerial vehicles (UAVs). From 2005 to 2012, one study found that Israel sent out UAVs worth $4.6 billion. At least half of these exports went to European countries, such as the UK, which bought a lot of Israeli Hermes 450 UAVs. By 2017, it was thought that Israel exported about 60% of all UAVs around the world. At least 50 countries use UAVs made in Israel. Reports say that at least $500 million, or 6% of total sales, of Israeli military exports in 2020 came from unmanned aerial vehicles (UAVs). This means that UAV exports made up at least 2% of all sales. In October 2021, the Israel Air Force will celebrate 50 years of using UAVs in operations. With such long-term use, strong investments in R&D, and a focus on innovation-led growth, there is no doubt that the Israeli defence industrial base will continue to grow in value and help promote defence exports as well.

Critics of The Defence Relationship

When it comes to defence cooperation between India and Israel, many governments put a lot of emphasis on keeping things secret. When asked in the Rajya Sabha in November 2001 if India had signed defence contracts with Israel worth $2 billion, Defence Minister Fernandes said that India did sign defence contracts with Israel, but it would be "not in the interest of national security" to say what those contracts were for.

Defence Minister Antony told the Lok Sabha in November 2007 that:

> *Procurement/acquisition of items to meet defence requirements of the armed forces is made from various indigenous as well as foreign sources including Israel. ... Divulging details in this regard would not be in the interest of national security*

Responding to a query from Sitaram Yechury of the CPI (M) on the purchase of missiles from Israel, Antony insisted that 'divulging details ... would not be in the interest of national security'. Anthony, again, six years later in 2013, repeated the same national security argument when the government was asked by Chandan Mitra if India and Israel were jointly developing anti-missile defence systems.

Anthony's successor, Manohar Parrikar, in December 2014, when asked whether the Government had signed a new defence equipment purchase with Israel, stated that while two capital procurement contracts were signed with Israeli vendors during the financial year, 'divulging of details will not be in the interest of national security'. As noted earlier, the Government only on two occasions–in August 2005 and May 2007–disclosed data relating to the estimated financial volume of the India-Israel defence relationship.

Successive government's policy positions on not divulging detail about the nature and quantum of the India-Israel defence trade, is, no doubt, justified on account of national security considerations. There is, however, a better appreciation of the financial volume of India's other critical defence relationships, like the India-US defence relationship. The opacity surrounding the India-Israel defence relationship, specifically on aspects relating to financial volume, therefore, leaves space for critics to raise issues about the nature of the relationship.

After the Indian government cancelled the Spike ATGM deal in 2017, just ahead of Prime Minister Netanyahu's visit to India in January 2018, critics of India's defence engagement with Israel stated that the decision was a 'huge blow' to the Israeli weapons industry. Such critics, though, discount the fact that the Spike ATGM is currently in the inventory of the armed forces of more than 30 countries. India, has also subsequently re-entered into contracts with the Israeli defence company, Rafael, for the supply of the Spike ATGM, to fulfil critical operational requirements.

During the discussion in the Indian Parliament about Israel's 2014 military operation in the Gaza Strip, called "Protective Edge," some lawmakers asked that India stop working with Israel in the military. This was because the opposition wanted to pass a Resolution that was critical of Israel. Asaddudin Owaisi, a member of parliament from Hyderabad, and Sitaram Yechury, a member of the CPI(M), both called for the defence ties with Israel to end. But Foreign Minister Sushma Swaraj turned down the opposition leaders' request and instead asked them if they had made the same request during Israel's previous military attacks on the Gaza Strip. She was probably talking about Operation Cast Lead, which took place when a coalition led by Congress was in power. Swaraj insisted that the government would still support the Palestinian cause in international forums, even though it was against rocket attacks from the Palestinian side of the border that hurt Israeli civilians.

US Factor

Israel is very dependent on the US, not only for political and economic support, but also for military support. A lot of Israeli military gear has parts made in the US. Israel needs permission from the US to export these things. Israel joined the Missile Technology Control Regime (MTCR) in 1991, which made it very hard for Israel to send sensitive technologies to India. For example, the US and Israel have an agreement about technology rights. This covers the Arrow anti-missile project, which was made by Israel and paid for by the US. Since India is not a close US ally, this would make it hard for Israel to send Arrow missiles or other technologies to India if India needed them. The US also tried to stop Israel from selling AEE to India, even though it didn't have any US technology in it.

Defence Joint Ventures

Israeli companies have set up defence joint ventures with both state-owned and private Indian companies in order to work together in more areas. HALBIT, the joint venture between Hindustan Aeronautics Limited (HAL) and Elbit, was set up in 2007 to not only take care of the maintenance of avionics, simulators, and training systems bought from the Israeli company, but also to work together on the design and development of these systems. HALBIT makes products for simulation, avionics, and computer-assisted learning systems (CALS). As was already said, BDL, which is owned by the government, is the lead integrator for the MRSAM and LRSAM missile systems, along with Rafael, BEL, and Larsen and Toubro (L&T).

India's private sector defence companies have entered into significant joint ventures with Israeli companies to address the requirements of the Indian armed forces. HELA Systems Private Limited, formed by Tatas with IAI's subsidiary, Elta Systems Ltd (74-24 per cent share), was set up in 2004 and has solutions in electronic warfare and homeland security, among other niche areas. The JV had a turnover of Rs. 54. 2 crores in 2020-21. Rafael Advanced Defence Systems Ltd. 's proposal for a JV with the Indian company, Mahindra and Mahindra in 2012 did not get regulatory approvals of the Foreign Investment Promotion Board (FIPB). As part of the JV, Rafael was to invest in the naval systems division of Mahindra and Mahindra in Pune.

The JV between Adani Defence and Aerospace and Elbit Systems, meanwhile, set up an advanced UAV manufacturing facility in Hyderabad. The Adani group also signed a Letter of Award (LoA) with Elbit-ISTAR and Alpha Design Technologies Pvt Ltd in March 2016 to work together on UAVs for Indian requirements as well as for export opportunities.

The Adani-Elbit UAV Complex was inaugurated in December 2018. The Adani-Elbit JV secured the distinction of supplying Indianmanufactured UAVs to an unnamed Southeast Asian country. Other reports had mentioned that the country in question was Philippines, and that the value of the deal was over $180 million, for a range of UAVs produced by Elbit, including Hermes 900, Hermes 450 for long-range missions and Skylark I and III for tactical missions. Both Adani and Elbit agreed to set up a Design and Development Centre at Hyderabad in February 2020 to focus on co-developing defence technologies. The Adani Group has another JV with Israel Weapons Industries (IWI) through PLR (Precise, Lethal, Reliable)

Systems Limited. The company in November 2021 secured an order from the MoD, for its Masada 9 mm pistols, for the Indian Navy's marine commandos (MARCOS).

The Adani Group acquired a majority stake in September 2020 in PLR Systems, which itself was incorporated in 2013. PLR Systems manufactures the Tavor assault rifles, the Galil sniper rifle, the Uzi submachine gun, among a host of niche products increasingly being used by the Indian armed forces and the central armed police forces (CAPF). The company is the first private sector entity to be given a license by the Government to manufacture small arms and ammunition.

Wipro Infrastructure Engineering (WIN), set up in 2013 by Wipro Enterprises, acquired an Israeli aerospace company, HR Givon in 2016, which manufactures metallic parts and assemblies for the aerospace industry. Wipro Aerospace has manufacturing sites in Israel, apart from India and the US. The IAI signed a Strategic Teaming Agreement with Wipro in July 2017 – one of the four defence-related agreements signed by the Indian private sector during the visit of Prime Minister Modi to Israel with his Israeli counterpart. Apart from the Wipro-IAI agreement, other defence-related agreements that were signed by the private sector companies, at the first meeting of the India-Israel CEO Forum, included those between Mahindra Aerostructures and Elbit Systems, Mahindra Telephonics and Shachaf Engineering for strategic electronics, Kalyani Strategic Systems Limited and IAI for opportunities in air defence systems, radars, among others, and Dynamatic Technologies, Elcom Systems with the IAI for collaboration in the field of unmanned systems.

Industry groups like the Society for Indian Defence Manufacturers (SIDM) and the Defence Cooperation Directorate of the Israeli Ministry of Defence (SIBAT) are working hard to build partnerships between Indian and Israeli defence companies. At a MoD, SIDM, and SIBAT webinar in September 2020, Indian MoD officials talked about the country's large modernization needs for artillery guns, multi-role fighters, helicopters, and other equipment, as well as the opportunities for Indian and Israeli defence firms to work together. During the event, it was said that at least nine Indian companies have signed 23 MoUs with IAI, Rafael, Elbit, and Elta Systems. There have also been MoD-SIDM teams that went to Israel to look for business opportunities.

Indian Defence and Aerospace Exports to Israel

India sends a small amount of arms and ammunition as well as helicopters and airframe structures to Israel as part of its defence and aerospace trade. Israel was interested in the Lakshya pilotless plane and paid for test flights, but they did not buy the plane. In November 2004, HAL and IAI signed a contract for one Dhruv helicopter. An MOU was also signed for joint marketing of the Dhruv helicopter, which had IAI's avionics built into it. However, not much was done on this front.

HAL's export business encompasses work packages, conversion kits, among others, for jet aircrafts. HAL secured a contract from the IAI in 2002 for the conversion of Boeing 737 passenger jets to cargo aircraft. This was HAL's first foray in the international civil aviation market. HAL also bagged an order from IAI to make airframe structures for transport aircraft in 2018.

India has sent at least US$ 200 million worth of arms and ammunition (HS Classification Code 93) to Israel. At the same time, it has bought nearly US$ 80 million worth of goods with the same code. The private sector in India is also working with Israeli firms and government agencies to meet their security needs. Tonbo Imaging, for example, is a niche Start-Up that started eight years ago with Rs 220 crore in private funding and has now made Rs 400 crore in sales. In February 2021, the CEO of the company told people at a seminar on Atmanirbhar Bharat that one of his clients was the Mossad, which is Israel's foreign intelligence agency. Earlier, in October 2016, Elbit Systems gave the private company Alpha Design Technologies a contract worth several million dollars to make VHF communication devices for export. As was already said, the Adani-Elbit UAV joint venture has sent UAVs to a country in Southeast Asia.

The Atmanirbhar Bharat Abhiyan and Implications For India-Israel Defence Trade

The Ministry of Defence (MoD) is putting a lot of emphasis on defence indigenisation, domestic procurement, and defence exports. From 2015 to 2021, more than 60% of the MoD's capital procurement contracts (190 out of 304) and 43% of their value (Rs 1,39,038 crore out of Rs 3,21,376 crore) went to companies in India. The goal of the Government's Atmanirbhar Bharat Abhiyan (ABA) is to help domestic industry and manufacturers reach their full potential and meet the growing needs of the country. The ABA call is especially important for the defence industry because the country has relied on imports for a long time to meet most of its platform and niche equipment needs.

To encourage innovation-led technology development in the defence and aerospace sector, the iDEX—Innovation for Defence Excellence, was launched in April 2018. Four Defence India Start-Up Challenges (DISC) have been held so far, in which over 1,000 Start-Ups have participated. Budgetary support of Rs 500 crore has been earmarked for iDEX till 2025–26, for Start-Ups, MSMEs and individual investors, through the Defence Innovation Organisation (DIO), an umbrella organisation formed with financial contributions from the aeronautics major, Hindustan Aeronautics Limited (HAL) and Bharat Electronics Limited (BEL).

In the 2021–22 defence budget, an amount of Rs 1,000 crore has been exclusively earmarked for procurement from Start-Ups. The 2022-23 budget, meanwhile, set aside an allocation of 25 per cent of R&D budget for the academia, Start-Ups and the private industry. Over 80 Start-Ups are developing more than 30 cutting-edge products. The Government aims to double the number of products developed by Start-Ups to at least 60 by 2024. In order to more actively involve the stakeholders in developing cutting-edge products most suited to the requirements of the armed forces, iDEX4Fauji was also launched in September 2020.

The Strategic Partnership (SP) model, first promulgated as part of the Defence Procurement Procedure 2016, is an effort to energise the domestic defence industrial ecosystem. The model seeks to encourage domestic industry to enter into tie-ups with global original equipment manufacturers (OEMs) to set up manufacturing and infrastructure supply chains with transfer of technology (ToT). The Defence Acquisition Council (DAC) approved the issue of Request for Proposal (RfP) for construction of six conventional submarines, in June 2021, the first such project pursued under this model.

Up to forty-nine per cent foreign direct investment (FDI) is permitted through the automatic route while investment beyond that requires Government approval. The FDI limit was raised from 49 to 74 per cent in August 2020. The total FDI in the defence sector till January 2021 was Rs. 4,191 crore. It is pertinent to note that a significant portion of this, Rs. 2,871 crore, was received after 2014. The Government has approved 44 FDI proposals in the defence sector.

The Government has introduced a separate domestic capital expenditure (CAPEX) budget of Rs 51,930 crore in 2020–21, nearly half of the total CAPEX budget. In 2021–22, this figure increased to Rs 71,438 crore, or 64 per cent of the total capital expenditure budget of Rs 1,11,463. 21 crore. In the 2022-23 defence budget, the domestic capital expenditure budget rose to Rs. 84,598 crore, or nearly 68 per cent of the total capital budget of about Rs 125,000 crore.

The Policy for Indigenisation of Components and Spares used in defence platforms, which was notified in March 2019, had actually suggested that this domestic CAPEX be increased by 15 per cent every year. The actual increase in 2021–22, which was close to 30 per cent, therefore, was double of that suggested. In August 2020, a 'positive' list of indigenisation, of 101 items, was released. The list included mostly major platforms like armoured fighting vehicles (AFVs), conventional submarines, light combat helicopters (LCHs), artillery guns and also items like radars. Going forward, the aim is to procure such items from the domestic industry, within specific periods, while embargoing their imports. The cumulative value of imports of these items over the past decade was Rs 140,000 crores.

Another list released in May 2021, comprised 108 items, including sensors, weapons and ammunition, radars, tank engines, AEW&C systems, which will only be sourced from the domestic industry by 2025. 131 The DRDO also released a list of 108 systems and sub-systems in August 2020, which can be designed, developed and produced exclusively by the domestic industry. The contract for 83 Light Combat Aircraft (LCA), valued at over Rs 48,000 crores, is the biggest domestic procurement contract ever. More than 500 MSMEs will be involved in executing the project.

India has also made rapid strides in defence exports. India was listed at the 23rd position as the global arms exporter by SIPRI in 2020, the first time that India made it to the list. The aim is to achieve a defence exports target of US$ 5 billion by 2025. With a strong domestic defence industry and a strong exports profile, India aims to become an essential part of the global defence value chain. At the same time, the aim is to reduce the country's dependence on defence imports. India has spent over US$ 36 billion (SIPRI TIV) on imports during 2010–20. Over 90 per cent of imports were from Russia (accounting for 63 per cent), the US (11 per cent), Israel (8 per cent), France (7. 5 per cent) and the UK (3 per cent). During 2015–19, India accounted for more than 9 per cent of global arms imports. India's cumulative arms imports during 2016–20, though, were 33 per cent lower than the imports during 2011-15.

So, the government has recently made important policy decisions to boost domestic defence manufacturing, make it easier for defence to be made by people from the country, cut down on imports, and increase exports. The Indian government is very serious about making Indian defence companies "Vishwa Vyapi" companies, which means "world-encompassing."

Srijan Defence Indigenisation Portal

What will happen to India's key defence relationships with strategic partners like Israel as a result of this policy framework? The Srijan defence indigenisation portal, which went live in August 2020, can teach us a lot. The portal has a list of all the things that DPSUs, ordnance factories, and Service headquarters have bought from foreign original equipment manufacturers (OEMs). The private sector and the domestic industry are encouraged to work together to help the MoD with its efforts to make more things in the country. The domestic industry can design, develop, and make these things on its own, or it can work with the OEMs to do so.

The Srijan portal flows from the March 2019 Policy for the Indigenisation of Components and Spares used in Defence Platforms for DPSUs/ OFBs. The Policy document notes that the value of components imported by the DPSUs/OFBs during 2017–18 was nearly Rs 14,000 crores. The aim is to reduce the import bill of the DPSUs on this count. The MoD specifically pledges to support the development of capabilities relating to engine technology, materials technology and electronic chip technology. It will also give priority to indigenised components for testing and evaluation and encourage their exports.

More than 19,000 products, imported during the period 2018–22, have been listed for indigenisation, by the target year 2025–26. By July 2021, the Indian industry had shown interest for indigenisation of nearly 3,000 items. The portal lists, as of end of January 2022, nearly 90 products worth Rs. 50 million (Rs. 5 crore) and above, which have been imported during 2020–21, for a cumulative value of Rs. 20,000 million (Rs 2,000 crores or about US$ 270 million). These include components like data link transmitters, guided missile components and navigation instruments, imported by the Bharat Dynamics Limited (BDL), from Israeli OEMs like Elbit Systems and the Israel Aircraft Industries (IAI). The cumulative value of the imported components, from 2019 onwards and projected requirement till 2023, is close to Rs 1,000 million (Rs 100 crores or about US$ 14 million).

Earlier in September 2021, at least four such parts and equipment imported by the electronics major, Bharat Dynamics Limited (BDL) and the aerospace major, Hindustan Aeronautics Limited (HAL), from Israeli OEMs like Elbit Systems and the IAI, were listed. These include equipment for the beyond visual range (BVR) 'Astra' weapon system produced by the BDL, and display head assembly by HAL Avionics Division, Korwa. The cumulative value of imports of these equipment till 2025 is expected to be more than Rs. 1,300 million (Rs. 130 crore/ US$ 18 million). The projected value of imports by HAL's Korwa unit from Israeli companies of products valued between Rs 10–50 million (Rs 1 crore–Rs 5 crore) till 2025 is expected to be nearly Rs 700 million (Rs 70 crore/US$ 9 million). The projected value of imports by HAL's Korwa unit, apart from BDL, BEL and the HAL, from Israeli companies of products valued between Rs 0. 5–5 million (Rs 0. 05 crore–Rs 0. 5 crore) up to 2025, is expected to be nearly Rs 138 million (Rs 13. 8 crore/US$ 2 million).

Previously, the portal had also listed equipment and parts being imported from Israeli OEMs related to the Akash missile system (by BDL) and electronic and niche items by BDL and HAL. In September 2020, for instance, at least 23 products, worth over Rs 10 million (Rs 1 crore) each, were being sourced from Israeli companies. In September 2021, this number has reduced to eight. Items like the pressurised container system and sensor package unit for the Akash missile system made by the BDL, printed circuit boards and voltage control oscillators imported by the HAL, are no longer listed on the portal, perhaps signifying success in the indigenisation of such parts. In March 2016, Defence Minister Manohar Parrikar had informed Parliament that the imported content in the Akash missile system—touted as an indigenous system– was around 10 per cent. If the BDL was no longer importing some parts for the Akash missile system, the imported components percentage would have surely come down.

So, the Srijan defence indigenisation portal is a big deal because it shows how India's efforts to make its defence more self-sufficient affect key defence relationships. If the efforts of the MoD, the DPSUs, and the ordnance factories to make defence products and equipment in India work, the amount of defence products and equipment imported from Israel will decrease by at least Rs 9,000 million (Rs 900 crores, or about US$ 120 million) in the future. Even though this amount isn't that big compared to the size and scope of the Indo-Israeli defence trade right now, it's important to point it out because of the MoD's strong efforts to make defence equipment in India. If India's policies in the defence sector to achieve self-reliance and promote indigenization are carried out to their logical conclusion, they will have a negative effect on the amount of defence trade with key partners like Israel, less so in the short term but more so in the medium to long term.

Table 1: Annual Import Value of Equipment from Israeli OEMs Rs 10 million (approx. US$ 130,000) and Above

DPSU	Imported product	Import Value of product (since 2017-18) and Projected requirement (2025-26) (Rs in Million)
AWEIL	AWEIL Buffer recoil mechaNism	91
	Barrel extension assembly	139.7
	Slide assembly retracting	60.6
	Cover assembly	129.4
	Plate assembly with safety	158.2
	Barrel machine gun	182.6
	Yaw Bearing Assembly	16.47
BEL	Electronic modem for ETC	701.2
	MFSTAR-Antenna	497
	Radio Interface Adapter for ETC	142.2
	Radio Interface card	60
	Monitor Sync Unit (MSU) Electronic module	45
	Yaw Bearing Assembly	16.47
BDL	Data link transfer for Astra launcher (Elbit systems)	330.7
	RF Front end (Astra) (Elbit Systems)	361.9
	Inertial measuring unit (Astra) (IAI Ltd)	703.9

DPSU	Imported product	Import Value of product (since 2017-18) and Projected requirement (2025-26) (Rs in Million)
	Sensor package unit	1015.7
	Ring laser gyro	535.2
	Pressurised missile container	637.5
	HAL Display head assembly	320
	Radar processer	1077.7
	Transmitter	239.57
	Combiner assembly	261.77
	Beam Combiner	93.41
	Electronic components assembly	76.87
	Voltage control oscillator	60.21
	Portable solid state memory 64 GB	24.57
	Flash Disc Code	
	Printed Circuit Board Acct.box.kit electronic	42.1
	components assembly	97.9
	TWT Specification P/NO: 1020H012-001	15.57
	Electronic components assembly	
	Radio Frequency Interference filter	14.84
	Filter box assembly	23.74
	Tilt motor	13.51
	Video/Audio Coder/Encoder	11.97

Source: 'Opportunities for Make in India Defence', Department of Defence Production, Ministry of Defence, at https://srijandefence. gov. in/ProductList (Accessed September 2020, September 2021 and April 2022).

Conclusion

Lastly, India and Israel are two relatively new democracies with ancient civilizations. Their relationship is shaped by a complex interplay of geopolitical and geostrategic interests, but they continue to manage it very well. Even if you don't know anything about the Bible, the fast pace of progress and development in the last 25 years almost makes you feel like you need to make up for the "four decades spent in the wilderness." In the time since the end of the Cold War, both have been able to change their goals and priorities with little trouble. The fact that there has been some consistency and predictability in the relationship's growth shows how both parties have worked on it and how effective diplomats and defence officials have been.

India is likely to need more military equipment. There are a lot of things that make it hard to improve and modernise the military. Even though India's policymakers have decided to be self-sufficient in core technologies like missiles, tanks, and aeroplanes, there is a huge need for inputs, importing components, and working together. Also, the cost of research and development can be so high that it hurts the economy.

Indigenously developed weapons have a lot of problems. First, they often need technical help from other countries. Second, they take a long time to research and develop, so by the time series production started, the weapons were already out of date. So far, the goal of moving away from importing arms and towards developing and making them on their own through licenced production has not been reached. There is a good chance that new companies could make money by selling military equipment to the Indian military. Here, along with other countries, Israel is giving India equipment and technologies that are at the cutting edge. The military can get the most out of working with Israel in electronics, missile technology, and intelligence. Israel has fought in both rocky and sandy wastelands for a long time. Since India is also mostly desert, it can be helpful for the two armies to talk to each other often.

In the end, relations between India and Israel have become more important because they are based on very practical concerns. Israel is a source of high technology for India in many fields, including those related to the military, and this is even more important now that India has been punished for Pokhran. Pakistan's military and political moves could be balanced out by building ties with Israel. India is a big market with a lot of money for Israel. India and Israel are more likely to work together on research, make things together, and share technology if they have a strong relationship.

References

'Battle of Haifa, September 23, 1918', NDTV, September 26, 2010, at http://www. ndtv.com/ article/india/battle... 1918-54867 (Accessed November 20, 2016).

Rajendra Abhyankar, 'The Evolution and Future of India-Israel Relations', Research Paper No. 6, March 2012, Tel Aviv University, at http://www.tau.ac.il/humanities/ abraham/india- israel.pdf (Accessed November 20, 2016).

J. N. Dixit, My South Block Years: Memoirs of a Foreign Secretary, UBS Publishers' Distributors Ltd, New Delhi, 1996.

P.R. Kumaraswamy, 'India and Israel: Emerging Partnership', Journal of Strategic Studies, 25(4), 2002, p. 202.

Rajendra Abhyankar, No. 2.

P. R. Kumaraswamy, No. 4, p. 203.

Rahul Bedi, 'Moving closer to Israel', Frontline, 20(4), February 2003.

Y. S. Shapir, 'Israel's Arms Sales to India', Strategic Assessment, 12(3), 2009, p. 29.

Kaiser Tufail, 'Kargil Conflict and Pakistan Air Force', January 28, 2009, at http:// kaiser-aeronaut.blogspot.in/2009/01/kargil-conflict-and-pakistan-air-force.html (Accessed November 30, 2016).

A. Barzilai, 'Israel, India Sign Space Programme Cooperation Agreement', Haaretz, November 11, 2002. Cited in Efraim Inbar and Alvite Singh Ningthoujam, Indo-Israeli Defence Cooperation in the Twenty-First Century, December 22, 2011, at http://www.rubm center.org/2011/12/indo-israeli-defense-cooperation-in-the-twenty-first-century/ (Accessed November 30, 2016).

Neeta Lal, 'India's Eye in the Sky Takes Aim', Asia Times, April 21, 2009, at http:// www. worldsecuritynetwork.com/India-Israel-Palestine/Lal-Neeta/Indias-eye-in-the-sky-takes-aim (Accessed November 20, 2016).

Efraim Inbar, 'The Indian-Israeli Entente', Orbis, Winter 2004, p. 103.

Ritu Sarin, 'From Israel, Lessons of fighting Terror', Indian Express, July 21, 2009, at http:// archive.indianexpress.com/news/from-israel-lessons-on-fighting-terror/492051/ (Accessed November 25, 2016).

P. R. Kumaraswamy, No. 4, p. 202.

Efraim Inbar, No. 12, p. 100.

P. R. Kumaraswamy, 'Beyond the Veil: Israel-Pakistan Relations', JCSS Memorandum 55, Jaffee Centre for Strategic Studies, Tel Aviv, 2000.

The non-relations phase in India-Israel ties (from 1950-1992) could be compared to the 40 years the people of Israel are supposed to have spent while in 'Exodus' in the Sinai desert after their release from captivity in Egypt and their journey towards the 'promised land' in the Biblical narrative.

Poem / Lyrics "Acceptance" by Nissim Ezekiel published in Asian Jewish Life-India Issue December 2010, pg. 13 (https://issuu.com/asianjewishlife/docs/ajl-aut2010-whole-final)

Stockholm International Peace Research Institute (SIPRI) Year Book, 1994, (New

York: Oxford University Press, 1994), pp. 344-345. Indian leaders and technology managers distinguish between self-sufficiency, which they see as unattainable and self-reliance, which implies more modest goals.'

Ibid., See also p. 352.

Strategic Digest, vol. 23, no. 9, September 1993, p. 1543.

Jane's Defence Contract, June 1997, p. 7.

Observer of Business and Politics, March 9, 1998.

Jason Sherman, "Niche Carving: Subsystem Upgades Catapult Israel Defence Industries to New Heights", Armed Forces Journal, vol. 134, no. 12, July 1997, p. 34.

Bishara Bahbah, Israel and Latin America: The Military Connection, (London: The Macmillan Press Limited, 1986), p. 7.

Ibid., p. 8.

"Special Focus: Indo-Israeli Defence Cooperation", Indian Defence Year Book 1998-99, (Dehradun: Natraj Publishers, 1998), p. 119.

Ibid., pp. 119-120.

The Hindustan Times, May 15, 1980.

Ibid.

Moshe Dayan, Breakthrough, (New Delhi: Vikas Publications, 1981), pp. 26-27.

For details see, P.R. Kumaraswamy, India and Israel: Evolving Strategic Partnership, Security and Policy Studies no. 40, (Ramar Gan (Israel): Begin and Sadat Centre for Strategic Studies, 1998), p. 5.

Indian Express, September 19, 1990, Pioneer, April 1, 1993, and Bidanda Chengappa, "Indo-Israel Relations: the Great Leap Forward", Indian Defence Review, 1993, p. 108.

The Statesman, February 28, 1992.

The Times of India, February 22, 1992.

The Statesman, n. 16.

Telegraph, May 29, 1992.

Strategic Digest, vol. 23, no. 12, December 1993, p. 2014.

The Times of India, March 2, 1993.

The Pioneer, n. 15.

The Hindu, May 19, 1993.

The Hindustan Times, April 8, 1995.

The Hindustan Times, July 8, 1995.

Observer of Business and Politics, n. 5, and MEA Report 96-97 (New Delhi, Government of India).

Ibid.

International Herald Tribune, June 10, 1998.

The Hindu, February 5, 1997.

Annual Report, Ministry of External Affairs, 1997-98 (New Delhi: Government of India) p. 54.

Observer of Business and Politics, n. 5.

SWB/MEO552, August 25, 1998, p. 10.

Ibid., pp. 10-11.

The Statesman, August 20, 1998.

Asian Recorder, vol. 45, no. 22, May 28-June 3, 1999, p. 28151.

Ha'aretz, August 12, 1999.

Ibid.

Ibid.

The Times of India, August 25,1998. See also, P.R. Kumaraswamy, n. 14, p. 37.

"Indian Industry offers MiG-21 Upgrades", Strategic Digest, vol. 23, no. 10, October 1993, p. 1765.

"Israel intensifies efforts to bag MiG-21 upgradation contract". Strategic Digest, n. 20, pp. 2086-87.

Jane's Defence Weekly, vol. 25, no. 4, January 24, 1996, p. 13.

The Hindu Business Line, April 22, 1996.

"Technical and Cost Problems Stall India's LCA", Jane's Defence Weekly, vol. 33, no. 6, February 9, 2000, p. 14.

Ibid.

"India Rolls out LCA", Jane's Defence Weekly, vol. 24, no. 22, December 2, 1995, p. 18.

Kumaraswamy, n. 14, p. 27.

"Extra Fighter Aircraft for India", Jane's Defence Weekly, vol. 33, no. 21, May 26, 1999, p. 15.

Indian Defence Year Book, 1998-99, n. 9, p. 122.

Asian Recorder, vol. 45, no. 37, September 10-16, 1999, p. 28387; The Hindustan Times, April 6, 2000.

Ibid.

"The Unmanned Air Vehicles Comes of Age", Jane's Defence Weekly, vol. 24, no. 3, July 22, 1995, p. 21 and "UAVs take off into a multifunction future," Jane's Defence Weekly, vol. 24, no. 6, August 12, 1995, p. 33.

Indian Defence Year Book 1998-99, n. 9, p. 123.

The Hindu, May 22, 1998.

Ibid.

Newstime, February 12, 2000. A UAV is ideal for surveillance on the 704 km long LoC, 140 km of which falls in high altitude ranging from'13,000 ft to 19,000 ft.
Ibid.

Newstime, December 28, 1998. See also, Indian Defence Year Book 1998-99, n. 9, p. 124. RPVs are small computerised aeroplanes capable of sending intelligence via visuals even from hundreds of miles away from their control base. Their mission profile also includes gathering real time reconnaissance, guiding artillery fire during war and designating laser guided bombs. The MoD opened negotiations with the IAI as the DRDO was anxious to utilise the accompanying transfer of technology not only to develop Falcon but also Lakshya, the locally developed Pilotless Target

Aircraft (PTA).

Indian Defence Year Book 1998-99, n. 9, pp. 517-18. '

Jane's Defence Weekly, vol. 31, no. 13, March 31, 1999, p. 14.

Kumaraswamy, n. 14, pp. 29-31.

Observer of Business and Politics, n. 5.

The Hindustan Times, February 13, 1997.

Observer of Business and Politics, n. 5, and Indian Defence Year Book, 1998¬99, p. 123.

Indian Defence Year Book 1998-99, p. 123.

The Hindu, May 22, 1998.

Observer of Business and Politics, n. 5.

For details see, Indian Defence Year Book 1998-99, n. 9, pp. 122-23.

The Statesman, August 20, 1998.

SWB/ME/3246, June 6, 1998, p. 7.

SWB/ME/3247, June 8, 1998, p. 10.

SWB/ME/ n. 70.

The Hindu, May 14, 1998.

Internal Paper, Ministry of External Affairs, (New Delhi, Government of India), and Ibid.

Jerusalem Post, May 14, 1998.

International Herald Tribune, May 30, 1998.

The Hindu, June 13, 1998.

P.R. Kumaraswamy, "Indo-Israel Military Relations: Prospects and Limitations", Indian Defence Review, vol. 8, no. 3, July 1993, p. 50; and SWBfMEW/0556, September 22, 1998, p. 7.

Chapter 4
India–Israel Relations: U.S. Factor

Introduction

In the summer of 1947, when many people were watching the Partition of the Subcontinent, India was making one of its first big moves in diplomatic and international politics at the UN in New York. India tried to join the UN Special Committee on Palestine at the request of Prime Minister Jawaharlal Nehru (UNSCOP). This may have seemed like a logical step for a newly independent India that wanted to show it wanted to be a big player in world politics, especially in the new global institutions that were being built after World War II. However, India also took this step knowing it would lead to one of its first big fights with the US. This less well-known historical debate, which happened at the UN from April to September 1947, set up a major disagreement between India and the US that would last for decades.

As India's policy towards Israel changed over time, from its initial opposition to the partition of Palestine in September 1947 to its recognition of the state of Israel in September 1950, and then from its decision to put off establishing diplomatic relations for 42 years to its strong trade and military ties after normalisation in 1992, the US has always been involved, but not in a consistent or predictable way.

Scholars have said, for example, that the US has had a long-term effect on India's policy of not having any ties with Israel. Some people pointed out that leaders like Nehru thought of Israel as an imperialist state that had been set up with help from the US. These especially point to Prime Minister Nehru's criticism of the US government's role in the Palestine debate at the UN in 1947. Others said that the reason India and Israel didn't get along for so long, until 1992, was because of the Cold War. India and Israel were thought to be pretty much part of the two opposing Cold War blocs, which made it hard for them to get closer.

But neither individual nor international arguments take into account how the US's influence on India's Israel policy has changed over time, depending on who was in charge in New Delhi and Washington, what was happening in West

Asia, and how international factors like the Cold War affected both subcontinental and West Asian politics. Also, this chapter goes against traditional state-centered approaches, which ignore a lot of the transnational activities that have happened between the policy systems and societies of India, Israel, and the US. For example, it doesn't say that the US put direct and constant pressure on New Delhi to improve its relationships with Israel. In fact, the US foreign policy towards South Asia and West Asia did not focus directly on this issue until the late 1980s. State-centric arguments have therefore ignored the indirect but decisive influence and transnational networks of certain historical figures who were not in the executive branch or the foreign policy bureaucracy, like US Congressmen Emmanuel Celler in the 1940s or Stephen Solarz in the 1980s, as well as influential Jewish interest groups in the US political system, like the Anti-Defamation League (ADL) and the American Jewish Committee (AJC).

For example, Nehru didn't agree with US policymakers at first about the conditions that led to the creation of the state of Israel. However, he did keep lines of communication open with Israeli leaders, which were made easier by American actors who weren't part of the government. This long-term conversation can help explain why India finally recognised Israel in 1950. During the Suez crisis in 1956, both India and the US said that Israel shouldn't have helped France and the UK. Even though the end of the Cold War and US lobbying for a change in India's attitude towards Israel led to the establishment of diplomatic relations in January 1992, the story of US influence is more indirect and gradual. It can be traced back to the mid-1980s in the form of mediation by American Jewish organisations. Lastly, the US encouraged defence ties between India and Israel at first, but now its defence companies are in direct competition with Israeli companies.

So, it's important to figure out how dependent India-US and India-Israel relations have been since 1947. It's also important to figure out when and how American influence, both direct and perceived, has slowed or sped up the growth of India-Israeli relations. Here's how the rest of the chapter is put together: First, I talk about the first talks between Indian and Jewish nationalists in the 1930s, which were made easier by the fact that some US actors were involved. Second, I look at the fight between the US and India over the creation of the state of Israel, which lasted until September 1950. In the third section, I talk about how, from the 1950s to the 1980s, India and the U.S. became more and more at odds over the different conflicts in West Asia. Fourth, I talk about how US domestic politics, especially certain US politicians and interest groups, helped bring India and Israel closer together and get their relationships back to normal in January 1992. Then, in the fifth section, I look at the changing role of US support for defence ties between India and Israel, as well as any problems that might come up as the US and Israeli defence industries compete more and more for some markets. Lastly, I'll say what I think might happen in the future with India, Israel, and the US.

Pre India's Independence

India's policy towards Israel was formed before independence, especially in the 1920s and 1930s, when the Indian National Congress (INC) made its first statements about the Israel–Palestine conflict. So, even before Israel became independent, members of the INC met regularly with people who wanted Israel to become a state. Many of these people were Jewish agency representatives based in the US.

Because most of the people who moved to Palestine in the 1930s came from Europe and North America (mainly Britain, Eastern Europe, and the US), Indian nationalists at first connected Zionism with its countries of origin. Most of the money and political support for the Zionist movement came from Europe and the United States. This made the leaders of the INC think that the Zionist movement was directly controlled by British and American interests. Since the main goals of the Zionist movement were to get arms, raise money, and make it easier for Jews to move to Palestine, the INC was not seen as a priority in its diplomatic efforts. The Zionist movement also tried not to be associated with other nationalist movements in Asia. Instead, it made a strategic decision to focus its diplomatic efforts on getting material and political support from the United Kingdom and the United States.

But US-based Zionists talked with Indian nationalist leaders all the time. By the early 1930s, the Jewish agency was trying to get in touch with Gandhi and Nehru, who they thought were important people in India and around the world. By the early 1930s, the Jewish Agency also realised that it had to fight back against the anti-Zionist message that Mufti al-Husayni was spreading in India. In 1937, Hayim Greenberg, the editor of the US-based Jewish Frontier newspaper, wrote to Gandhi to tell him that he was worried about the spread of anti-Zionist feelings among Indian Muslim communities.

American Zionists tried over and over to get Gandhi to talk about Palestine in public, and they finally succeeded in 1938. But his claims that Palestine belonged to the Arabs and his criticism of Zionists who worked with Britain's imperialists in his famous 1938 Harijan article showed how hard it was for the Jewish Agency to win over the Indian nationalist leader. Americans like Hayim Greenberg said that Gandhi was unfair to Jews and had a bias against them. He said that Gandhi had missed the fact that the Jews needed a home country to survive. Gandhi wrote a response to this accusation in another column of Harijan. He included a short version of Greenberg's letter and said that he didn't see any reason to change his mind.

Nehru said that the main problem in Palestine was the fight between Arab nationalists and the British Empire. The Jewish issue, on the other hand, was a religious minority problem that was mostly caused by British policies. He came up with the idea of a federal system that would protect the religious rights of Jews in

Palestine. Before and after independence, Zionists sent messengers to Nehru to ask for his help in making a Jewish state, just like they did to Gandhi.

Gandhi's views seemed to have changed after World War II. Even though he was very angry about how Jews were treated in Europe, he insisted that giving the Jews all or part of Palestine as their national home would be a crime against humanity and the Muslims. Even though he said this, Gandhi met John Haynes, an American Unitarian minister and pacifist who had been sent by Stephen Wise, a well-known Zionist from New York. Gandhi also met the American journalist Louis Fischer in 1946. When Fischer asked him if the Jews had a "prior claim" to Palestine, Gandhi said that they did. But in a later article published in Harijan in July 1946, Gandhi explained his point of view. He said that the Jews had been "wronged by the world," but he also said that they shouldn't have relied on American and British help or on terrorist tactics.

These different statements show that Gandhi and Nehru did not have a fixed opinion on the Palestine issue. Instead, they had a complex and changing view of the situation, which was influenced in part by their meetings and conversations with American Zionists and members of the Jewish Agency. Gandhi died a few months before Israel was made, so he had no direct effect on India's policy towards Israel. Nehru, on the other hand, was both the prime minister and the minister of external affairs after India got its independence. This gave him a key role in making decisions about foreign policy. In the early years after independence, his early contacts with American Zionists were important.

Establishment of Israel

From April to September 1947, the British brought up the Palestine question at the UN General Assembly. This was India and the US's first big diplomatic fight (UNGA). Nehru agreed with the British idea that the UN should deal with the Palestine issue, and he chose Asaf Ali, India's first ambassador to the US, to be its first representative at the Special UNGA Session on Palestine. Ali was given very clear instructions, like supporting the end of the Mandate and making sure that India would be on any committee that looked into Palestine. Ali was also told not to commit the government to any position without first getting permission from New Delhi and not to bring up issues that might "affect" India's relationships with other countries. The instructions showed that India's position wasn't set in stone and was still up for discussion. Nehru also knew that India's international partners, especially the US, would look very closely at the decisions India made.

Ali fought hard at the UN to stop big countries like the US and UK from getting involved in the Palestine issue or having too much power over it. After a heated discussion that lasted until May 15, 1947, it was decided that the five major powers that were permanent members of the UN Security Council (UNSC) would not be allowed to join the special committee that was set up to look into the Palestine issue. Ali pushed for India to be a part of the UNSCOP after Nehru told him to. But India had trouble adding the first list of neutral members of the Committee, which was suggested by Warren Austin, the US Ambassador to the UN.

Nehru was upset with Ali's performance, which went against his orders to stay out of trouble. Ali tried to get a proposal on the Agenda of the Special Palestine Committee that called for the end of the Mandate and the proclamation of Palestine's independence right away. Ali also asked Mufti Hussayni, who was part of the Arab Higher Committee, to talk to the Special Committee. But he also agreed that the Jewish Agency should be asked to testify. Ali's open support for Arabs caused him to fight with other Committee members. Nehru was worried that Ali's position could hurt India's relationships with its Western allies. He told Ali not to bring up divisive topics like the Arab proposal for immediate independence. Nehru said that he had heard "negative comments" in response to Ali's words, and he suggested that "fewer commitments" be made on the issue. Nehru wanted India to still care about Arab problems, but he also thought it was best to keep a cautious and open-ended policy so as not to upset relations with the US.

Last but not least, the UNGA decided to make the UNSCOP more diverse. Two more people from the South Pacific and Asia were added to the committee because those areas were underrepresented in the first group of nine people. India was able to get in because of the growth. After the first reactions to Ali's comments, Nehru made it a top priority to change India's position so that it was a more neutral observer of the conflict. Sir Abdur Rahman was chosen as India's representative to the UNSCOP. This was the first thing that was done. Nehru asked Rahman to back a federal solution that had to be okayed by the Arabs. But because people had very different ideas about this issue and the outcome of the talks was unclear, Nehru also suggested keeping a "vague" position and being "friendly" to both sides. Nehru didn't want Rahman to make the same mistakes as Ali and point India in one direction with his words.

However, significant disagreements emerged between Rahman and Nehru. Rahman, for example, had doubts about India's legal standing in the UN structure after the Subcontinent was split up. So, Rahman defended India's federal solution at the UNSCOP, but on August 14, 1947, he also wrote a note of disagreement. Rahman agreed with Nehru that partition was not a good idea because it would not lead to a peace plan between Arabs and Jews that would last. But in his personal note, he said he didn't agree with the federal solution, which he thought was just as impractical because all parties were against it. In the end, Rahman supported a single, unified state where a clear majority of Muslim Arabs (three-quarters) had the right to decide for themselves. Rahman thinks that a plan to divide the country would go against the idea of self-determination. But Rahman also said that the constitution of a new Palestinian state should protect religious, cultural, linguistic, and educational rights, and that there should be quotas for the number of Jews in government and other public offices.

Since the Jewish Agency thought Rahman would side with the Arabs in the UNSCOP, it kept a close eye on these disagreements between New Delhi and its representative. There were many attempts to tell Nehru about Rahman's supposed bias. In a cable he sent to Nehru, American Congressman and Zionist Emmanuel Celler played an important role by telling Nehru directly about his worries about Rahman. Celler was well-liked in India because he fought for India's right to be independent in the U.S. Congress. In the 1940s, Celler also pushed for more flexible US immigration laws to help Jewish refugees fleeing the Holocaust. Celler had also helped make it possible for a Jewish delegation to be invited to the Asian Relations Organisation Conference in New Delhi in March and April 1947. At first, India had invited 32 delegations, one of which was from Palestine. In the INC, there was a lot of opposition to inviting a Jewish delegation. But Sarojini Naidu and, especially, Vijaya Lakshmi Pandit, Nehru's sister and India's representative to the UN, who had talked about the issue with Celler in Washington, made a big difference. After the conference, the Jewish delegation talked about how important it was to get help from US politicians like Congressman Celler who had supported both Indian nationalism and Zionism. So, in his answer to Celler, Nehru said that he had told Rahman to make sure that the quasi-judicial nature of the inquiry was clear and that India's position was fair.

When the UNGA vote on the Palestine issue was coming up in October 1947, Celler tried to get the Indian vote by talking to Pandit, who was the Indian representative to the UNGA. The US liked the idea of partition, but India liked the idea of a federal plan. Pandit had her own doubts about what Nehru was saying. She wrote a letter to the Ministry of External Affairs (MEA) on October 8, 1947, letting them know that India's plan for a unified country had little support because both sides, including the Arabs, didn't like it. Also, a report was sent to Ben-Gurion that said there had been a debate about the voting within the Indian delegation and that Pandit had told Nehru that he should not vote on the partition plan.

Celler tried to get India to support the partition plan, but he failed because Pandit didn't directly go against Nehru's orders from New Delhi and the Indian delegation stuck to its support for the federal plan on November 29, 1947. India and the US didn't agree on the partition plan, and they also didn't agree on whether or not to recognise Israel as a state after it declared independence on May 14, 1948. Even though the Harry Truman administration had some disagreements, the US recognised Israel within a few hours of the proclamation. On May 17, 1948, Moshe Sharret, who was in charge of foreign affairs for Israel's temporary government, sent a cable to Nehru asking India to officially recognise Israel as a state. Eliyahu Epstein, who was the representative of Israel's provisional government in the US, sent another cable to the Indian chargé d'affaires in Washington.

Since there was no official response from New Delhi, Israel used the channels of communication between Eilat and Indian diplomats in Washington and New York to push for recognition. Israeli diplomats also tried to get India to change its policy by pointing out how close it was to the US. At the time, Indian leaders thought that the US financial support was necessary for the success of India's first five-year plan. This meant that diplomatic pressure, or at least the appearance of it, was important. Congressman Celler was often asked to help convince Indian diplomats at meetings between Israeli diplomats and Indian diplomats.

After the second Arab-Israeli peace treaty was signed in September 1948, India's Ambassador to the US, B. N. Rau, met with his Israeli counterpart, Eliahu Eilat, in Washington to talk about the possibility of recognition. In a later conversation in May 1949, Pandit, who was now the Indian Ambassador to the US, told Eilat in Washington that the situation in Kashmir had caused the recognition to be put off. After the UN accepted Israel as a full member in September 1949, Pandit told Eilat that India was moving towards recognising Israel. When Nehru went to Washington in October 1949, he met with Ambassador Eilat and Congressman Celler. Nehru said that the delay in recognising Israel was because there was opposition in India that had to be dealt with carefully. Nehru did say, though, that recognising Israel could not be put off indefinitely. Eilat also told Sharett in a letter that Nehru had talked directly about how the "painful" partition affected the "30 million Indian Muslims" and that the Palestine question was a "constant source of agitation" for this group. Celler said that Nehru also told him it would be "unwise" to recognise Israel while he was in the US because it could be seen as "American pressure."

Even though they met regularly, India didn't recognise Israel as a state until September 1950, and it decided to put off establishing diplomatic relations with Israel for good. So, with a few exceptions, India and the US were usually on opposite sides of the Israel–Palestine conflict for the next 40 years.

Dissecting India and the U.S. during Soviet Era

India and the US were on different sides of the religious and/or political fights that split West Asia for 30 years. For a while, their goals also went against each other. This changed India's policy towards Israel in a big way. In the early 1950s, for example, the US started an alliance that became official with the Baghdad Pact in 1955. This alliance included Pakistan and was meant to stop Soviet expansion in

West Asia. This alliance was seen as a direct threat to India's security because it gave Pakistan the chance to build up its military and refuse any diplomatic solution to the Kashmir dispute. To fight against this new military alliance plan and the spread of Cold War politics into West Asia, Nehru decided to strengthen India's ties with other Arab countries like Egypt and Syria.

Because of this, Nehru was hesitant at the time to make diplomatic ties with Israel. India thought it was important to stress that Arab states and it had similar views on most issues in West Asia, including the conflict between Israel and Palestine. Other Arab states, besides Egypt, praised India for not joining the Baghdad Pact and criticised Pakistan for joining. Two years after he had visited Pakistan and helped them with the Kashmir problem, King Saud of Saudi Arabia was upset that the "Islamic State of Pakistan" had joined a "Western Military Pact" with countries that work with Zionist Jews. The warming of relations between India and key Arab states helped to stop Pakistan's diplomatic efforts to form a coalition of Muslim Arab states and dispel the idea that the Indian government was pro-Zionist after it recognised Israel.

Even though India and the US have different diplomatic relationships in West Asia, they both agreed to condemn Israel's actions during the Suez crisis. In July 1956, Gamal Abdel Nasser, the president of Egypt, decided to take over the Suez Canal. A long-running political dispute between Egypt, the United States, and the United Kingdom over a plan for funding the building of the Aswan High Dam led to this sudden and drastic move. As the Suez Canal was an important trade route that had stayed under British control even after Egypt became independent, the decision to nationalise it was seen as a direct challenge to European powers that had a lot riding on the Canal.

India's first response was to agree with Nasser's choice. In August, Nehru said that the Egyptian decision was in line with the laws of a sovereign Egypt. But Nehru also wanted to support international legal principles, so he talked about how the Anglo-Egyptian Agreement of 1954 said that the Suez waterway had "international character." Nehru hated both how "sudden" the decision was and how it was carried out, because it hurt European economic interests. India's argument was that Egypt had the right to nationalise the Suez Canal, but it should have done so in "the normal way of international expropriation." So, Nehru was upset that the UK and Egypt hadn't talked about this issue through UN-led mechanisms.

During the Suez crisis, India's position was shaped not only by moral and legal considerations, but also by what was best for India as a country. Nehru was worried about what would happen in the long run if the Canal was closed to international traffic. India was not a "disinterested party"; it was the "principal user of this waterway" and its "economic life and development" were directly affected. So, India told all the countries involved to stop making threats, using violence, and acting on their own in order to keep the conflict from getting worse and turning into a crippling war in the region. Even though each country had its own interests, Nehru wrote directly to US President Dwight Eisenhower and British Prime Minister Anthony Eden about a conference of canal users that would be held in London. Nehru strongly agreed with Eisenhower's plan to have as many people as possible attend the conference. Nehru also talked Nasser out of skipping the conference and into sending one person with the Indian representative to the London Conference, Krishna Menon.

Even though India tried to be a mediator at the London conference, the different groups could not come to an agreement. Nehru was worried that things could get worse because European countries wouldn't negotiate any further after Egypt turned down the American offer. Nehru sent a message to John Foster Dulles, who was the Secretary of State, asking the US to stop British troops from landing in Egypt. Dulles replied that the US wouldn't back anyone who didn't respect Egypt's rights, but it wasn't clear what those rights were. India thought that the Suez Canal was of "vital importance," so Nehru kept pushing for a "peaceful negotiated settlement."

So, Nehru kept asking Eisenhower and Eden to think about the Egyptian ideas. In New York, the Foreign Ministers of Britain, France, and Egypt started private talks. Krishna Menon was there to act as a mediator. India was hopeful that things would end peacefully, but on October 29, 1956, Israel attacked Egypt without warning. The Suez Canal was taken over by British and French troops two days later. Along with the US and the USSR, India was very critical of the operation by the UK, France, and Israel. Nehru asked the US to get involved. The Anglo-French ultimatum about the Suez Canal was called a "flagrant violation of the UN Charter" by India. In a letter to Dulles, Nehru called the Israeli military operation "clear, naked aggression" and said that "the whole future of relations between Europe and Asia hangs in the balance." Arthur Lall, India's UN ambassador, also asked the US UN ambassador, Henry Cabot Lodge, to stop what the UK, France, and Israel were doing to Egypt.

India's main goal was to end a war that had stopped people from getting to the Suez Canal. India supported the UNGA's efforts during a Special Emergency Session to get all sides to stop fighting right away and pull their troops back from the armistice line. On November 2, 1956, India backed a US-sponsored resolution at the UNGA that called for an immediate ceasefire and asked all sides to move back behind the armistice lines. This plan became known as "the Eisenhower-Nehru formula," and Eisenhower was eager to meet Nehru as soon as possible, "just the two of them," because he thought that if they worked together, they would be able to get more respect from the rest of the world. India also agreed to help fund the UN Emergency Force (UNEF) along with 10 other countries, but only if Egypt agreed to have such forces based on the 1949 border between Egypt and Israel.

India got involved in the Suez crisis and then sent in the UNEF because it wanted to be a mediator between the European powers (France and the UK), the great powers (the US and the USSR), and Egypt. During the crisis, Nehru and Eisenhower wrote to each other often. They found that their interests were similar, so they agreed to condemn the Israeli military attack on Egypt.

But the events in Suez and the fact that the use of military force was condemned were one of the few times when Arab, US, Soviet, and Indian positions were all the same. In the years that followed, the US got closer and closer to Israel, while Nehru and India changed their position, which had always left the door open for diplomatic talks. After 1956, diplomatic ties were ruled out because it was thought that they could hurt India's relationship with Arab states and make it harder for India to act as a peacemaker in the area. So, when there were wars in 1967 and 1973, India and the US were on different sides. New Delhi always sided with Egypt and Syria, while Washington supported Israel.

Nehru met with Israeli diplomats like Abba Eban, Israel's ambassador to the US, in Washington in December 1956, even though they had decided to put off building diplomatic ties. In 1957, Nehru met with Nahum Goldmann, who was the president of the Jewish World Congress. This meeting was set up by an American diplomat named Chester Bowles. Goldmann was not able to convince Nehru that having diplomatic ties with Israel was important. He was said to have thought that Nehru's feelings about Israel were "ambivalent." The US stopped letting Indian and Israeli officials talk to each other through a back channel. This was because Lal Bahadur Shastri and Indira Gandhi, who came after Nehru, didn't want it to continue. It was also because of India's international alignment policies after the Indo-Soviet Treaty of Peace, Friendship, and Cooperation was signed in 1971. The US would not have an indirect effect on the relationship between India and Israel until the 1980s.

During the end of Cold War

In the 1980s, when the Cold War was coming to an end, Rajiv Gandhi brought back the diplomatic channels that his grandfather had built in the US to talk with Israeli officials. The Rajiv Gandhi government was also looking for ways to improve India's relationship with the US, especially in terms of business. Since the Soviets invaded Afghanistan and the US gave Pakistan military aid afterward, relations between the two countries had been getting worse. Another bad thing was that the Jewish community in the US, especially the powerful ADL, complained more and more about India's "discriminatory" treatment of Israel. In May 1987, the ADL released a report that criticised India for being unfair to Israel. Since the mid-1960s, India hasn't given visas to Israeli citizens, and the report talked about that and quoted many anti-Israeli statements. The report made it clear that the US should put sanctions on India.

So, the Indian government became aware that it needed to work to stop pro-Israel American groups from getting in the way of new diplomatic efforts to work with the US. Even before the ADL report came out, Rajiv Gandhi's government took some steps to improve relations with Israel. A few days before the annual meeting of the UNGA in 1985, Israel bombed the headquarters of the Palestine Liberation Organization (PLO) in Tunis. Rajiv Gandhi spoke out against the attack and said he was worried about Yasser Arafat's safety. India's Minister of External Affairs, Bali Ram Bhagat, also criticised Israel's "aggressive and expansionist policies" at the UN and called the air raid a "threat to peace and security." At first glance, this position seemed to be in line with how India has always stood with the Arabs and Palestinians against Israel. In October 1985, though, things were different. In response to the raid, 18 Arab states put their names on a UNGA resolution that called for Israel to be kicked out of the UN. India usually votes for resolutions backed by Arab countries, but this time it decided not to. During the 40th session of the UNGA, Rajiv Gandhi even met with Shimon Peres, who is the prime minister of Israel. This was the first time that the two countries' current prime ministers met in public. As another sign of change, India decided to make it easier for Israeli citizens to get visas. In July 1987, for the Davis Cup Tournament, the government of Rajiv Gandhi let an Israeli tennis team play against the Indian team in New Delhi.

Rajiv Gandhi also seemed to know that pro-Israel groups and people in Congress like Stephen J. Solarz have a lot of power over US policy in that area. Solarz was a member of the US Congress from New York. In the 1980s, he was in charge of the House Foreign Affairs Committee's Asian and Pacific Affairs Subcommittee. Solarz was a representative in the House for a district that had one of the largest Jewish populations in the country. He had been a supporter of Israel for a long time. He was also interested in India, and he helped get the US Department of State's South Asia Bureau set up. So, in June 1988, Rajiv Gandhi set up a meeting in New York with Solarz and people from different American Jewish groups. Solarz, the Chairman of the Conference of Presidents of Major Jewish Organizations (and former President of the American Jewish Committee), Morris Abram, the Conference's Executive Vice Chairman Malcolm Hoenlein, the President of the American Jewish Congress Robert Lifton, the Executive Director of the ADL Abe Foxman, and the Executive Director of the American Jewish Committee Ira Silverman were all at the meeting in Rajiv Gandhi's hotel suite. Gandhi is said to have said that he wanted to improve the US's economic and political ties. The Jewish groups asked the Indian Prime Minister to change India's policy towards Israel and its people, especially about visa restrictions. They also asked India to put pressure on the Palestinians to stop calling for Israel to be destroyed and to do what Egypt did. Some Israeli news outlets later said that Prime Minister Rajiv Gandhi had promised to improve relations with Israel during the meeting.

Soon after these talks, India let an Israeli diplomat work as vice-consul in Bombay, which is now called Mumbai. This was an important diplomatic move because, ever since Indira Gandhi kicked out the Israeli consul in Bombay in 1982, India had always turned down requests to fill the position. Also, in 1989, a group from the ADL and Congressman Solarz went to New Delhi. Two of the people on this delegation had signed the ADL report from 1987. The delegation met with Narasimha Rao, the Minister of External Affairs, Alfred Gonsalves, the Foreign Secretary, and P. K. Singh, the Joint Secretary of the MEA to the Prime Minister. One report said that the ADL delegation pushed for better relations between India and Israel but was told that things would not change soon. After the meeting, the Government of India made another diplomatic move towards Israel by making it official that the Israeli consulate could now work in the southern state of Kerala, which had a historically large Jewish population.

Even though the Rajiv Gandhi government talked with pro-Israel groups and took a number of important steps towards change, it was not able to completely change India's foreign policy towards Israel. Instead, in November 1988, India was one of the first countries that wasn't Arab to recognise Palestine as a state. Political and electoral issues at home and events in the region, like the Palestinian Intifada of 1987, made it hard to get closer to Israel. In the early 1990s, especially after the Gulf War, the US had a bigger say in India's policy towards Israel. The fact that India changed its mind about Iraq and agreed to let US military planes refuel at Indian airports was the first important sign that India had to deal with the increased American presence in West Asia.

India's economy was in trouble in 1991, and India's traditional partner, the Soviet Union, was no longer there. This made New Delhi more reliant on US economic aid. In June 1991, Prime Minister Rao took over from his predecessor, who had left him an important economic crisis. India has always been self-sufficient, so the crisis gave it a chance to liberalise and open its economy to the rest of the world. Rao and his Finance Minister Manmohan Singh changed India's economic policies in a big way. Rao famously tried to get investments and loans from the US and from international organisations like the International Monetary Fund (IMF) and the World Bank. The goal for Rao and Singh was to get rid of any problems in Washington that stood in the way of the loans India needed right away. As Minister of External Affairs in 1988, Narasimha Rao had also talked with Solarz and American Jewish groups. He knew that not having good relations with Israel made it harder to get along with the US, whose financial help was needed for India's economy to get better.

So, India first joined the US-led effort in December 1991 to get rid of UNGA Resolution 3379, which said that Zionism was the same as racism. In the second week of January 1992, Joseph Hadass, who was in charge of the Israeli Ministry of Foreign Affairs, met with Lalit Mansingh, who was in charge of the Indian Embassy in Washington. Reports say that Hadass made it clear to Mansingh that if India wanted to be invited to take part in the new peace process in West Asia, it was up to India to start diplomatic relations first. The next day, just before he went to the UN in New York to meet with US President George H. W. Bush, Narasimha Rao said that diplomatic ties would be made with Israel. After the announcement, Congressman Stephen Solarz also sent out a press release saying that he was happy about the new diplomatic move.

Post Establishment of India and Israel Diplomatic Ties

After India and Israel established diplomatic ties in January 1992, defence ties, especially arms sales from Israel to India, became an important part of their growing relationship. But the US has not played a direct or consistent role in how defence relations have grown. In fact, the Bill Clinton administration at first didn't want Israel to sell weapons to India because of rules about how technology was transferred and an embargo that was put in place after India did nuclear tests in 1998. This situation started under the George W. Bush administration, which at the time openly encouraged defence cooperation between two partners it was trying to include in its global War on Terror. The current situation is uncertain because both the American and Israeli defence industries are now openly competing for access to the growing Indian market.

In the 1990s, there were problems on the international level with sharing defence technology. Some of the tech that Israel and the US worked on together couldn't be shared without first getting permission from Washington. For example, the US had stopped Israel from giving China Lavi, Patriot, and Phalcon technologies in the past. Still, after the nuclear tests in India and Pakistan in May 1998, the US indirectly helped Israeli defence companies get a foothold on the Indian market. In the days after the tests, the US put economic sanctions on both India and Pakistan. Among the sanctions was a ban on US economic aid and the export of defence technology and materials.

Israel, unlike the US and even Russia, did not condemn the nuclear tests and did not join the weapons embargo against New Delhi. Instead, a few days after the tests, a group from Israeli Aerospace Industries (IAI) went to India to try to speed up the sale of Unmanned Aerial Vehicles (UAVs) made in Israel (UAVs). A few weeks later, the IAI also made a big deal with India to sell high-tech electronics for warplanes. Since this equipment was only made and developed in Israel and didn't use any American technology, it was able to get around the existing sanctions. However, the US still opposed the deal, saying that it broke international arms control agreements. Even though Israel was criticised, it stuck to the deal it had made in 1996. In fact, Israel also gave India a promise that all contracts and joint ventures that had been talked about before the tests would be kept.

In the early 2000s, though, Americans got over their initial worries. At the time, the Bharatiya Janata Party (BJP) government was trying to buy the Phalcon Airborne Warning and Control System from Israel for $1.1 billion (AWACS). This deal changed the game because of two main things. First, the Phalcon system gave Indo-Israeli defence operations a new edge in terms of quality. Second, the deal changed the way the US felt about the transfer of technology between Israel and India. In 2000, the Clinton administration put a lot of pressure on Israel to cancel the sale of the Phalcon radar system to China. This meant that Israel had to give up a billion-dollar contract. India and Israel were worried that China would set a bad example, so they worked together with high-level US officials during the negotiations. In 2003, after four years, Washington finally gave the go-ahead for the sale of Phalcon.

The BJP in Washington came up with a new way to lobby for political change, which helped the Phalcon deal go through. Since Rajiv Gandhi's time in office, Indian policymakers, including those in the BJP government, have known that they need to work with Jewish groups in the US to get the US to support defence ties with Israel. India and Israel have talked about defence exchanges on a regular basis since 1992, but India could only buy Israeli-made weapons and technologies. As some of the technology for the Phalcon AWACS and ballistic missile defence systems came from the US, there were institutional and legal problems with buying them. India was still a target of US sanctions and bans on technology that were put in place after the nuclear tests in 1974 and 1998. So, India worked hard to get the support of the US government by working with American Jewish groups. Indian-American groups like the US–India Political Action Committee have modelled themselves after the American–Israel Political Action Committee (AIPAC) and the American Jewish Committee (AJC) to try to bring India and the US closer together. They have also made institutional links with AIPAC and the AJC.

India's National Security Adviser Brajesh Mishra's trip to the US and speech to the AJC in May 2003 must be seen in the context of this goal of improving relations with both Israel and the US. In his speech, Mishra talked about how the US, Israel, and India could work together as a three-way axis. Noting that all three were democracies that shared a "common vision of pluralism, tolerance, and equal opportunities," he said that stronger ties between the three countries made "natural sense." He also said that the three democracies faced similar security threats and should work together to fight the threat of "global terrorism," which they all faced. Even though these statements haven't been followed up with any concrete actions, the appearance of a change in ideology has made it possible for India and Israel to work together on defence without the US getting in the way.

In other high-tech niches, like missile defence, where India hadn't been able to build up strong capabilities on its own, Israel provided key equipment and expertise. For example, India bought Barak-I point-defense systems from Israel in 2001. Israel was also a way for the US to get defence technology to other countries (such as subelements of the Arrow system like Green Pine Radar). But the growing defence partnership between India and Israel has also caused problems for some US defence companies, which are increasingly going after niche Indian defence contracts. Even though Israel is only the fourth largest supplier of arms to India after Russia, the US, and France, and even though Israel and the US won't be competing directly for major platforms like combat aircraft, US and Israeli firms have competed over specific tenders.

India and Israel are getting more and more competitive in some areas, and a recent event shows how this could cause problems. India was going to buy US-made "Javelin" anti-tank guided missiles at first (ATGM). The two countries were "nearly done" with talks about making the ATGM together by the end of 2016. But in the end, the talks broke down because Washington didn't want to share technology with India and wouldn't let India make the "tank killer" missiles on its own. India also talked with Israel about getting third-generation ATGMs called "Spikes." Reports say that India is almost done making a deal with Rafael Advanced Defence Systems in Israel to buy the ATGMs. This has shown that Israel is flexible when it comes to transferring technology and that, unlike the US, it doesn't put too many restrictions on its dealings with India.

Over the last 20 years, Israeli defence industries have shown that they are good partners for India because they are willing to share technology and work together on making high-tech military equipment and doing research and development. On the other hand, India-US defence ties have been held back by distrust when it comes to making joint defence platforms. Even though they signed the Defence Trade and Technology Initiative (DTTI) and talked about working together to build India's next-generation aircraft carrier, India is still wary of the US as a defence partner because of the embargoes that have happened in the past. On the other hand, American defence industries are still trying to figure out how to meet India's defence offset policy.

Conclusion

The main goal of this chapter was to show that, contrary to what most Indians and even some Indian academics think, the US factor in relations between India and Israel has never been the same. Instead, it has changed over time based on who was in power in India and what was going on in West Asia. Most people who study the relationship between India and the US point out that one of the first things that made them disagree was the US's support for Pakistan. However, few people bring up the early disagreements over the creation of the state of Israel. Rarely is it also brought up that India and the United States worked together to condemn Israel's actions during the Suez crisis of 1956.

Another important finding is that non-state and sub-state actors, such as Congressmen Celler and Solarz and pro-Israel interest groups based in the US, have played an important role in shaping the nature of relations between India and Israel. This is something that state-centric approaches often miss. The US government has never tried to change India's policy towards Israel in a consistent or direct way. In fact, it was Congressman Solarz's help and mediation in the 1980s that made it possible for Rajiv Gandhi to talk to Jewish groups in the US in a roundabout way. This made it possible for diplomatic relations to be established in 1992.

Also, India, Israel, and the US may have had similar goals at some points in history, like in 2003, but their policies and strategies rarely match up. As was already said, India and the US worked together in 1956 to stop Israeli actions and interests. As was explained in the last section, the US has both supported Israeli arms sales to India and directly opposed them. This is because of worries about technology transfer and also because of worries about competition. Another important thing to keep an eye on is whether or not Israel's "clear and purposeful" engagement with Asian partners like China and India is not also a response to the US's less enthusiastic or uncertain support of its policies over the last decade. Whether it was President Barack Obama's direct criticism of Israel's settlement policies or President Donald Trump's mixed messages about a two-state solution, it seems clear that Prime Minister Benjamin Netanyahu's government has been leaning towards building new partnerships in Asia, especially with India, which remains its main market for defence exports. Still, it's not clear yet if closer ties between Israel and India will hurt the third party in this tricky strategic equation.

The trilateral relationship between India, Israel, and the US has its roots in the Cold War era when India and Israel maintained a low-profile strategic partnership, and the US was the primary patron of Israel. However, India's foreign policy approach, which emphasized non-alignment and support for the Palestinian cause, limited the scope for closer ties with Israel. Following the end of the Cold War, India began to reassess its foreign policy priorities and sought to diversify its strategic partnerships. Israel, which was also looking for new allies in the region, saw India as a promising partner. The US, which had been engaging India since the early 1990s, recognized the potential of a trilateral partnership and encouraged closer collaboration. The trilateral relationship has evolved significantly over the past two decades, driven by shared strategic interests and growing economic and technological ties. The three countries have deepened cooperation in a range of fields, including defense, counter-terrorism, cyber security, energy, agriculture, and space exploration. In the defense sector, Israel has emerged as one of India's top defense partners, supplying advanced weapons systems and technologies. The US, which has also been a major defense partner of India, has supported the trilateral partnership by facilitating defense technology transfer and joint military exercises. The three countries have also collaborated on counter-terrorism initiatives, sharing intelligence and best practices to combat the growing threat of global terrorism. In the economic realm, India, Israel, and the US have sought to enhance trade and investment ties, with a particular focus on technology and innovation. The three countries have launched several joint initiatives to promote entrepreneurship, innovation, and start-ups, including the India-Israel Innovation Bridge and the US-India-Israel Innovation Summit. It is driven by several factors, including shared strategic interests, complementary capabilities, and mutual respect. All three countries face common threats and challenges, including terrorism, radicalization, and regional instability, which require close cooperation and coordination. Moreover, each country brings unique capabilities and strengths to the partnership, which allows for greater synergy and collaboration. For example, India's large market and skilled workforce provide attractive opportunities for Israeli and American companies, while Israel's expertise in defence and innovation complements India's needs in these areas. The US, with its global reach and technological prowess, can facilitate the trilateral partnership by providing access to cutting-edge technologies and expertise.

The trilateral relationship between India, Israel, and the US has significant implications for regional and global security, economic growth, and technological innovation. The partnership can help to promote stability and security in a volatile region and counter the growing influence of China and Russia. It can also create new economic opportunities and promote entrepreneurship and innovation, which can drive job creation and economic growth. Moreover, the trilateral relationship can serve as a model for other countries and regions seeking to build stronger partnerships based on shared interests and values. The trilateral relationship between India, Israel, and the US is a dynamic and evolving partnership that reflects the changing global geopolitical landscape. The partnership has grown from a low-profile strategic alliance to a multifaceted and strategic partnership that is helping to shape the future of the region and the world. The partnership is driven by shared strategic interests.

References

For more on the historical background of the relationship, see Nicolas Blarel, The Evolution of India's Israel Policy: Continuity, Change, and Compromise since 1922, Oxford University Press, New Delhi, 2015; P. R. Kumaraswamy, India's Israel Policy, Columbia University Press, New York, 2010.

Michael Brecher, 'Israel and Afro-Asia', International Journal, 16, 1961, pp. 107-137; Michael Brecher, The New States of Asia; A Political Analysis, Oxford University Press, London, 1963, pp. 129-130; Michael Brecher, India and World Politics: Krishna Menon's View of the World, Oxford University Press, Oxford, 1968; P. R. Kumaraswamy, no. 1; B. R. Nanda (ed.), Indian Foreign Policy: The Nehru Years, University Press of Hawaii, Honolulu,1976; Gideon Shimoni, Gandhi, Satyagraha and the Jews: A formative Factor in India's Policy towards Israel, Leonard Davis Institute for International Relations, Hebrew University of Jerusalem, Jerusalem, 1977.

Stephen P. Cohen, India: Emerging Power, Oxford University Press, New Delhi, 2001; P. R. Kumaraswamy, 'Israel-India Relations: Seeking Balance and Realism', in Efraim Karsh (ed.), Israel: The First Hundred Years: Israel in the International Arena, Frank Cass, London, 2004; C. Raja Mohan, Crossing the Rubicon: The Shaping of India's Foreign Policy, Penguin, London, 2005.

Nicolas Blarel, 'Indo-Israeli Relations: Emergence of a Strategic Partnership', in Sumit Ganguly (ed.), India's Foreign Policy: Retrospect and Prospect, Oxford University Press, New Delhi, 2009, pp. 143-161.

Nicolas Blarel, no. 1, Chapter 1.

Ariel Glucklich, 'Brahmins and Pharisees: The Roots of India's Anti-Zionism', Midstream, 34, 1988, pp. 12-15.

Michael Brecher, 'Israel and China: An Historic "Missed Opportunity"', in Michael Curtis and Susan Aurelia Gitelson (eds), Israel in the Third World, Transaction Books, New Brunswick, 1976.

P. R. Kumaraswamy, no. 1, pp. 31-35; Gideon Shimoni, no. 2.

Joseph Schechtman, 'India and Israel', Midstream, 12, 1966, pp. 48-71.

Gideon Shimoni, no. 2, p. 49.

Jawaharlal Nehru, Glimpses of World History, Penguin, New Delhi, 2004 [1934], p. 891.

Shimoni, no. 2, pp. 39, 51.

Ibid., pp. 58-59.

Mohandas Karamchand Gandhi, The Collected Works of Mahatma Gandhi, vol. 84, Publications Division, New Delhi, 2000, pp. 440-441.

Cited in P. R. Kumaraswamy, no. 1, p. 87.

Sarvepalli Gopal (ed.), Selected Works of Jawaharlal Nehru, Series II, vol. 2, Orient Longman, New Delhi, 1988, p. 494.

Itzhak Gerberg, The Changing Nature of Israeli-Indian Relations: 1948-2005, University of South Africa, Pretoria, 2008, p. 193.

Sarvepalli Gopal, no. 16, p. 497.

Ibid., pp. 474-475.

United Nations Special Committee on Palestine (UNSCOP), Report to the General Assembly, vol. 1, ch. IV, United Nations, New York, 1947, p. 44.

Gopal Krishan and Sarabjit Sharma, India and Israel: Towards Strategic Partnership, Authors Press, New Delhi, 2007, pp. 122-123.

UNSCOP, Report to the General Assembly, Vol. 2, A/364, Add. 1, United Nations, New York, 1947, p. 44.

P. R. Kumaraswamy, no. 1, p. 64; Gideon Shimoni, no. 2, p. 57.

Nicolas Blarel, no. 1, p. 88.

Ibid., p. 94.

Benny Morris, 1948: A History of the First Arab-Israeli War, Yale University Press, New Haven, 2008, p. 56.

P. R. Kumaraswamy, no. 1, p. 104.

Itzhak Gerberg, no. 17, pp. 194-195; Prithvi Ram Mudiam, India and the Middle East, British Academic Press, London, 1994, pp. 144-147.

Michael J. Devine (ed.) Harry S. Truman, The State of Israel, and the Quest for Peace in the Middle East, Truman State University Press, Kirksville, 2009; Evan M. Wilson, Decision on Palestine: How the United States Came to Recognize Israel, Hoover Press, Stanford, 1979.

G. Parthasarathi (ed.), Jawaharlal Nehru, Letters to Chief Ministers, vol. 1: 1947-1949, Oxford University Press, Delhi, 1987, pp. 127-128.

P. R. Kumaraswamy, no. 1, p. 109.

Paul McGarr, The Cold War in South Asia: Britain, the United States and the Indian Subcontinent, 1945-1965, Cambridge University Press, New York, 2013, ch. 1.

Itzhak Gerberg, no. 17, pp. 77, 209-210, 215.

Shimon Avimor (ed.), Relations between Israel and Asian and African States: A Guide to Selected Documentation, Maor-Wallach Press Ltd, Jerusalem, 1991, p. 172.

P. R. Kumaraswamy, no. 1, p. 112.

Shimon Avimor (ed.), no. 33, p. 172; Itzhak Gerberg, no. 17, pp. 230-231.

Itzhak Gerberg, no. 17, pp. 230-231.

Cited in P. R. Kumaraswamy, no. 1, p. 119.

Paul McGarr, no. 31, pp. 16-25.

Donald Eugene Smith, South Asian Politics and Religion, Princeton University Press, Princeton, 1966, p. 440.

The Canal Corporation was an Egyptian company subject to Egyptian law, and the nationa¬lisation was therefore considered to be within the competence of Egyptian law. See Lok Sabha Debates, vol. 7, pt 2, Lok Sabha Secretariat, New Delhi, August 8, 1956, pp. 2536-2544.

Quote by Krishna Menon at London Conference, in Foreign Relations of the United States, 1955-1957, Suez Crisis, July 26-December 31, 1956, vol. 16, US Government Printing Office, Washington,1956, pp. 159-178.

Lok Sabha Debates, no. 40.

Ibid.

Swapna Kona Nayudu, The Nehru Years: Indian Non-Alignment as the Critique, Discourse and Practice of Security (1947-1964), Doctoral Thesis, King's College London, 2015, pp. 135-136.

Quoted in ibid., p. 141.

Lok Sabha Debates, vol. 8, pt 2, September 13, 1956, pp. 6963-6968.

Swapna Kona Nayudu, no. 44, p. 143.

Foreign Affairs Record, vol. 2, no. 10, Ministry of External Affairs, October 10, 1956.

M. S. Rajan, India in World Affairs, 1954-1956, Asia Publishing House, London, 1964, p. 151.

Ibid., p. 144.

Ibid., p. 145.

Dwight D. Eisenhower, The White House Years: Mandate for Change 1953-56, Doubleday, Garden City, 1963, p. 83.

Nahum Goldmann, Sixty Years of Jewish Life, Holt, Rinehart and Winston, New York, 1969, p. 310.

India's Campaign against Israel, Anti-Defamation League of BnaiBrith, New York, 1987.

Annual Report, External Publicity Division of the Ministry of External Affairs, New Delhi, 1985-1986, p. 20.

The Times of India, October 3, 1985.

Richard E. Ward, India's Pro-Arab Policy: A Study in Continuity, Praeger, New York, 1992, p. 124.

P. R. Kumaraswamy, 'India, Israel and the Davis Cup Tie 1987', Journal of Indo-Judaic Studies, 5, 2002, pp. 29-39.

It is important to note here that I am referring to perceptions of the Indian Government of the influence of Jewish-American organisations in the US context on US foreign policy which led to the engagement of these organisations. The US political system is widely regarded as very favourable to interest groups, and particularly ethnic interest groups' influence, as argued by Allan J. Cigler and Burdett A. Loomis, Interest Group Politics, CQ Press, Washington, 2007; Patrick Haney, 'The Role of Ethnic Interest Groups in US Foreign Policy: The Case of the Cuban American National Foundation', International Studies Quarterly, 43(2), 1999, pp. 341-¬361; Henriette M. Rytz, Ethnic Interest Groups in US Foreign Policy-Making: A Cuban- American Story of Success and Failure, Palgrave Macmillan, New York, 2013; Tony Smith, Foreign Attachments: The Power of Ethnic Groups in the Making ofAmerican Foreign Policy, Harvard University Press, Cambridge, 2000; and John J. Mearsheimer and Stephen M. Walt, The Israel Lobby and US Foreign

Policy, Farrar, Straus and Giroux, New York, 2007. However, this scholarship has generally found that ethnic interest groups' influence over US foreign policy has not been consistent over time. Even the most influential coalition of pro¬Israel organisations, loosely referred to as the 'Jewish Lobby' by Mearsheimer and Walt, has not always been successful at shaping US policy towards the Middle East. The sale of AWACS aircraft to Saudi Arabia in the 1980s or the Iran nuclear deal of 2015 were pushed through by two different US administrations, against the will of the American Israel Public Affairs Committee (AIPAC).

Itzhak Gerberg, no. 17, p. 246.

P. R. Kumaraswamy, no. 57.

Robert Lifton, An Entrepreneur's Journey: Stories from a Life in Business and Personal Diplomacy, Author House, Bloomington, 2012, pp. 255-256.

Los Angeles Times, June 10, 1988.

Robert Lifton, no. 61, p. 256.

Los Angeles Times, June 10, 1988.

P. R. Kumaraswamy, no. 1, p. 227.

The Hindu, January 6, 1988.

Richard E. Ward, India's Pro-Arab Policy: A Study in Continuity, Praeger, New York, 1992, pp. 128-129.

Itzhak Gerberg, no. 17, pp. 113-114.

'Economic Crisis Forcing Once Self-Reliant India to Seek Aid', New York Times, June 29, 1991.

Interview with Ambassador Lalit Mansingh, October 12, 2011, New Delhi.

Itzhak Gerberg, no. 17, p. 336.

Yitzhak Shichor, 'Israel's Military Transfers to China and Taiwan', Survival, 40, 1998, pp. 68-91.

'Clinton Imposes Full Sanctions on India', Business Standard, May 14, 1998.

International Herald Tribune, June 10, 1998.

Farah Naaz, 'Indo-Israel Military Cooperation', Strategic Analysis, 24, 2000, pp. 969-985.

The Statesman, August 20, 1998.

P. R. Kumaraswamy, 'Israel-China Relations and the Phalcon Controversy', Middle East Policy, 12, 2005, pp. 93-103.

'US Approves Israeli Phalcon Sale to India', Indian Express, May 23, 2003.

For more on the Indian lobby, see Jason A. Kirk, 'Indian-Americans and the US-India Nuclear Agreement: Consolidation of an Ethnic Lobby?', Foreign Policy Analysis, 4 (3), 2008, pp. 275-300.

NSA Brajesh Mishra's speech at the American Jewish Committee dinner,May 5, 2003, at http://www.mea.gov.in/Speeches-Statements.htm?dtl/4526/ Address +by+Shri+Brajesh+Mishra national+Security+Advisor+ at+the+American+Jewish+Committee+Annual+Dinner (Accessed April 10, 2017).

Ibid.

Shishir Gupta, 'India to Buy Missile Defence Systems from Israel', Hindustan Times, February 11, 2001.

Ninan Koshy, 'US plays Matchmaker to India, Israel', The Asia Times, June 10, 2003.

Vivek Raghuvanshi, 'US, India Said to be Nearing Javelin Co-Production Agreement', DefenceNews.com, September 21, 2016, at http://www.defensenews.com/articles/us-india- said-to-be-nearing-javelin-co-production-agreement (Accessed April 10, 2017).

Rahul Singh, 'India, Israel seal $2 billion missile deals: What it means for New Delhi?', Hindustan Times, April 7, 2017.

Elizabeth Roche, 'India Calls for Broadening of Defence Ties with Israel', Livemint, November 16, 2016.

Seema Sirohi, 'The US Defence Secretary's Visit to India Is about One Thing—Technology', Quartz India, June 3, 2015, at https://qz.com/418514/the-us-defence-secretarys-visit-to-india- is-about-one-thing-technology/ (Accessed April 10, 2017).

Herb Keinon, 'Israel Is Clearly Pivoting to Asia, Netanyahu Announces in Singapore', Jerusalem Post, February 21, 2017.

Leslie Shaffer, 'Israeli Prime Minister Netanyahu: We Are Pivoting toward Asia', CNBC, February 20, 2017, at http://www.cnbc.com/2017/02/20/israel-prime-minister-netanyahu-we- are-pivoting-toward-asia.html (Accessed April 10, 2017).

Chapter 5

Reactions in India to Israeli Actions in Gaza

Introduction

After Israel left Gaza in August 2005, legislative elections were held in January 2006. Hamas won those elections. After a very bloody fight with Fatah in June 2007, it took full control of the area. Since then, Israel has sent in big military forces three times to the Gaza Strip. These were "Operation Cast Lead" (December 27, 2008–January 18, 2009), "Operation Pillar of Defence" (November 14, 2012–November 21, 2012), and "Operation Protective Edge" (July 8-August 26, 2014).

Israel took these steps to stop the constant rocket attacks from the enemy, which made the country feel less safe. The Israel Defence Force (IDF) says that between 2005, when Israel left the Gaza Strip, and July 2014, when Israel returned, more than 11,000 rockets were fired at Israel from the Gaza Strip. Even though military action did bring some relief, the enemy always rebuilt their military infrastructure, which led to the situation getting worse again and again.

Over 3,600 Palestinians, both militants and civilians, have died in these fights, and about 100 Israeli soldiers and civilians have also died. People have questioned Israel's military strategy because so many people have died compared to what they should have. United Nations agencies and other international observers have said that both Israel and its enemies have done things that "go against customary international humanitarian law." Israel disagrees with this last comparison, saying that the IDF did things that had never been done before to protect civilian lives while its enemies put civilian lives in danger on purpose. It says that Hamas has turned the Gaza Strip into a "fortress for terror activity," putting the lives and safety of its people and infrastructure at risk. Israel also says that since 2000, more than 1,200 Israelis have been killed in terror attacks by Hamas and other armed Palestinian groups.

This book is an attempt to look at how India reacted to Israel's big military moves in the Gaza Strip after the disengagement. Strategically, this evaluation is based on the fact that Israel has become one of India's most important sources of defence technology and equipment. At the same time, India remains consistent in its support for the creation of a Palestinian state and for negotiations between Israel and the Palestinians to achieve that objective.

The conflicts we're looking at happened in New Delhi when two different political parties were in charge. The Indian National Congress (INC) led the United Progressive Alliance (UPA), which was in power from 2004 to 2014. Since June 2014, the Bharatiya Janata Party (BJP) has led the National Democratic Alliance (NDA), which is also in power.

The BJP secured an absolute majority in the Lok Sabha (Lower House of Parliament) in the general elections conducted in May 2014, securing 31. 34 percent of the total valid votes polled and winning 282 of the 428 seats it had contested. This was the first time a single party had crossed the absolute majority mark (272 out of a total 533 seats) since the massive victory of the INC in 1984, when it won 404 seats of the 491 seats it had contested with 49. 1 percent of the vote. In 2014, the INC won just 44 of the 464 seats it contested, securing 19. 52 percent of the vote.

The monograph begins by sketching the contours of the burgeoning India- Israel strategic partnership and the historical depth of the India-Palestine engagement. The next section is the main focus of inquiry, examining the Indian responses to the three major Israeli military interventions in the Gaza Strip in the aftermath of disengagement. The reactions of the Ministry of External Affairs (MEA) to these conflicts are discussed, and the robust parliamentary debate on 'Operation Protective Edge' and the stances of representatives belonging to different political parties are covered in detail. The next section looks at how the Indian parliament has dealt with the Israel-Palestine conflict and other issues related to the relationship between India and Israel in recent years.

The next section looks at the broad outlines of the Modi government's Middle East policy, which has shown a greater willingness to work with the countries in the region at the highest political levels. The study ends with what the Modi government's strategic priorities mean for India-Israel relations and India's policy towards Palestine.

India-Israel: Strategic Alliance

The growing strategic partnership between India and Israel since full-scale relations began in January 1992 is one of the most important parts of India's foreign policy since the end of the Cold War. Several important things brought the two countries closer together: the end of the Cold War and the fall of the Soviet Union, which was India's most important strategic ally; positive changes in Israel's relationship with the Palestinians; and important changes in domestic policy, especially economic reforms. Israel's export-focused defence industry and India's need to update its Soviet-era equipment in a more dangerous world are both things that keep the relationship going in the right direction. So is the political will in Israel and the non-partisan nurturing of the relationship by successive governments in Delhi.

The partnership includes working together on high-tech and agricultural projects, getting to know each other, and, most importantly, strong strategic engagement.

Strategic Partnership

The most important thing about India and Israel's relationship is that they work together strategically. India's Ministry of Defence (MOD) says that along with the US, Russia, France, and the UK, Israel is one of the country's top five "defence partners." In its Annual Report 2006-07, the MOD says it hopes that the "rapidly expanding defence cooperation and ties" with these partners "will improve not only the security situation in the region, but also the security situation around the world."

India's Defence Research and Development Organisation (DRDO) and the Israeli Directorate of Defence Research and Development signed a Memorandum of Understanding (MoU) in July 2005. (DDR&D). Under the direction of the Indo-Israel Management Council (IIMC), DRDO and DDR&D get together once a year to work on R&D projects related to defence. In March 2015, Defence Minister Manohar Parrikar told the Lok Sabha that "Israel shares technology information, know-how, and know-why" with India. He also said that "joint R&D" and "collaborative research projects" are done within this institutional framework.

Defence Purchases

After the Kargil War in 1999, when Israel gave important ammunition for artillery guns, India and Israel started to work together strategically. Since then, India has bought specialised defence equipment like airborne warning and control systems (AWACS), unmanned aerial vehicles (UAV), surveillance radar for the Indian Air Force (IAF), anti-missile defence (AMD) systems for naval warships (including aircraft carriers), beyond visual range (BVR) missiles for light combat aircraft (LCA), and more. More than 150 Searchers and Herons made by Israel Aerospace Industries are among the Israeli UAVs India has (IAI). '

The Phalcon AWACS deal with Elta Systems Ltd., which is a part of IAI, was for three planes and cost $1.1 billion. It was one of the biggest deals that either country has ever made. The first two AWACS planes were given to the military in May 2009 and March 2010. In March 2011, the third one joined. On March 1,

2016, the Cabinet Committee on Security (CCS) approved a plan to buy two more Phalcon AWACS from Israel for more than $800 million. The planes would come from Russia. Elta-made radars mounted on aerostats are being used to keep an eye on India's borders.

The Indian Navy (IN) has successfully put the Barak-I AMD system on many ships, including the aircraft carrier INS Viraat. In September 2014, the Cabinet Committee on Security (CCS) gave the go-ahead to buy $164 million worth of Barak-I missiles. This came after the Central Bureau of Investigation (CBI) closed a case about alleged problems with the original deal in October 2000, which included nine of these systems and missiles worth about $272 million.

India has also bought from Israel Tavor assault rifles, Galil sniper rifles, forward-looking infrared (FLIR) cameras for the Coast Guard, and Spyder low-level quick reaction missiles for the IAF to use to protect high-value assets (HVA). In October 2014, India's Defence Acquisition Council (DAC), which is led by Defence Minister Manohar Parikkar, agreed to spend over $525 million on 8,000 anti-tank guided missiles (ATGM) made by Spike instead of the US-made Javelin. India needed a lot of these third-generation ATGMs. It had more than 380 infantry battalions and needed more than 2,000 launchers and 24,000 missiles to replace its second-generation ATGMs, like the "wire-guided" Russian Konkurs-M and the French MILAN. The first contract went to Rafael Advanced Defence Systems Ltd. of Israel, putting it in charge of meeting India's military needs.

India's work on similar systems like the Nag missile has been all over the place. During tests in a hot desert, the Nag's infrared seeker guidance system didn't work well. The system was tweaked, and in 2010, the Army put in an order for more than 400 of these missiles. But it is not clear when these missiles will be put into service.

Reports from the end of June 2015 say that Rafael will form a joint venture (JV) with India's private sector Kalyani Group to make the Spike ATGM in a factory near Hyderabad in South India.

Swaping of Defence Tech and Joint Alliance

India and Israel signed a contract worth more than $350 million in January 2006 to work together on making long-range surface-to-air missiles (LRSAM) for the Indian and Israeli navies. The system was supposed to be finished by 2012, but the project kept getting pushed back. So, the Barak-1 system was put on the INS Kolkata, India's largest guided missile destroyer, which was put into service in August 2014. Reports say that the boosters made by the DRDO to fire the LRSAM missiles did not work.

Unlike the Barak-I system, which has a range of 9–10 km, the LRSAM system "has a range of 70 km using dual pulse rocket motor and active radar seeker in terminal phase and inertial/mid-course update for guidance." Even though there have been delays, the system has made some progress. For example, in July 2012, there were two successful control and navigation flight tests in Israel. After the system was put on one warship, "home-on-target" flight tests were done in August 2013. On November 10, 2014, the missile was tested against a moving target in Israel. Former DRDO Chief Avinash Chander was there and said it was a "milestone" in the way the two countries worked together to make advanced weapons systems. In December 2015, the LRSAM was successfully tested from the INS Kolkata. In addition to the guided missile destroyers INS Kochi and INS Chennai, the system will be added to more than ten other upcoming destroyers and frigates of the IN.

IAI and the Indian Air Force (IAF) signed a contract in 2009 for the joint development of Medium-Range Surface-to-Air Missiles (MRSAM) worth more than $1 billion. MRSAM is a land-based air defence system "capable of neutralising a variety of targets, such as Fixed Wing Aircraft, Helicopters, Missiles (subsonic, supersonic, and tactical ballistic missiles) within a range of 70 km and up to a height of 20 km. The Firing Unit has the tools to stop threats from many different targets at the same time.

Along with IAI, Bharat Dynamics (BDL) is in charge of putting the missile together. The MRSAM systems won't be put into use until 2017, which is three years later than planned. India and Israel are also said to have agreed to make changes to the MRSAM system so that the Indian Army can use it instead of the Russian systems it bought in the 1970s and 1980s. The Army's initial need for these kinds of systems was around $1.5 billion, but the total cost is expected to be close to $6 billion.

Other programmes include 130mm artillery ammunition made by India's Ordnance Factory Board (OFB) in technical collaboration with Israel Military Industries (IMI); advanced electronic warfare (EW) suites for light combat aircraft (LCA) made by DRDO in collaboration with Elisra, Israel; dual colour missile approach warning systems (DCMAWS) for Su-30 MKI fighter planes made by DRDO and Elisra; and efforts to improve the accuracy of Pinaka multi-barrel rockets

Members of the armed forces see these kinds of joint development projects as "symbiotic" and "a win-win for both countries." For example, retired Lt. Gen. Prakash Katoch said that Israel gave India "the best technology compared to other countries." Former Navy Chief Arun Prakash said that the LRSAM agreement was a "milestone," and he also said that the weapons system was "modern" and "top of the line." Admiral Prakash said that in 2004 and 2005, when the Israeli Navy made the first offer to the Indian Navy to work together on the LRSAM (Barak-8) project (along with the multi-function phased array radar, which he called the "cherry on the cake"), the small amount needed by the Israeli Navy would have made the project too expensive without a trusted joint development partner. He said that "Israel couldn't trust many countries with such sensitive technology."

Even though there were delays, MRSAM and LRSAM are good examples of how to work together. Less successful examples include the work done by Israel's Elta and India's Defence Avionics Research Establishment to make EW suites for Mig-27 fighters (DARE). As tested, the system didn't meet many technical requirements, and it couldn't be improved quickly enough to be financially or technically viable, especially since the aircraft itself was being phased out. India's watchdog for audits said that the joint development effort was a bad idea.

India is thought to have bought \$8 billion to \$10 billion worth of military gear from Israel. In August 2005, Deputy Defence Minister B. K. Handique told the Rajya Sabha, which is the upper house of the Indian Parliament, that "the total value of the purchase contracts concluded [with Israel] during the last three years [2002-2005] is 11882.54 crores," which is about \$2.7 billion. In May 2007, A. K. Antony, who was the Defence Minister at the time, told the Rajya Sabha that the country had bought more than \$5 billion worth of weapons from Israel from 2002 to 2007. Antony told the Lok Sabha in August 2013 that Israeli goods made up 29% of the Indian Army's total capital spending from 2010 to 2013.

Motivation for Cooperation

India and Israel work together on defence because India has had trouble making its own niche technologies, like UAVs, AWACS, and AMD systems. It took until August 2012 for Bengaluru to get a homegrown AWACS system mounted on a smaller Embraer aircraft from Brazil. This is different from the Israeli systems, which are mounted on the Russian IL-76 heavy-lift aircraft. India chose the Israeli Barak-I AMD only after the DRDO Trishul system, which was being made at the same time, failed. Israel, on the other hand, has shown that it has the political will to give India specialised equipment like AWACS. In 2000, the United States put pressure on Israel to stop giving China similar equipment, even though the two countries had agreed to do so in 1998.

India and Israel have worked together on defence because they don't have any other good options. In 2000, Fernandes, who was the Defence Minister at the time, told the Rajya Sabha that the IAF's demonstrations of the Russian A-50 AWACS did not meet Indian requirements. The lower price of Israeli equipment is another reason why India and Israel should work together. In May 2007, Antony said that

Elta was the "lowest bidder" for medium-power radars for the Indian Air Force (IAF).

Israel's army has been using special equipment for a long time. In October 2011, the IDF celebrated 40 years of using unmanned aerial vehicles (UAVs). Israel's defence industry has a long history and invests a lot in research and development. These factors continue to appeal to India as it meets its most important defence needs. That doesn't mean that the Israelis are telling everyone what to do. In June 2015, the parties had a hard time agreeing on how to make the Spike ATGM deal work.

Strong Intercommunication

Aside from buying important equipment and working together on research and development projects, the two armed forces have strong institutional interactions. The different parts of national security get together to talk about internal security, non-proliferation, and other problems. Since 2001, up to eight defence chiefs from each side have gone to the other's country to talk and learn more about each other. The last person from India to visit Israel was then Chief of Army Staff General Bikram Singh in March 2014. The last person from Israel to visit India was Chief of the Israeli Navy Vice Admiral Ram Rothberg in August 2015. In a statement about Admiral Rothberg's visit, the Ministry of Defence said it hoped that India and Israel would "reap strategic benefits" by using the Modi government's "Make-in-India" programme.

Service-to-service staff talks are a regular part of these interactions, and port visits by IN warships are an important part of defence diplomacy. In June 2006, the INS Mumbai and INS Brahmaputra went to Haifa. These two warships, along with INS Betwa and INS Shakthi, were part of "Op Sukoon," an operation led by Rear Admiral Anup Singh that successfully evacuated nearly 1,500 Indian and South Asian citizens from Beirut on June 21–23, 2006, just before the Israel–Lebanon War. In September 2007, the INS Sujata and INS Shardul, which are training ships for the Indian navy, went to Haifa.

In 2009 and 2010, the Indian Navy did "passage exercises" (PASSEX) with the Israeli Navy. In July and August 2012, Rear Admiral A. R. Karve, Flag Officer Commanding Western Fleet, led the INS Mumbai, INS Trishul, INS Gomati, and INS Aditya on a friendly visit to Haifa Port. The Indian Navy's front-line frigate, the INS Trikand, stopped at the port of Haifa on August 19, 2015, and stayed there for four days. The MOD said that these kinds of events "strengthen the existing mechanisms of maritime cooperation between the two countries while working towards the same goal of safe and secure seas."

In September 2002, Tel Aviv was the site of the first meeting of the India-Israel Joint Working Group (JWG) on Defence Cooperation. According to the Annual Report of the MOD for 2014-15, the eleventh meeting of the JWG took place in Tel Aviv in June 2014, two years after the last meeting. The two countries are also members of a Sub-Working Group (SWG) on Defence Procurement, Production, and Development (DPPD), which held its eighth meeting in May 2013. There is also a Joint Working Group (JWG) on Counterterrorism (CT), and there are ongoing talks about issues related to not spreading weapons. In July 2015, the Foreign Office (FO) held its fourteenth round of consultations in Tel Aviv.

Strategic Alliances

No Indian Minister of Defence has ever been to Israel. Given how well the two countries work together on defence, this is a bit surprising. Since September 1999, when NSA Brajesh Misra went there on business, no other Indian National Security Advisor (NSA) has gone there on business. Misra went back to Israel in 2006, but this time it was on his own time to give a lecture at Tel Aviv University. Shiv Shankar Menon was the Indian Ambassador to Israel from 1995 to 1998. During his time as Foreign Secretary (2006–2009) and NSA (2009–present), he never went to Israel (January 2010-May 2014). When Foreign Minister S. M. Krishna went to Israel in January 2012 to celebrate the 20th anniversary of diplomatic ties between the two countries, Israeli Foreign Minister Avigdor Lieberman said in public that he hoped India would send more high-level political visits in the future.

Israeli NSAs have been going to India more often. Six Israeli NSAs have been on at least seven of these trips since 2001. Yaakov Amidror went there in March 2012 after a bomb attack in New Delhi the month before, which happened in the car where the wife of the Israeli Defence Attaché was riding. In October 2014, Joseph Cohen, who is the current head of Mossad, talked with Indian leaders like Interior Minister Rajnath Singh and Indian NSA Ajit Doval about a wide range of topics.

Even though the lack of high-level engagement hasn't hurt the relationship between the two countries, it does suggest that the Indian political leadership thinks its policies towards the Palestinians make it impossible to do so. Even with this reason, India's policy on high-level visits to Israel seems to be the norm rather than the exception when you look at the region as a whole. There haven't been many high-level political trips to the Middle East by Indian leaders. India does not have the same kind of defence ties with most of the other countries in the area. Still, its huge energy imports do add a strategic element to its relationships with other countries in the region.

After 28 years, India's Prime Minister Dr. Manmohan Singh went to Saudi Arabia in 2010. Saudi Arabia is India's largest source of energy. When the Saudi

King went to India in 2006, he was the Chief Guest at the Republic Day parade. This was fifty years after the last time a Saudi King went to India. In November 2008, Egyptian President Hosni Mubarak and Turkish Prime Minister Recep Erdogan went to India. This was 25 years after the last time a leader from either country went there. After Mubarak was removed from power, Egyptian President Mohamed Morsi went to India in March 2013.

Even though Indian policymakers have said that CT cooperation is one of the main goals of bilateral engagement (Defence Minister Sharad Pawar said this as far back as February 1992), this part of the relationship doesn't seem to have taken off based on how often the JWG on CT meets. The JWG on CT was set up in 2002, and since then, it has met eight times. The most recent meeting was in February 2013 in New Delhi. Ashok Tandon, head of India's elite counterterrorism unit the National Security Guard, went to Israel in 1995. This was one of the first times a top Indian security official went there after diplomatic ties were made (NSG). On September 11, 2001, the day Al Qaeda attacked New York, an Israeli delegation led by the then-NSA Uzi Dayan was having a strategic dialogue with their Indian counterparts. They were talking about CT measures and other things.

Why is cooperation between India and Israel in CT on hold? One reason could be that Israeli and Indian analysts have different ideas about how dangerous Islamic fundamentalism is. Israeli analysts say that "radical offshoots of Islam in the greater Middle East" are a threat to both countries. On the other hand, Indian analysts say that fighting Islamic fundamentalism, which is often mentioned as a possible common enemy, doesn't seem like a good idea and that both countries have been careful not to show that they are working together against militant Islam.

Former MEA official Rajendra Abhyankar says that India and Israel have different ideas about how to fight terrorism and how dangerous terrorists are. He says that Pakistan is a "Islamic threat" to India, while Iran, Syria, Hezbollah, and Hamas are part of a "concentric circle of threats" to Israel. Abhyankar, who was in charge of the Indian delegation at one of the JWGs on terrorism with Israeli officials when he was in the military, says that the two countries have shared "practical experiences" on border security, suicide terrorism, aviation security, terror financing, information security, and cyber warfare.

People have also said that the lack of focus on CT cooperation is due to "the nature of domestic political sensitivity in India," which made it hard for India and Israel to work together on CT after the Mumbai attacks in November 2008. This theory, however, doesn't seem to fit with the overall direction of bilateral relations, which have been moving away from the idea that the Indian political establishment needs to take into account how India's Muslim population feels about Israel.

In 1992, the INC had more freedom to establish full diplomatic relations with Israel because "prominent Muslim leaders of North India... backed the Janata Dal led by V. P. Singh" in the general elections that put the INC in charge. Kumaraswamy also says that "Muslims at home have started to change their minds about Israel." Israel's outreach and public diplomacy activities have shown Indian audiences the Israeli way of life and point of view. This has helped reduce the negative feelings about Israeli policies towards the Palestinians.

Strategic Cooperation

This section looks at the other important areas of bilateral cooperation, such as trade, working together on agriculture, tourism, and high-tech.

Economic Relationship

Since diplomatic ties began in January 1992, the relationship has grown by a factor of ten. In 1992, trade between the two countries was worth about $200 million. In 2011-12, it was worth over $6 billion. In 2014-15, it was worth about $5.7 billion. Notably, between 2008 and 2015, the top three imports from Israel were natural and cultured diamonds, electrical machinery, and fertilisers (USD 11,739. 12 million out of USD 15,861. 18 million). Mineral fuels and natural/cultured diamonds (after polishing) were India's top two exports during the same time period. Together, they made up more than 72 percent of the country's total exports (USD 15,363. 01 million out of USD 21,163. 94 million).

Even though this shows that a small number of products make up most of the trade basket, the two countries are working on a free trade agreement (FTA) to boost their trade even more. In May 2015, India's Commerce Minister Nirmala Sitharaman told the Rajya Sabha that there had been eight rounds of talks between January 2010 and November 2013 and that India wanted to reach an agreement with Israel that was good for both countries.

Table 5.1

Year	2008-09	2009-10	2010-11	2011-12	2012-13	2013-14	2014-15
Exports (by India)	1,458.55	1,968.59	2,919.78	4,040.52	3,739.71	3,746.94	3,289.85
Imports (from Israel)	2,090.41	1,885.06	2,253.51	2,635.34	2,356.66	2,311.58	2,328.04
Total Trade	3,548.96	3,853.65	5,173.29	6,675.86	6,096.37	6,058.52	5,617.89

Source: Government of India, Ministry of Commerce and Industry, Export-Import Data Bank, at www.commerce.nic.in

Israeli ministers and officials have been optimistic about the chances of an FTA. After meeting Indian Finance Minister (now President) Pranab Mukherjee in October 2010 in Washington, Finance Minister Yuval Steinitz said that Israel "cannot rely only on the markets in the US and Europe. We need new markets". A month later, Steinitz told a group of business people in Israel that "the huge Indian market is full of endless opportunities for Israeli companies." When Steinitz went to India in December 2011, it was the first time an Israeli Finance Minister had been there in 15 years. He said that he hoped that trade between the two countries would "double or triple" in the six to seven years after an FTA was signed.

Agriculture

Cooperation in agriculture has become the most important part of the relationship between India and Israel. The majority of people in India depend on agriculture for their living, but both the tools and methods used in agriculture aren't very good. So, Israel's knowledge of agriculture is a key part of the two countries' partnership. In 1993, India and Israel signed an MoU to work together in agriculture. In 2006, a "Work Plan" for agricultural cooperation was signed. It called for cooperation in "energy-efficient greenhouses, recycling of waste water for irrigation, post-harvest management for horticulture and dairy products, dairy development through genetic improvement, extension services, training, and visiting facilities in respective countries."

In 2008, a "Action Plan" was made, and in the states of Haryana, Maharashtra, Rajasthan, Gujarat, Punjab, Bihar, Karnataka, and Tamil Nadu, "Centers of Excellence" (CoE) were opened with technical help from Israel. At these centres, you can see the latest Israeli technologies for making horticultural crops, like subtropical fruits, more productive.

In August 2015, the latest CoE for vegetables opened in Gujarat, which is Prime Minister Narendra Modi's home state. Carmon said at the event in Gujarat that the next step in the partnership would be to build more centres and work together in new ways. In September 2015, the third phase of cooperation began, which will last until 2018. As of December 2015, 15 CoE were running in nine Indian states, and nine more will start soon. This cooperation is being led by the Department of Horticulture in the Indian Ministry of Agriculture and the Israeli Agency for Development and Cooperation (MASHAV). Before becoming the Israeli ambassador to India, Daniel Carmon was in charge of MASHAV.

Tourism

Strong tourist connections are another important part of the two countries' relationship. Officials and ministers from both Israel and India have said that tourism helps people get along better and learn more about each other's culture and way of life. Many Middle Eastern tourists who visit India are Israeli. In 2014, 49,312 Israeli tourists went to India. This was about 12 percent of all tourists from the Middle East. In 2012, 16 percent of Israelis went to the country, when 47,649 Israelis went there. India, on the other hand, is one of the top places where Asian tourists go to visit Israel. In 2014, 34,900 Indians went to Israel. By 2017, Israel hopes to have more than three times that many.

Modern Tech

High technology is another area where Israel and India still work together. In Uttar Pradesh, for example, the Israeli company Tower Jazz is working with the Indian company Jaiprakash and Associates Ltd. and the American company IBM to set up Semiconductor Wafer Fabrication (FAB) facilities. In March 2014, the project was given the green light to move forward. A French/Italian company, a Malaysian company, and an Indian company are working together to build another FAB facility.

In January 2015, the Modi government, while reconstituting a committee of experts to help advise the government regarding these projects, noted that the FAB project

> *"is a critical pillar required to promote Electronics System Design and Manufacturing in India which will stimulate the flow of capital and technology, create employment opportunities, help higher value addition in the electronic products manufactured in India, reduce dependence on imports, and lead to innovation".*

Water management and recycling are two other areas where cooperation could grow. The Indian Ministry of Urban Development has agreements for technical cooperation with Israel, Japan, China, and the Netherlands in the area of waste water management. In the fields of waste water and sewerage management, the parameters for cooperation include pilot studies and the possibility of setting up "commercial demonstration centres."

The Modi government has a lot of ideas for improving cities. It has started national programmes like "Swacch Bharat" (which means "Clean India") and said it wants to clean up "sacred" rivers like the Ganga, which runs through Varanasi, which is PM Modi's parliamentary district. The group in charge of carrying out these plans, the National Mission for Clean Ganga (NMCG), wants to put waste water treatment facilities in more than 100 towns that the Ganga flows through, as well as other towns. The Indian Chief Ministers have been to Israeli networking events like the Water Technology and Environment Control (WATEC) exhibitions many times.

India-Palestine: Insights

High-level visits between India and the Palestinian National Authority (PNA) have been going on all the time. Mahmoud Abbas, the president of the PNA, has been to India many times. He was there in May 2005, October 2008, February 2010, and September 2012. Both visits, in 2008 and 2012, were state visits.

India has always stood up for the rights of the Palestinian people. In 1975, India was the first country that wasn't Arab to agree to work with the Palestine Liberation Organization (PLO). It gave the PLO full diplomatic recognition in 1980, and it recognised the State of Palestine after the Palestine National Council said it was a state in 1988. In 1996, the Indian Foreign Ministry opened a Representative Office in Gaza. In 2003, it was moved to Ramallah.

In an interview with Saudi journalists before he went to Riyadh in February 2010, India's then-Prime Minister Dr. Manmohan Singh said that India's support for the Palestinians was "an article of faith for us." Before we got our own country, we stood with the people of Palestine. At a meeting of the Non-Aligned Movement (NAM) Committee on Palestine, which was started at the 1983 NAM Summit in New Delhi, Foreign Minister Sushma Swaraj said that India's "commitment to the Palestinian cause has been a core part of its foreign policy." This meeting took place in September 2014 on the sidelines of the UN General Assembly (UNGA).

India's Position at the United Nations

India's support for the Palestinian cause is most clear at the UN, where it regularly votes for resolutions that call for the creation of a Palestinian state, criticise Israeli settlements, and support the work of the UN Relief and Works Agency (UNRWA) for Palestinian Refugees in the Near East. In September 2011, India backed Palestine's bid to become a full member of the UN. In November 2012, India co-sponsored and voted for Resolution 67/19, which changed Palestine's status from "Observer Entity" to "Non-Member Observer." In 1974, the Palestine Liberation Organization had been given the status of "Observer Entity." 138 countries voted for this resolution, while 9 countries voted against it and 41 countries didn't vote at all. China, France, and Russia, which are permanent members of the UN Security Council, voted in favour. The United States voted against it, and the United Kingdom didn't vote either way.

Ambassador Hardeep Puri, who was India's Permanent Representative to the UN at the time, called the vote a "milestone" and said that the situation in the occupied Palestinian territories was getting worse because of settlement activities, which were threatening the idea of a two-state solution. On November 30, 2011, Puri said that Israeli settlements were "the biggest thing standing in the way of direct negotiations."

In an interview with Asian Age in January 2013, then Foreign Minister Salman Khurshid stated that Israel did not want India to vote for the November 2012 resolution

> *"...but we did. We've found the right sort of balance between our legitimate concerns about Palestine and our growing relationship with Israel. It's important that we keep in mind popular perceptions in the country that, historically, have been strongly in favor of Palestine".*

Analysts like the former Special Envoy for the Middle East Peace Process, Ambassador Chinmaya Gharekhan, have noticed that India's position on the Israel-Palestine conflict has become more "moderate." They say this is because India and Israel have built strong strategic ties since the Kargil War. Gharekhan also says that India doesn't pay for "statements in favour of Palestine" anymore, but it still backs them.

India's behaviour at the UNGA, on the other hand, does not easily suggest that it is becoming more moderate towards Israel. Even after the Modi government took over, India still helped pass resolutions at the UNGA that were critical of Israeli policies. On November 4, 1976, "Palestinian Refugees in the Gaza Strip" was the first resolution at the UNGA that was about Palestine. India, Afghanistan, Cyprus, and Pakistan were all co-sponsors of this resolution.

India has been a co-sponsor of the "Right of the Palestinian People to Self-Determination" resolution since 1998, even when its government was in a different place. The 2015 resolution called for an end to the "Israeli occupation that began in 1967." It also cited the July 2004 opinion of the International Court of Justice (ICJ), which said that Israel's building of a wall, along with other actions, "severely hinders the right of the Palestinian people to self-determination." The Modi government did not stop co-sponsoring the 2014 resolution, but it chose not to co-sponsor the 2015 resolution (though it extended support to it). During those two years, India also backed a lot of other resolutions at the UNGA that helped the Palestinians.

Israel views these resolutions as "outdated" and "outrageous", and holds that they represent "anti-Israeli incitement and the defamation and delegitimization of Israel". In November 2014, an Israeli Foreign Ministry official named Israel-Nitzan Tikochinski said he was unhappy that the UN spends more than $6 million each year on the UN Division for Palestinian Rights, the UN Committee on the Exercise of the Inalienable Rights of the Palestinian People, and the Department of Public Information's special information programme on the question of Palestine. He questioned the purpose of these committees and programmes, as well as what the UN's 2014 International Year of Solidarity with the Palestinian People had accomplished. He charged that the solidarity so expressed was "with the culture of hatred and incitement... [and] with unilateral actions instead of direct negotiations".

Grants and Assistance

India had given the PNA $27 million in grants for development, humanitarian aid, and other projects up until the middle of 2008. India gives the UNRWA $1 million every year. Before 2009, it only gave $20,000 a year. At India's request, this money is being used to give additional food aid to 76,000 UNRWA school students for fifty school days starting in 2011. India said it would give the PNA $10 million in budgetary aid in 2008, 2010, and 2012. (during the visits of President Abbas). As for development aid, $5 million was promised at the Paris Donor Conference in December 2007, $10 million during Abbas's visit in October 2008, and $4 million at the Cairo International Conference on Gaza Reconstruction in October 2014. (transferred in January 2015). In October 2015, a budgetary aid of five million dollars was given.

India's government built the Palestine Embassy Chancery and Residence buildings in New Delhi as a gift to the State of Palestine. In 2015, the Indian Technical and Economic programme (ITEC) offered training courses to 80 Palestinian citizens (out of 8,360 civilian training slots for 161 partner countries). Anil Wadhwa, Secretary (East) to Palestine, opened the Jawaharlal Nehru Secondary School for Girls in Asera Al-Shamalyeh on July 8 and 9.

The Jawaharlal Nehru Secondary Boys School in Abu Dees, the India-Palestine Center for Excellence in ICT, the Digital Learning & Innovation Center at Al Quds University (with a satellite centre in Ramallah), and the supply of TVET (technical and vocational education training) equipment and services to seven vocational training centres in the PNA are all examples of other ongoing capacity-building activities by India.

The PNA also gets cars and medicines from India. In September 2004, for example, E. Ahmed, who was then the Deputy Foreign Minister, gave the PNA medicines worth two crores (about $500,000) and fourteen cars. 72 In May 2006, a programme to help people in need announced that it would give $2 million for medical aid. Together with IBSA, a sports complex was opened in November 2011. The IBSA Fund, which was started at the Paris Donors' Conference in December 2007 with an initial donation of $3 million for three years, promised $1 million to rebuild a hospital in Gaza that was destroyed during the July-August 2014 conflict. IBSA is also working on projects like fixing up the Al-Quds hospital in Gaza and building a "Center for People with Special Needs" in Nablus.

Indian Response to Gaza Conflict

Violence between Israel and its enemies in the Gaza Strip always gets a lot of attention around the world and leads to both government and non-government activism around the world. India has important strategic ties with Israel that make it dependent on them. At the same time, India has always stood up for the Palestinian cause. Because of this, how the Indian government, political parties, and civil society reacted to the fighting between Israel and Gaza is a unique case study of how other countries see these kinds of conflicts.

Even before Israel pulled out of the Gaza Strip in 2005 and Hamas won elections in January 2006, India's MEA was critical of Israeli military actions in the Gaza Strip that killed civilians. On May 20, 2004, for example, the MEA "condemned" the IDF for destroying homes and "using force without discrimination" in the Rafah refugee camp. In September and October 2004, Israel launched a military offensive in the Gaza Strip that killed more than 130 Palestinians. This was in response to rocket attacks that killed two children in Sderot. The Deputy Foreign Minister, E. Ahmed, "condemned" the "disproportionate and unjustified use of force," showed "deep concern" about the loss of "innocent civilian lives," and urged a return to the path of negotiations.

In August and September 2005, when Israel pulled out of Gaza, the cycle of violence got a lot worse. At the beginning of June 2006, the IDF killed a top Hamas official by firing missiles at him from an Apache helicopter. This led to more rocket attacks, which made Israel use more artillery and planes to hit back. On June 9, 2006, nine members of a Palestinian family were killed on a beach in Gaza. India was upset about this "unprovoked act and the killing of innocent civilians."

Israel started a military offensive in the Gaza Strip at the end of June 2006 after an IDF soldier was taken hostage. Seven Israelis, including five soldiers, and more than 400 Palestinians, including more than 250 "militants," died during the operation, which went on until August. The MEA "condemned" the kidnapping of Shalit, saying that it had "led to the threat of massive retaliation measures by Israel."

Hamas came to power when it won 74 of the 134 seats in the Palestinian parliament on January 25, 2006. At the time, India was happy with the result and hoped that the "new Government representing the will of the Palestinian people will continue on the path of peaceful negotiations." Of course, what happened next crushed those hopes.

In February 2008, Israel started a ground and air attack that killed more than 100 Palestinians. On March 1, India's government said it was "dismayed" by the continuing violence and criticised the "disproportionate use of retaliatory force" that had caused civilian deaths, including those of innocent children, that could have been avoided. This can't happen." On March 7, 2008, eight Israelis were killed in a terrorist attack at Merkaz Harav Yeshiva. The MEA condemned the attack and said, "The current cycle of violence, including disproportionate retaliation by Israel, must end if the people of the region are to stop suffering."

On April 18, 2008, India's Ministry of External Affairs (MEA) said that the country was saddened by the rise in violence in Gaza, which had killed many Palestinians and Israelis. On November 17, 2008, India spoke out against the Gaza blockade, which had been in place since January of that year. They said that there was "no justification" for keeping over a million civilians in Gaza from getting essential supplies.

The Gaza War

The IDF said that this operation was started "after all non-military and diplomatic moves to stop Hamas' rocket attacks had been tried and failed." As the graph below shows, 2008 was the year when the most rockets were fired from the Gaza Strip. During the years 2007 and 2008, rocket attacks hurt more than 1,200 Israelis and killed 25.

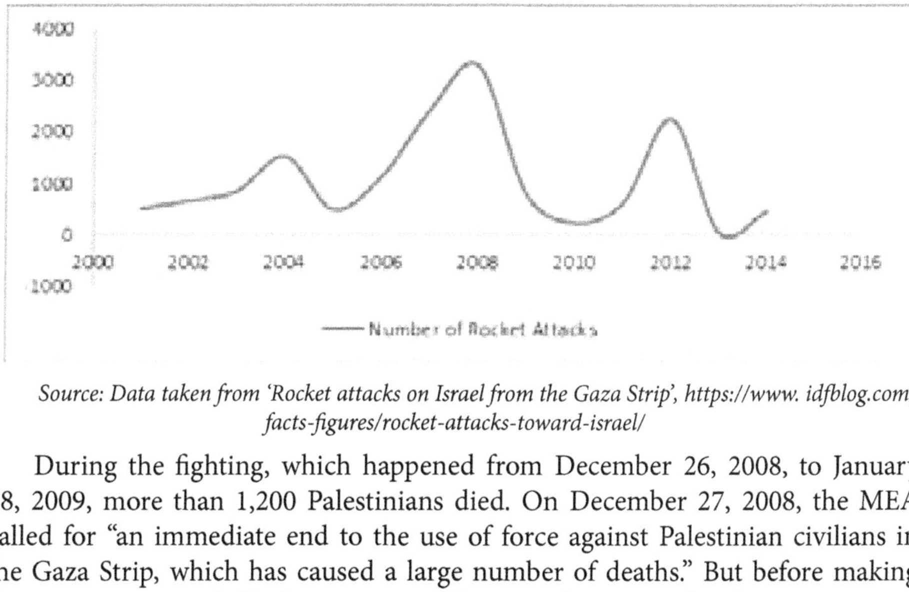

Source: Data taken from 'Rocket attacks on Israel from the Gaza Strip', https://www. idfblog.com/ facts-figures/rocket-attacks-toward-israel/

During the fighting, which happened from December 26, 2008, to January 18, 2009, more than 1,200 Palestinians died. On December 27, 2008, the MEA called for "an immediate end to the use of force against Palestinian civilians in the Gaza Strip, which has caused a large number of deaths." But before making the statement, it said, "India is aware of the immediate cross-border provocations caused by rocket attacks, especially on targets in southern Israel." After that MEA statement, the Israeli Deputy Chief of Mission (DCM) Eli Belotsercovsky told the Political Officer of the US Embassy that they were "not very depressed" and that it was "reassuring" that the MEA acknowledged the "cross-border provocations." This was shown in a Wikileaks cable.

Still, two days after the first statement, the MEA called Israel's "disproportionate use of force" "unjustified and unacceptable" and called for "utmost restraint." It also said that it was worried that Israel's attack in the Gaza Strip could hurt the peace process in a way that couldn't be fixed. In response to a sudden call for help from UNRWA on January 2, 2009, India gave a donation of $1 million. In another strong statement made on January 4, India "condemned the ongoing incursion into Gaza by Israeli ground and other forces... People in the area must no longer have to suffer."

On January 9, 2009, India said that the situation in Gaza was "heartbreaking." Even though Israel wasn't mentioned by name, the MEA said it was "strange" that there was no "sorrow or concern about the plight of the 1.5 million Gazan civilians who live in a permanent state of fear." In response to a question in the Lok Sabha on February 18, 2009, Deputy Foreign Minister E. Ahmed told the MPs that India had "consistently supported the peaceful resolution of the conflict in West Asia resulting in a sovereign, independent, viable, and united State of Palestine living within secure and recognised borders, side by side and at peace with Israel."

Later, in October 2009, India agreed with the UN report of the fact-finding mission led by South African judge Richard Goldstone. Danny Ayalon, Israel's Deputy Foreign Minister, said that India should have shown "more restraint" because the Goldstone report "denies democracies the right to self-defense." During the Gaza war, both the Israeli government and Palestinian militant groups did things that were called "crimes against humanity" by the report.

Later, at a special session of the UNGA in November 2009, the leader of the Indian delegation, B. K. Hariprasad, MP, said, "We have reservations about giving unqualified support to the various recommendations and some of the procedures adopted by the Goldstone report..." In the rest of his statement, he asks everyone involved to "take firm action against those who break international humanitarian law and human rights."

Later, Mr. Goldstone wrote an opinion piece for The Washington Post in which he acknowledged that Israelis were still looking into what happened that led to the deaths of Palestinian civilians. He also complained that Hamas hadn't looked into why they were firing rockets and mortars at Israel. Israel was very angry about what he said, and Prime Minister Netanyahu said, "Israel did not mean to hurt civilians..." The Israeli response was called "out of line" by an editorial in The Hindu, which also said that Goldstone's retraction "does not change the core fact that... more than 1,400 Palestinians and 13 Israelis were killed, and that half of the Palestinians and three of the Israelis were civilians."

As we've already said, after "Cast Lead," India helped the Palestinians get full membership in the UN General Assembly in 2011 and 2012 and hosted Abbas in 2010 and 2012. In the meantime, strategic cooperation between India and Israel continued and even grew. In May 2009, four months after the conflict, the first Phalcon AWACS was sent out. In the same year, the two countries signed the $1 billion MRSAM deal.

2012 Israeli Operation in the Gaza strip

The IDF started this eight-day operation on November 14, 2012, "in response to the Gaza Strip's constant rocket attacks." The Israeli Ministry of Foreign Affairs (MFA) said that between January and November 2012, more than 800 rockets were fired from Gaza into Israel. Ten days before the operation, more than 100 rockets were fired from Gaza into Israel. The operation started when the head of Hamas's military wing in the Gaza Strip was killed on purpose. The IDF hit more than 1,500 different places.

There were 174 Palestinian deaths and 6 Israeli deaths. Nearly 1,500 rockets were fired by Palestinian armed groups. They were aimed not only at the south, but also at Tel Aviv and Jerusalem. In her investigation of the conflict, the UN High Commissioner for Human Rights (UNHCHR) said that the IDF did not "respect the principles of distinction, proportionality, and precautions, as required by international humanitarian law." She also said that Palestinian armed groups broke international humanitarian law by firing rockets from "densely populated areas."

On November 18, 2012, half way through the conflict, India said it was "deeply concerned" by the sharp rise in violence, urged "both sides to exercise maximum restraint," and called for direct talks between Israelis and Palestinians to find a "comprehensive solution to the Palestinian situation." Some analysts have pointed out that this statement is different from previous Indian responses because the word "condemn" is not used to criticise the actions of either side, as it was in earlier statements. They say that this is because India and Israel are working together more strategically and because of the Arab Spring, which "took some of the attention away from the Palestinian struggle and caused a big rift between Arab countries and Iran-backed groups like Hamas and Hezbollah." This interpretation is true, but only as far as the MEA's specific responses go. This is because, just four days after the above statement, India, Brazil, and South Africa (IBSA) "strongly condemned" the ongoing violence between Israel and Palestine, urged both sides to "exercise maximum restraint," and repeated the "urgent need to lift the blockade on Gaza," which is making an already bad situation in Gaza even worse.

Members of the Rashtriya Swayamsevak Sangh (RSS), which is the parent group of the BJP, liked Israel's strong military responses in the Gaza Strip. One of its prominent members, Ram Madhav, who has since become a BJP General Secretary (a top organizational post in the political party), writing in a blog post published at the end of Israel's 2012 campaign, charged that:

> *"India is driven by an instinct of compromise. We may pay lip sympathy to Gaza by asking Israel not to use disproportionate force; but one has to be on the other side of the Gaza border to understand what it means to be a target of Hamas terrorism. ... Excessive force argument doesn't have any merit in a war; and Israel is in a perpetual war."*

During a speech at Chandigarh on November 24, 2012, Madhav criticized the government's advice to Israel regarding 'disproportionate force':

> *"'Don't use disproportionate force', our Government advised Israel. What does 'disproportionate force' mean? Should we first mutually agree upon the weapons that each one of us would use and then start the war? Does it happen that way? When the Chinese attacked us in 1962, did they use 'proportionate power'? ".*

2014 Gaza Wars

From January to July 2014, more than 450 rockets were fired into Israel, which made "millions of Israelis live in fear," according to the IDF. Even though this is a big reason why Israel doesn't feel safe, this number doesn't compare to the same numbers from 2007 and 2008, when Israel was hit by thousands of rockets.

During the 2014 summer escalation, though, nearly 4,600 rockets were fired at Israel. The Iron Dome antimissile defence (AMD) system stopped more than 80% of the 800 projectiles that were thought to be a threat to Israeli population centres. During the conflict, however, more than 3,800 rockets did land in Israel. Seven civilians were killed and 126 were hurt.

Israel says that more than 10,000 people had to leave their homes because of the rocket attacks during "Operation Protective Edge." Even though the Iron Dome system works pretty well, Israel says that "more than half a million Israelis had less than sixty seconds to get to safety after a rocket was fired from Gaza into Israel." People have estimated that the military operation in July and August 2014 cost more than 3.5 billion Israeli Shekels, which is close to $1 billion.

The IDF also points out that Palestinian rockets are getting more and more complicated and that their range is getting longer, which means that they can reach more Israelis. The IDF says that Hamas has rockets like the M-302, which can travel 160 km, the M-75, which can travel 75 km, the Grad rocket, which can travel less than 50 km, and the Qassam projectiles, which can travel less than 20 km. The IDF, on the other hand, hit almost 1,500 sites in the Gaza Strip. There were 72 Israeli deaths and over 2,300 Palestinian deaths.

On July 10, the MEA Spokesperson, responding to a media query on the latest military escalation between Israel and the Palestinians, stated: "

India is deeply concerned at the steep escalation of violence between Israel and Palestine, particularly, heavy air strikes in Gaza, resulting in tragic loss of civilian lives and heavy damage to property. At the same time, India is alarmed at the cross-border provocations [emphasis added] resulting from rocket attacks against targets in parts of Israel. India calls upon both sides to exercise maximum restraint".

The only official thing the MEA said about "Protective Edge" was what you just read. It also made a single statement during "Pillar of Defence." India's Foreign Ministry put out five statements during "Cast Lead." The unprecedented demand for a debate in the Indian Parliament, which was not made during either "Cast Lead" or "Pillar of Defence," brought the issue of Israeli military responses to provocations across its borders to the centre of the Indian political system. In the paragraphs that follow, you can read about the main points of the debates and the BJP government's response.

India's Parliament Response

In lower house of Indian Parliament on July 15, MPs from opposition parties were angry about the ongoing conflict and asked the government to explain where it stood on the issue. Mehbooba Mufti, a member of the People's Democratic Party (PDP), which has 3 MPs in the 545-member Lok Sabha and is based in India's only Muslim-majority province, Jammu and Kashmir, asked the House to "condemn" the Israeli attack. She said that the attack only came from one side because all of the people who died were from Gaza. She also said that Kashmiri schoolchildren were "on the streets" and that the situation was "very important for everyone."

Dr. Shashi Tharoor, a former Deputy Foreign Minister under the UPA government and a former UN Under Secretary General, supported Ms. Mufti's request and said, "When a tragedy is happening, we feel it is right for the Lok Sabha to express the concerns of the Indian people." He started his speech by saying, "India and the Congress Party have always stood for peace and justice in the Palestine area."

Former Deputy Foreign Minister of the UPA coalition E. Ahmed of the Indian Union Muslim League (IUML, Kerala, 2 MPs, who visited Ramallah four times from 2004 to 2013) said that "innocent people were being killed" and that "what is going on is a flagrant violation of human rights." He also said, "India should condemn the supposed atrocities and war crimes that Israeli forces are committing in Gaza." Ramadan is the holy month. Even so, Israel is at war with the innocent people of Palestine in a way that is unfair and disgusting. Ahmed ended by saying that India "cannot just go to sleep" about something so important to the whole world.

Saugata Roy of the Trinamool Congress (TMC, West Bengal, the fourth-largest party with 34 MPs) said, "The Zionists in Israel have been trying to kill the Palestinian people. In the most recent incident, the Israelis started firing missiles at Gaza Strip without being asked to. This killed men, women, and children. Roy said, "We don't deny Israel's right to exist, but we think the Palestinian people need to be treated fairly." He told the government, "Bring a Resolution that condemns Israel's aggression and the genocide they are committing in Gaza."

M. Thambi Durai from the All India Anna Dravida Munnetra Kazhagam (AIADMK, Tamil Nadu, third-largest party with 37 MPs), who is also the Deputy Speaker of the House, said that it was wrong for the Israeli army to kill innocent Palestinians. We ask the government to... come up with a solution." P. Karunakaran of the Communist Party of India-Marxist (CPI-M; 9 MPs) said, "Governments may change, but the country's foreign policy can't change based on what any government or party wants." Even if we don't ask, the government has to speak out against this."

Asaduddin Owaisi of the All India Majlis-e-Ittehadul-Muslimeen (AIMIM, Hyderabad, single MP) asked the government to send a delegation to the Gaza Strip and to "stop diplomatic relations with Israel and give humanitarian aid to poor Palestinians." Mulayam Singh Yadav of the Samajwadi Party (SP, which sees the Muslims of Uttar Pradesh as a key part of its vote bank) reminded the House that it has been India's policy since the time of Prime Minister Jawaharlal Nehru that when there is injustice anywhere in the world, India "does not keep quiet."

Venkaiah Naidu, the Union Minister for Urban Development and Parliamentary Affairs, spoke on behalf of the government, which has 282 MPs. He reminded the House that India has a "stated policy" about how it treats Israel and Palestine. So, anything the Indian government does at this point will affect our foreign policy. Naidu said, "As far as the government is concerned, we don't plan to move any Resolution." I would tell the Minister of External Affairs what the members had to say." Naidu also said, "Domestic politics shouldn't affect how we get along with other countries."

The Short Duration (SD) Discussion in upper house of Indian Parliament on "The unprecedented spike in violence in Gaza and the West Bank of Palestine, which has killed dozens of civilians" was first put on the House's agenda on July 16. This was after the Leader of the Opposition, Ghulam Nabi Azad (INC), gave notice on July 15 that he wanted such a discussion. But on July 16, Foreign Minister Swaraj wrote to Vice-President Hamid Ansari, who is in charge of the Rajya Sabha, and asked him not to let the discussion happen. She cited procedural problems and said that the topic "refers rudely to a friendly foreign country." Ansari turned down Swaraj's request, saying that "the notices given by the Leader of the Opposition and others did not have any flaws."

So, on July 17, the opposition asked for the Question Hour, which is the first hour of each Lok Sabha session and when members can talk about anything, to be cancelled so they could talk about the Gaza conflict. Ansari insisted that the government had to agree to a new date for the discussion to happen, while Sitaram Yechury of the CPI(M) pointed out that the topic was on the "Revised List of Business," which "cannot be circulated without the Government's prior agreement."

Anand Sharma (INC), who was Deputy Foreign Minister and Commerce Minister in the UPA government, said that the conflict got "half a page" in the BRICS Fortaleza Declaration, even though the government tried to avoid talking about it. Azad also said that the government shouldn't be afraid to talk about Israel and Palestine now that PM Modi had signed the BRICS Declaration, which says a lot about Israel and Palestine.

But the BRICS Declaration of July 15, which came out a week after the conflict began, doesn't even mention the ongoing conflict. Instead, it just restates positions that have been held for a long time. These include asking both sides to start talking again, speaking out against Israeli settlement policies, praising efforts to bring Palestinians together, and asking the rest of the world to keep supporting the work of UNRWA. (It's important to note that Brazil, one of the BRICS countries, called back its ambassador to protest Israel's actions, and on July 17, South Africa called the Israeli ambassador to protest strongly about the rise in violence.)

The discussion finally happened in the Lok Sabha on July 21. Three MPs from the ruling BJP (including the Foreign Minister) and two MPs from the INC took part. Most of the remaining 15 MPs were from regional parties or communist parties. The leader of the opposition, Ghulam Nabi Azad, started his speech by lamenting the fact that the subject had been on the agenda since July 15 but had not been talked about until then. He talked about the history of the "roots of the conflict" and said that the "fate of the Gaza Strip" was in the balance. He wanted to know what India thought about the conflict and said that the government should have spoken up first, even before the opposition.

Azad gave numbers about how many people had died and how much damage had been done in the Gaza Strip. He then said, "There is no comparison between the situation on the Palestinian side and the situation on the Israeli side." He reminded the government that former BJP Prime Minister Atal Bihari Vajpayee "fully supported the Palestinian cause" and asked if "this government's foreign policy has changed in any way." Azad said that India had a self-interest in the region as a whole, since there are more than 7 million Indians living abroad in the Middle East and India gets 70 percent of its oil from that area. He asked the House to pass a resolution that condemned "Israeli attacks" and demanded that the "massacre" of Palestinians stop. Notably, he also said, "Hamas's defiant rocket attacks on Israeli territory should also stop."

Anil Madhav Dave from the BJP wondered if the war in Gaza was the only fight going on in the world. He named the Sinai Insurgency, the wars in Sudan, Syria, Northern Kosovo, Northern Mali, the wars in the Central African Republic, Russia, and Ukraine as some of the other conflicts that are still going on, and he asked the House to talk about the whole picture. Ahmed Hasan of the TMC (West Bengal) called the conflict a "new Holocaust" and said that instability in the area was bad for India because so many Indians live in the Middle East. Sharad Yadav of the JD(U) (Bihar) compared Israel's offensive to Saddam Hussein's invasion of Kuwait and said that Israel was "trampling on a six square kilometre land." Yadav also said that there are a lot of people in India who follow the same religion (as those in Gaza).

A. Maitreyan of the AIADMK, which is based in the South Indian state of Tamil Nadu, spoke out against the violence and reminded the members that the House had not passed a single resolution to express sympathy for the suffering of Sri Lankan Tamils. Ram Gopal Yadav of the SP (Uttar Pradesh) said that this issue was important to India's national interests and that Israel was attacking the Palestinians with US-made weapons. He told the House that it should condemn what Israel did, just like it did when Iraq invaded Kuwait. Sitaram Yechury of the CPI(M) said that what was happening in Gaza was "genocide," and he asked the House to pass a resolution and "immediately stop all military purchases from Israel." He said that India, which buys the most weapons from Israel, was "paying Israel the profits that they are using to do this genocide in the Gaza Strip."

Majid Memon of the NCP (Maharashtra) said that the government's silence was "becoming criminal," and he asked the House to "express its outrage at Israel's behaviour." The Communist Party of India's (CPI) D. Raja started his speech by saying, "We Communists always stand up against genocide." He said that Hamas, which had the "popular support" of the Palestinians, was being "demonised" by Israel. He said that the conflict was between "an occupier and the occupied" and asked India to support the Palestinians. Like his countryman Yechury, Raja said that India should stop buying weapons from Israel.

Anand Sharma, the former deputy foreign minister of the INC, called attention to Israel's "arbitrary and disproportionate" use of force and said that the Congress had asked for a meeting because the government "had not reacted properly." Chandan Mitra of the BJP said, "India can't and won't support any violation of human rights anywhere in the world," but he also said, "Both of the countries involved in the conflict in Gaza are friendly to India." The way we lean in one direction or the other could affect our foreign policy and economic stability as a whole..." Mitra said that an INC government gave Israel diplomatic status in 1992 and that "India's relations with Israel have been strengthened, just as India has always supported the Palestinian cause." Also, he told the House not to "get too emotional about one issue," because "this kind of conflict has happened before."

Sharad Yadav of the Janata Dal (United) JD(U) said that Mitra was wrong to tell India to treat both sides the same when only one side was being killed. Mitra replied that a ceasefire was important and that the House should "not go into the merits, demerits, who is right, and who is wrong at this point in time." Kanimozhi

Karunanidhi of the DMK (Tamil Nadu), echoing A. Maitreyan of the AIADMK, said that the House "was silent" about the killing of civilians in Sri Lanka, but that it was "very good" that the House was coming together to pass a Resolution about it. Though Israel has a right to defend itself, this House must condemn the disproportionate attacks..." She also said that when Tamil Nadu members wanted to talk about the killing of Tamils, "we couldn't say anything bad about Sri Lanka" because it was a "friendly neighbour."

Tarun Vijay of the BJP said that Jews came to India "after being persecuted everywhere" and that PM Nehru "gave refuge to the Tibetans and the Dalai Lama." Vijay reminded the members of the BRICS Declaration, which called for efforts to bring Palestinians together. He said that the language was used because there are two groups in Palestinian politics—Hamas and Fatah—and asked if India could possibly support Hamas. He also said, "India can't be any more Arab than the Arabs." We can't be any more Indian than we already are." While asserting that Israel has a right to exist, he pointed out that Hamas had dropped twenty bombs on a UNRWA school. In response to the Communist members' demand that India stop trading arms with Israel, Vijay said that defence cooperation between India and Israel has "doubled in the last ten years." He thanked the INC for helping to make this happen, as it was in India's best interest.

K. C. Tyagi of the JD(U) said, "Once upon a time, praising Israel was considered a crime." He also said that the delay in having the discussion had led to a lot of wrong ideas. He didn't agree with Minister Naidu's statement from July 15 that domestic politics shouldn't affect foreign policy. He said that foreign policy has its roots in domestic politics. Tyagi disagreed with a Foreign Ministry statement from July 10 that said India was "alarmed" by the "cross-border provocation." He said that such statements don't reflect India's foreign policy and asked how India can compare Israel to the Palestinians. He also disagreed with the views of some members who said that similar resolutions condemning other countries had not been passed. He pointed out that the House had condemned Iraq's invasion of Kuwait.

Mohammed Adeeb (Independent from Uttar Pradesh) inquired why the government had hesitated to discuss the issue given India's historical support for the Palestinian cause. Equating Israel's occupation of Palestine with Pakistan's occupation of Kashmir, he charged that Israel's Ambassador (presumably referring to Daniel Carmon)—who he claimed had visited BJP Headquarters on "the day the Parliament wanted to discuss the issue" (July 15)—was influencing India's policy. This charge appears specious, as the Embassy of Israel in New Delhi has no record of any Israeli Embassy official visiting the BJP office on that day. The record indicates that it was on July 31 that Carmon presented his credentials to the President of India.

Hussein Dalwai of the Nationalist Congress Party (NCP) in Maharashtra said that India had nothing to gain from a relationship with Israel and that the country's interests were in the region as a whole. Baishnab Parida of Biju Janata Dal (BJD) from Orissa, while calling Israel and Palestine "two friends", went on to say that "[I] f one friend attacks another friend to kill him and if we stand as a mute spectator and let the two decide who will kill whom, then the stronger one will kill the weaker one".

Ramdas Athavale of the Republican Party of India (RPI) said that there was no need to cut ties with Israel, but that India should speak out against Israel for being unfair to the Palestinians. Mohammad Shafi of the Jammu and Kashmir National Conference (JKNC) charged that Israel was acting as an imperial country and that the issue was one of injustice and not solely a matter of Muslim concern.

In her response to the discussion, Foreign Minister Swaraj said that the government would not make any decisions based on religion. She also brought up the MEA statement from July 10 and the BRICS Declaration to refute the claim that India had nothing to say about the conflict. She answered Anand Sharma's question about whether or not PM Modi had talked about the issue with BRICS leaders by saying that the Joint Statement could only have been written after those leaders had talked about it. (However, as was mentioned above, the most recent rise in tensions was not even mentioned in the BRICS Declaration.) When asked about India's humanitarian aid, Swaraj pointed to the money India gave to the PNA's budget and the help it gave for development. She said that India's foreign policy wouldn't change because of the conflict. She said, "We support the Palestinian cause with all our hearts, but we want to keep working with Israel."

Swaraj pointed out that it was INC governments that had recognised Palestine (1988) and Israel (1992), adding that relations with Israel continued to grow after 1992 even under coalition governments. So, she was saying that it was India's "national" policy, not just that of the BJP or the INC, to support the Palestinian cause with all its heart while also getting along better with Israel. Members of the Left wanted the government to stop buying weapons from Israel. She asked them if they had made the same request in 2008 and 2012, when there was violence (presumably during operations "Cast Lead" and "Pillar of Defence"). She pointedly noted that in 2008, when the Communists were supporting the UPA coalition, 1,400 Palestinians had been killed.

Yechury interjected to say that his advice in 2008 to stop defence cooperation with Israel had not been followed, and he urged the Minister to listen to his advice now. Tapan Kumar Sen, a member of the Left party, said that the Communists had stopped supporting the UPA coalition because their advice to stop working with Israel on defence had not been taken. Swaraj admonished him not to misstate facts, as they had in fact withdrawn support on account of their opposition to the Indo-US nuclear deal. She also said that the Israel-Palestine problem was very complicated and pointed out that peace would have been reached during the most recent flare-up if Hamas had taken Egypt's offer to stop the fighting. She ended by saying that, according to the rules that the government had agreed to when it agreed to an SD Discussion, "there shall be no formal Motion before the Council, nor shall there be any voting." After a bit of chaos, the whole opposition left the meeting.

The MPs from the ruling party supported the government's response, while the MPs from the opposition tried to corner the newly elected government on a complicated foreign policy issue. No one else who took part in the discussions called for cutting diplomatic ties with Israel or ending the defence relationship, like Owaisi did in the Lok Sabha (as did Communist members Yechury and Raja in the Rajya Sabha).

It is important to remember that the leader of the opposition in the Rajya Sabha, Azad, called for an end to the "defiant rocket attacks" from Gaza even though he was very critical of Israel's actions. The member's comments show how hard it is for the government to handle these kinds of crises. Parida, a member of the BJD, said that both of India's enemies were "friends" of the country and told the government not to be a "mute spectator." Opposition MPs didn't talk much about differences between Palestinians, but BJP MP Vijay couldn't ignore the fact that Hamas was in charge in the Gaza Strip.

Representatives from local parties like the AIDMK and the DMK reminded the House that the demand for a resolution didn't make sense if Tamils in neighbouring Sri Lanka weren't also asking for the same thing. MPs from the ruling party also talked about the harsh reality of other conflict zones around the world.

Reaction of Indian Citizens

India's civil society was more affected by Israel's third military attack on Gaza than by the first two. Near a village in Srinagar, the capital of India's Muslim-majority province, police shot and killed a teenager who was protesting when the protests turned violent and people started throwing stones at security forces. Protests were also reported in Hyderabad, which is where the AIMIM is most powerful, and at the Israeli Consulate in Mumbai. Protests were held at the Israeli Embassy in New Delhi by 70–80 students from the Jawaharlal Nehru University, which is the best school in the country (JNU). After the war, at the end of August 2014, police in the city of Ahmedabad had to arrest a number of anti-Israeli protesters who had gathered without the proper permits.

There were also protests in favour of Israel, especially in the city of Kolkata. "Nearly 20,000" people went to a rally on August 16 to remember the Hindus who died in the 1946 Hindu-Muslim riots in the city. The rally was put on by a Hindu community group. The organisers shouted pro-Israel slogans and supported Israel's right to defend itself from the constant rocket attacks.

Some analysts said that supporting Israel's Gaza policy was the same as supporting "militarism and discrimination," but others praised the government for taking the "right approach" by not rushing into "foolish parliamentary resolutions" that wouldn't help solve the crisis or advance India's interests. Rajesh Rajagopalan said that the accusations of genocide were "ridiculous" because Israel took steps during the conflict that were meant to keep civilian deaths to a minimum. Former Ambassador Ranjit Gupta said that the "current hostilities in Gaza are essentially a war between Hamas and Israel and not a war between Israel and Palestine," and that Hamas was politically isolated in the Arab world except for Qatar. Gupta also said that parliamentary resolutions on complicated foreign policy issues "limit the flexibility and options of the government" and that the demand to stop working with Israel on military issues would be "an absolutely devastating wound we would inflict on ourselves."

UN Security Council Open Debate, 2014

At the UN Security Council Open Debate on July 23, 2014 , India's Permanent Representative voiced "deep concern" and said that India's "continuing commitment to Palestine is rooted in our modern history." At the twenty-first Special Session of the UN Human Rights Council, people said similar things (UNHRC). India supported the UNHRC resolution from July 23, 2014, that set up an International Commission of Inquiry to look into whether international humanitarian and human rights laws were broken in the "occupied Gaza Strip." In its first main paragraph, the resolution "strongly condemns [emphasis added] the failure of Israel, the occupying Power, to end its long occupation of the Occupied Palestinian Territory, including East Jerusalem, in accordance with international law and relevant United Nations resolutions."

This shows again that India did not stop supporting resolutions that use the word "condemn" in multilateral settings like the UNHRC, even though the word "condemn" seems to have been replaced by "deep concern" in its official statements made after November 2012. The US was the only member of the UNHRC to vote against the resolution. Of the 47 members, 29 voted for it, 17 didn't vote, and 17 abstained. In the wake of "Cast Lead," India and 33 other countries also voted for UNHRC resolution S-9/1 on January 12, 2009.

On July 1, 2015, however, India didn't vote at the UNHRC on a resolution that praised the report of the Commission of Inquiry (for which India had voted a year earlier) for calling on "parties concerned to cooperate fully with the preliminary examination of the International Criminal Court and with any subsequent investigation that may be opened." Fourty-one of the 47 members voted for this resolution. Gen. V. K. Singh (Ret.), India's Deputy Foreign Minister, said that India didn't vote because the resolution made a direct action-oriented reference to the International Criminal Court, which India is not a member of.

Senior Israeli officials were quoted as saying that India's reason for not cooperating with the ICC was "pretty weak" and that the Modi government's position was a "major change." A Jerusalem Post editorial also saw the ICC's reason for abstention as "an attempt to minimise India's purported pivot towards Israel" and said that such reasons were "motivated by a desire to avoid upsetting Muslims, including India's large Muslim population." This argument doesn't quite hold up when you think about it.

Many people think that the previous government's support for Palestinian-related resolutions at the UN or UNHRC was a sign that they understood how India's Muslim population felt. As was already said, this link was getting weaker and weaker. Even so, if the Modi government's reason for not voting was the same, it is hard to argue that India's position has changed significantly.

Experts say, "India still doesn't vote with Israel and the U.S., and both of its abstentions [in July 2015 and June 2015, both about an NGO with ties to Hamas] were about Hamas" (an Islamist terrorist organization). It remains to be seen if other Palestinian issues will also change in the same way. Inbar says something important: "The content of the bilateral relationship is more important than votes at the UN."

Parliament and India-Israel Ties

The unprecedented discussion in the Lok Sabha (July 15) and the Rajya Sabha (July 21), as well as the disagreements that led to the government agreeing to the discussion, was one of the few times the Indian Parliament spent a lot of time on the Israel-Palestine issue. The only other time the Lok Sabha talked in depth about India-Israel relations was on August 18, 2000. This was also when the BJP-led NDA government was in power. The talk happened after Foreign Minister Jaswant Singh and Interior Minister L. K. Advani made historic trips to Israel in June and July 2000, respectively.

Still, since 1992, MPs have asked a lot of questions about the relationship between India and Israel, their defence cooperation, and India's policy towards Palestine. They did this to find out more about or clarify government policy. On March 20, 2013, for example, BJP member Chandan Mitra asked if India and Israel could work together in more ways. Mitra wanted to know if India's Defence Research and Development Organization (DRDO) was working with Israel to make an Indian version of the Iron Dome missile defence system. This is because the Army has no protection against short-range rockets or artillery fire. Piyush Goel, who is currently India's Power Minister and a member of the BJP, asked if the government had responded to the offer of gas ventures in Israel. R. P. N. Singh, who is India's Deputy Minister of Petroleum and Natural Gas, said that no such offer was on the table.

On the other hand, MPs from Left parties like Owaisi (in Lok Sabha) or Adeeb (in Rajya Sabha) were worried about the growing ties between India and Israel. On April 21, 2010, Owaisi asked if the government's policy towards Israel had changed because India was no longer "condemning" Israel for building settlements or for "repression and violence in Gaza." Owaisi asked about whether a Congress-led government would change its policy towards Israel. In July 2014, the Congress-led opposition asked the BJP-led government the same questions.

In March 2012, Adeeb asked the government if the All India Muslim Majlis-e-Mushawarat had expressed concern about the growing ties between India and Israel. Deputy Minister Ahmed said that the government had seen a report claiming to be from the group and expressing worry. In December 2012, Adeeb asked what the growing trade between India and Israel would mean for India's trade with the Middle East. Anand Sharma, India's Minister of Commerce and Industry, told the member, "India's relations with Israel stand on their own and do not affect our long-standing and close ties with Middle Eastern countries."

Members of Left parties have almost always been the ones to raise questions about corruption in defence deals between India and Israel. On November 24, 2010, for example, Brinda Karat asked the government if they were "aware that the multi-billion dollar defence deals with Israel have become a major source of corruption and kickbacks, corroding the integrity of the Indian defence establishment." Minister Antony told her, "Some Israeli defence companies have been found to have done things that aren't right, so dealing with these companies has been made harder."

In August 2007, D. Raja and Syed Azeez Pasha, both of the Communist Party of India (CPI), asked about the idea of making missiles together with Israel. For good measure, they asked, "Is it true that most people in the country don't want military ties with Israel because it will upset the Muslim countries that India gets along well with?" Minister Antony told them that the LRSAM contract was signed in January 2006 and that working with Israel "does not get in the way of the warm and mutually beneficial cooperation we have with friendly Muslim countries."

MPs have the right to ask the government of the day about any issue and get more information, but the general direction of the questions they ask shows a clear link between their political views and the questions they ask. The only other time Parliament (Lok Sabha) "condemned" Israel was on July 31, 2006, when a resolution was unanimously passed criticising "the large-scale and indiscriminate Israeli bombing of Lebanon." The House sent the people of Lebanon "the deepest condolences, sympathy, and support of the people of India at this difficult time" and asked "all parties to the conflict to avoid violence."

A few days earlier, on July 27, 2006, Prime Minister Dr. Singh told Parliament that India "condemned in the strongest possible terms Israel's excessive and disproportionate military response." He also said that India had "condemned" the "unjustified arrest and continued detention" of "representatives of the Palestinian people who were elected by the Palestinian people."

During a Rajya Sabha debate on December 10, 2001, air strikes against Palestinian leader Yasser Arafat were given a "Special Mention." This was again when the BJP-led NDA was in power. Eduardo Faleiro, a member of Congress, asked the government to tell Israel to "immediately stop the aggressive strikes." Faleiro was the Deputy Foreign Minister who made the first official contact with Israel in September 1993 when he met with Foreign Minister Shimon Peres in New York. He also said that Gaza and the West Bank should have a "international protection observer force." Manoj Bhattacharya, a member of the Revolutionary Socialist Party, agreed with what he said (RSP). Foreign Minister Jaswant Singh said, "Air strikes, especially at President Arafat's home, are unacceptable and wrong. India supports the Palestinian people's inalienable rights without a doubt. Singh also said that he had talked to both Arafat and Foreign Minister Peres. He said that both of them "appreciated India's position and...asked India to help restart the peace process."

Modi's Middle East Strategy

After the Modi government took over in June 2014, there was a concerted effort to fix the strange fact that India's top political leaders didn't talk to each other much. In August 2015, for the first time in 34 years, Prime Minister Modi went to the United Arab Emirates (UAE). The relationship between India and the UAE was changed to a "Comprehensive Strategic Partnership" with agreements and understandings on a wide range of issues, from the economy to security. For example, the two countries agreed to set up a $75 billion fund to invest in infrastructure in both countries. They also agreed to work together to make defence equipment in India. This is part of their plan to strengthen the defence relationship they already have.

The India-UAE Joint Security Committee is part of the existing institutional framework for defence cooperation. This is a place where all aspects of security cooperation are talked about. (So far, the forum has held two meetings, in March 2013 and December 2014.) Since March 2013, there has been a permanent Defence

Adviser (DA) at the Embassy in Abu Dhabi. The DA's job is to improve defence cooperation by coordinating things like visits by naval ships and exchanges of military education.

In November 2015, India's Finance Minister Arun Jaitley went to the United Arab Emirates (UAE) to try to get more money to flow into the country. During his trip, Jaitley met the Managing Director of the Abu Dhabi Investment Authority (ADIA), which has the second-largest sovereign wealth fund in the world and is worth more than $800 billion. India wanted the UAE to put money into the National Infrastructure Investment Fund, which had just been set up.

There have also been a lot of high-level visits to India from the UAE, with the Crown Prince of Abu Dhabi and the Deputy Supreme Commander of the UAE Armed Forces, Sheikh Mohammed bin Zayed Al Nahyan, being the most recent ones in February 2016. India and the UAE did nearly $60 billion worth of business with each other in 2014-2015. Since 2000, the UAE has sent over $3.3 billion in foreign direct investment (FDI) to India. Over 35% of the 7 million Indians who live in the region live in the UAE. These people send home more than $15 billion in remittances. India-UAE relations have gotten a boost from the Modi government's renewed focus on reviving the Indian economy and from the fact that the UAE is home to the largest Indian diaspora outside of India after Saudi Arabia.

Foreign Minister Swaraj went to Israel, Palestine, and Bahrain in September 2014, the UAE in November 2014, Turkey in January 2015, Oman in February 2015, and Egypt in August 2015. (January 2016). Compared to the above visits, which happened in the 20 months after the NDA took office in June 2014, UPA Foreign Ministers Salman Khurshid and S. M. Krishna made a total of eight trips to the region during the entire second five-year term of the Congress-led coalition from 2009 to 2014. During that time, Dr. Manmohan Singh's only trips as Prime Minister were to Riyadh in February 2010 and Iran in August 2012 for the NAM Summit. Modi, on the other hand, has been in office for 17 months and has already made a successful bilateral trip to the UAE and a multilateral trip to Turkey (for the G20 Summit).

After Modi's trip to Antalya, Minister Swaraj went to Ankara in January 2015 for a bilateral meeting. Turkey's Finance Minister Mehmet Simsek went to India in February 2015, Foreign Minister Mevlut Cavusoglu went there in March 2015, and Deputy Prime Minister Ali Babacan went there in June 2015.

India and Turkey have been talking to each other more because of both economic and political needs. During Babacan's trip, for example, business groups in India and Turkey signed a deal to work together. India also asked Turkey for help in June 2014 to find 39 of its citizens who had been taken hostage in Iraq. Before PM Modi went to Antalya in November 2015, the Turkish Ambassador to India,

Burak Akcapar, was asked if the Indian PM's possible trip to Israel would affect relations between India and Turkey. Akcapar said that India and Turkey "have a very concrete agenda with India as a friendly country and...any third country does not figure into that."

Not only the Crown Prince of Abu Dhabi, but also the Foreign Minister of Bahrain (February 2015), the Emir of Qatar (March 2015), the Iranian Foreign Minister (August 2015), and the UAE Foreign Minister have visited India since Modi took office (September 2015). As was the case with the UAE, the Qatari Emir's visit focused on security cooperation. The two countries agreed to work together more to fight terrorism and to share intelligence information. India also agreed to train Qatari security forces. During the visit of the Bahraini Foreign Minister in February 2015, the first meeting of the "High Joint Commission" between India and Bahrain took place.

India and Iran are currently changing their energy ties from a buyers-sellers relationship to a real energy partnership that includes both upstream and downstream projects. India thinks that Iran's share of its oil imports, which had been cut because of unilateral US and EU sanctions that have since been lifted, will go back up. In 2009-10, India bought more than 13 percent of its oil from Iran, both in terms of quantity and value. By 2014-15, that number had dropped to about 6 percent. (While Iran cut back on oil supplies, India got oil from Iraq, which is now the second-largest crude oil supplier after Saudi Arabia, as well as from markets in Africa and Latin America.) India also hopes to see more progress on Chahbahar and the International North South Transport Corridor, which are both important projects for connecting to Iran (INSTC).

The Modi government has also made a big difference in the way India talks to Israel and the PNA on a political level. After Modi won the election in May 2014, Israeli PM Benjamin Netanyahu called him and met him in September 2014 at the UNGA. When asked if the leaders had talked about the Gaza conflict, the MEA Spokesperson said no, since the meeting took place less than a month after "Operation Protective Edge." In a statement, the Prime Minister's Office said that the talks were mostly about defence ties and ways to work together in software, cyber security, water management, and farming in dry areas.

In November 2014, India's Interior Minister Rajnath Singh went to Israel to improve cooperation on homeland security. Unlike other Indian cabinet ministers, he did not make the usual trip to Ramallah. The Defence Minister, Moshe Yaalon, went to India three months later. He went to the Israel Pavilion at the Aero India 2015 show in Bengaluru and met with Indian leaders like Prime Minister Modi and Interior Minister Singh in New Delhi. Both sides said again that they wanted to keep up their strategic cooperation and start working together on homeland security.

In March 2015, when Modi was in Singapore for the state funeral of Lee Kwan Yew, the leader of Singapore, he met with Israeli President Reuven Rivlin. In 2015, Modi and Netanyahu talked on the phone several times. For example, Netanyahu called Modi to thank him for the help that Indian agencies gave to Israelis after the April 2015 earthquake in Kathmandu. In December 2014, Modi sent a tweet in Hebrew to the Jewish people to wish them a happy Hanukkah. In March 2015, he sent a tweet in Hebrew to congratulate Netanyahu on his election win.

Foreign Minister Swaraj told reporters on May 31, 2015, when the Modi government had been in power for one year, that Modi was planning to visit Israel, but that "no dates have been set." If the visit goes ahead, Modi will be the first Indian prime minister to ever go to Israel. This will make up for the visit that Ariel Sharon made in September 2003.

President Pranab Mukherjee made a path-breaking visit to the PNA and Israel in October 2015. In his speech to the Knesset on October 14, he emphasized that

> *"India's consistent policy has been to build a strong, substantive and mutually beneficial relationship with Israel. We will continue to do so through high-level visits and exchanges so that India-Israel relations are accorded the utmost priority".*

When Minister Swaraj went to Israel and the PNA in January 2016, the MEA said again that India's relationship with Israel was "part of its engagement with the wider West Asian region" and was "independent of its relations with any country in the region." Swaraj met with President Rivlin and talked with Prime Minister Netanyahu, Defence Minister Yaalon, Deputy Foreign Minister Tzipi Hotovely, and Chair of the India-Israel Parliamentary Friendship Group Tzipi Livni about a wide range of topics. Swaraj had been to Israel once before, in 2008, when she was the Indian Chair of this group.

During her trip to Ramallah, where she opened a Digital Learning and Innovation Center, Minister Swaraj spoke again about the "three core dimensions" of India's policy towards Palestine. These were "solidarity with the Palestinian people, support for the Palestinian cause, and support for Palestine's efforts to build a nation and improve its capabilities." Her comment was important because, in July 2014, the Modi government was accused of changing India's policy towards the Palestinians, which had been in place for decades. As it did in Parliament, the government has tried to show that it is still a strong supporter of the Palestinian cause when talking to people from other parts of the region. On August 21, 2014, at the First India-League of Arab States Media Symposium, Minister Swaraj said that "India's policy of giving strong support to the Palestinian cause while keeping good relations with Israel" has not changed.

A meeting between President Mahmoud Abbas's Special Envoy Nabil Shaath and Minister Swaraj in November 2014 is another example of the Modi government working with top Palestinian leaders. Shaath was in New Delhi to celebrate the 125th anniversary of the birth of Jawaharlal Nehru, India's first Prime Minister. This event was put on by the INC, the BJP's political rival. On November 21, 2014, the International Day of Solidarity with the Palestinian People, PM Modi released a statement reiterating "India's support for the cause of Palestine" and expressing hope that "talks and negotiations between the Palestinians and the Israelis will resume soon." In November 2007, Dr. Singh made the last statement from the Prime Minister on this topic. In 2013, Deputy Foreign Minister Ahmed made a statement. In April 2015, Foreign Minister Swaraj met Palestinian Prime Minister Rami Hamdallah at the Asian-African Conference in Jakarta, Indonesia. The conference was held to celebrate the 60th anniversary of the Bandung Conference. The first talks between India and Palestine took place in May 2015.

On September 28, 2015, PM Modi met with President Abbas on the sidelines of the 70th UNGA session. At the time, the official spokesperson for the MEA tweeted that India and Palestine were "bonding." In September 2013, Foreign Minister Salman Khurshid met with his Palestinian counterpart at the UNGA. This was another high-level meeting. As we already said, Abbas's most recent trip to India was in September 2012, which was his fourth trip there since 2005. Modi's meeting with Abbas can be seen as more proof that the government is committed to keeping India's policy towards Palestine the same. In his speech in Ramallah on October 12, 2015, President Mukherjee said, "India's sympathy for the Palestinian cause and its friendship with the people of Palestine have become an important part of our foreign policy."

PM Modi has been to 37 countries since he took office, but only two of them were in the Middle East. These were the UAE and Turkey. Modi is expected to go to both Riyadh and Jerusalem in 2016, though. In August 2015, when he met with Modi, Iranian Foreign Minister Javad Zarif repeated the invitation that Iranian President Hassan Rouhani had given to Modi at the SCO Summit in Ufa in July 2015. All three of these trips will be closely watched, though the trip to Iran may not happen until after 2016.

In 2015, things got tough between India and Saudi Arabia. In September 2015, a Saudi diplomat in New Delhi was accused of being cruel to his Nepalese maids, which led to a diplomatic row. In another case, an Indian maid working in Saudi Arabia was hurt when her employer allegedly "chopped off" her hand. On October 9, 2015, Foreign Minister Swaraj said that the maid's injury was "unacceptable" in a tweet.

Even during this time of tension, high-level meetings between India and Saudi Arabia did happen. In November 2014, during the G20 Summit in Brisbane, Modi met with Salman Bin Abdul Aziz, who was then the Saudi Crown Prince and is now the King. Modi talked to King Abdul Aziz by phone on March 30, 2015, and told him that India was worried about the 4,000 Indian citizens who lived in Yemen. In December 2015, the MEA said that Ahmed Javed, a police officer, would be the new Indian Ambassador to Riyadh. This job had been open since April 2015, but Javed was the first person to fill it.

Under the Modi government, India's interactions with the wider region have been focused on protecting India's core interests, such as the safety and security of its citizens and the need for infrastructure investment in India by countries in the region. The Joint Comprehensive Plan of Action (JCPOA), which went into effect on January 16, 2016, made it easier for India and Iran to work together again on energy. Even though there is still a lot of trouble in the region, and the tension is made worse by the political rivalry between Tehran and Riyadh, India's "Look West" policy, which includes relations with key Gulf Cooperation Council (GCC) countries like Saudi Arabia, the UAE, and Qatar, as well as with Iran, is about to pick up speed.

Way Forward

The BJP has always pushed for closer ties between India and Israel, and its leaders have often (especially when they were in the opposition) praised the Israeli government's strong policies against terrorism and for protecting national security. When the Modi government took office, they said they were going to be tougher on national security issues. Modi was sworn in as Prime Minister on May 26, 2014. One of the first things he did was board the aircraft carrier INS Vikramaditya (which used to be the Russian Navy's Admiral Gorshkov) on June 13, 2014, and dedicate it to the country. This showed how important national security issues are.

The government has also said that India's defence procurement processes will be sped up to meet the urgent needs of the Indian armed forces to modernise and improve. In its year-end review in December 2014, the MOD said that the Defence Acquisition Council (DAC), the Ministry's highest decision-making body, had set a "scorching pace" by approving procurement proposals worth nearly INR 150,000 crores, or about $24 billion at the average exchange rate at the time. 205 Between May 2014 and February 2015, the MoD signed 18 contracts, two of which were with Israeli companies (relating to Barak-I missiles and Spike ATGM). In 2015, the amount of approved procurement proposals went up to INR 200,000 crores, which is about $29 billion. In 2015, Israel got new equipment like medium-power radars for air defence and Rafael-made "smart" bombs called SPICE that can be dropped from fighter planes on fortified or underground command centres.

All of these factors, which cover a wide range of ideas and strategies, have led to a stronger political and defence relationship between India and Israel, which will be completed by Modi's visit. Counter-terrorism cooperation, which both governments seem to have put at the top of their to-do lists, is one area of strategic engagement that could grow. India and Israel have the institutional tools they need to keep working together on CT/HLS, such as the HLS agreement signed in February 2014 at the end of the previous government's term. In September 2014, Israel was the site of the first meeting of the India-Israel Joint Steering Committee on Homeland Security.

Minister Rajnath Singh went to the HLS show in Tel Aviv in November 2014, as was already said. Since L. K. Advani's visit in June 2000, this was the first time an Indian Home Minister had come to the UK.

As part of its efforts to improve its HLS capabilities, India will continue to look for niche expertise in Israel. In August 2014, the Minister of State for Home, Kiren Rijiju, told the Rajya Sabha that one of the main goals of the India-Israel HLS agreement was to make sure that technologies and equipment used by security agencies were safe. India can benefit from using Israeli assault weapons, sniper rifles, and surveillance platforms like UAVs. India can also learn how to improve aviation security from Israeli training. These and other parts of bilateral cooperation can make it easier for India to deal with terrorist attacks.

Israel, for its part, seems to be putting a lot of thought into increasing cooperation between internal security and HLS. A person at the Israeli Embassy, the Deputy Defence Attaché for HLS Defence Cooperation, is in charge of these kinds of things. The issue is also on the list of things to talk about when Ambassador Daniel Carmon meets with leaders from the region. In December 2014, when Carmon met with the chief minister of Andhra Pradesh, they talked about the possibility of working together on internal security. During his trip, he also met with the heads of police in the two Telugu-speaking states.

Carmon said on April 1, 2015, at a public lecture at the United Services Institution of India (USI) that four working groups had been set up to improve CT cooperation. This suggests that institutional communication has been improved in this area. Carmon said again on the seventh anniversary of the Mumbai attacks that Israel "stands with the Indian people, government, and security forces in their never-ending fight against and eradication of terror."

In July and August 2014, when Israel attacked the Gaza Strip, it was the first real chance for the opposition, which had lost the election, to make the Modi government look bad on a sensitive foreign policy issue. Since no one asked the parliament to pass a resolution that was critical of Israel between December 2008 and January 2009 or in November 2012, the government was able to avoid this request.

India's support for a two-state solution hasn't changed, but people of all political stripes now agree that Israel is a key partner in meeting India's strategic and development needs. During the debates in Parliament, even people from the Left wanted to stop working with Israel on defence instead of breaking off diplomatic ties. (As was said, Owaisi of the AIMIM, the only MP for his party in Parliament, made this request.)

The lack of Palestinian or Arab-Palestinian solidarity is a key factor that can continue to affect how India responds to future Israeli-Palestinian fights. Chinmaya Gharekhan, a former Indian special envoy to the Middle East, says that "Hamas's rocket and missile activism only brings more support for Israel." However, he adds, "Israel's overreaction cancels out this advantage." As long as there are still disagreements between Palestinians and as long as Israel keeps saying that it has to use force to stop Hamas and other armed Palestinian groups from making trouble, the next round of violence will be just around the corner. The shape of India's response will stay the same as in the past, with all the problems that come with it. However, with a BJP-led government in power, there will be more politic al jostling at home.

References

See "A/HRC/22/35/Add.1", March 6, 2013, http://www.ohchr.org/ Documents/ HRBodies/HRCouncil/RegularSession/Session22/A.HRC.22.35. Add.1_AV.pdf

See "Operation Protective Edge", https://www.idfblog.com/operation gaza2014/#Terror

Ministry of Foreign Affairs (MFA), "Background to the 2014 Gaza Conflict", June 14, 2015, http://mfa.gov.il/MFA/ForeignPolicy/IsraelGaza2014/Pages/ Background-to-the-2014-Gaza-Conflict.aspx

For an examination of related issues, see P.R. Kumaraswamy, "India and Israel: Emerging Partnership", Journal of Strategic Studies, 25(4), pp. 192-206. See also Efraim Inbar, "The India-Israeli Entente", Orbis, 48(1), Winter 2004, pp. 89-104.

Portions of this section draw from my chapter "Equipping to Play the Role: India-Israel Strategic Engagement", in S.D. Muni and Vivek Chadha (eds.), IDSA Asian Strategic Review 2015: India as a Security Provider (New Delhi: Pentagon Press, 2015), pp. 312-326.

Ministry of Defence (MoD), Annual Report, 2006-07, p. 11, www.mod.nic.in

Lok Sabha, Unstarred Question No. 3994, "Indo-Israel Co-operation in Defence Sector", March 20, 2015, http://164.100.47.132/LssNew/psearch/QResult16.aspx?qref=14096

"Indian Government Approves Israeli Barak Missile Procurement", September 29, 2014, http://www.naval-technology.com/news/newsindian-government- approves-israeli-barak-missile-procurement-4387626

Dinakar Peri, "Kalyani Group Ties Up with Rafael to Make Spike Missiles", June 30, 2015, http://www.thehindu.com/news/national/kalyani-group-ties-up- with-rafael-to-make-spike-missiles/article7478207.ece

Pallavi Sengupta, "INS Kolkata, the Biggest Naval Destroyer, is the Weakest Link in Defence", August 14, 2014, http://news.oneindia.in/india/ins-kolkata- the-biggest-naval-destroye-is-the-weakest-link-in-defense-1502404.html

MoD, Annual Report 2006-07, p. 73, www.mod.nic.in

MoD, "Defence Research and Development", Annual Report 2012-13, Chapter 8, p. 104, www.mod.nic.in

MoD, Annual Report 2013-14, p. 89, www.mod.nic.in

Press Information Bureau (PIB), "Successful Flight-Testing of LR-SAM Missile", November 10, 2014, http://pib.nic.in/newsite/AdvSearch.aspx

Ajai Shukla, "Indian Navy Successfully Tests Long-delayed Air Defence Missile", December 31, 2015, at http://www.business-standard.com/article/ current-affairs/indian-navy-successfully-tests-long-delayed-air-defense- missile-115123000664_1.html

MoD, Annual Report 2011-12, p. 97, www.mod.nic.in

Vivek Raghuvanshi, "India, Israel to Build Missile Defence System", February 26, 2015, http://www.defensenews.com/story/defense/land/weapons/2015/02/26/ india-israel-mrsam-missile-army-air-force-air-defense/24050363/

See Lt. Gen (Retd.) Prakash Katoch,"Indo-Israel Relations", November 23, 2014, at http://www.indiandefensereview.com/news/indo-israel-relations/

Admiral Arun Prakash, "Planning for Tomorrow's Navy", excerpted from his book From the Crow's Nest: A Compendium of Speeches and Writings on Maritime and Other Issues (New Delhi: Lancer Publishers, 2007), at http:// www.indiandefensereview.com/spotlights/planning-for-tomorrows-navy/

Arun Prakash, "India needs a dedicated Defence Minister", August 23, 2014, at http://southasiamonitor.org/detail.php?type=sl&nid=8833

Report of the Comptroller and Auditor General of India for the year ended March 2012, "Union Government (Defence Services) Air Force and Navy, No. 4 of 2014 (Compliance Audit)", July 18, 2014, at http://www.saiindia.gov.in/ sites/default/ files/audit_report_files/Union_Compliance_Defence_Air_force_ Navy_4_2014_ Chapter_2.pdf, pp. 19-20.

Rajya Sabha, Unstarred Question 1786, "Establishing Chemical Plants in Bihar by Israel", August 10, 2005, http://164.100.47.5/qsearch/QResult.aspx

Prevalent exchange rate of I USD = 44 Indian Rupees; See Reserve Bank of India, "Reference Rate Archive", https://rbi.org.in/scripts/ReferenceRateArchive.aspx

Rajya Sabha, Unstarred Question No. 4481, "Defence Deals between India and Israel", May 16, 2007, http://164.100.47.5/qsearch/QResult.aspx

PIB, "Import of Defence Products", August 12, 2013, http://pib.nic.in/newsite/ AdvSearch.aspx

Rajya Sabha, Unstarred Question No. 1093, "Contracts for Defence Equipment from Israel", November 28, 2001, http://164.100.47.5/qsearch/QResult.aspx

Rajya Sabha, Unstarred Question No. 1105, "JV with Israel on Production of Missiles", August 22, 2007, http://164.100.47.5/qsearch/QResult.aspx

Rajya Sabha, Unstarred Question No. 2514, "Joint Development Programme with Israel to Develop Iron Drone", March 20, 2013, http://164.100.47.5/ qsearch/ QResult.aspx

Rajya Sabha, Unstarred Question No. 1098, "Procurement of Surveillance System from Israel", August 2, 2000, http://164.100.47.5/qsearch/QResult.aspx

Rajya Sabha, "Defence Deals between India and Israel", n. 24.

Pradip R. Sagar, "Defence Deal with Israel Hits a Roadblock", June 5, 2015, http://www.newindianexpress.com/nation/Defence-Deal-With-Israel-Hits-a-Roadblock/2015/06/05/article2850156.ece

PIB, "Commander-In-Chief of Israeli Navy Calls-on chief of the Naval Staff at New Delhi", August 24, 2015, http://pib.nic.in/newsite/AdvSearch.aspx

"Operation Sukoon", http://www.bharat-rakshak.com/NAVY/Galleries/ News/ Sukoon/

MoD, Annual Report 2009-10, p. 38, www.mod.nic.in

PIB, "INS Trikand Enters Haifa, Israel", August 19, 2015, http://pib.nic.in/ newsite/ AdvSearch.aspx

For an exploration of related aspects, see S. Samuel C. Rajiv, "The Delicate Balance: Israel and India's Foreign Policy Practice", Strategic Analysis, Vol. 36, No. 1, January 2012, pp. 128-144.

Inbar, "The India-Israeli Entente", p. 93.

Kumaraswamy, "India and Israel: Emerging Partnership", p. 202.

See Rajendra Abhyankar, "The Evolution and Future of India-Israel Relations", S. Daniel Abraham Centre for International and Regional Studies, Research Paper No. 6 (2012), p. 20, at http://www.tau.ac.il/humanities/abraham/india- israel.pdf (accessed on December 26, 2015).

Ibid.

Monika Chansoria in "Countering Terrorism through International Cooperation" in Gurmeet Kanwal and N. Manoharan (eds.) India's War on Terror (New Delhi: Knowledge World, 2010), pp. 189-190.

P.R. Kumaraswamy, India's Israel Policy (New York: Columbia University Press, 2010), pp. 240-241.

Kumaraswamy, India's Israel Policy, p. 268.

The former Indian Special Envoy to the Middle East Peace Process Ambassador Chinmaya Gharekhan brought this aspect to the attention of the audience during the 11th IDSA-BESA Bilateral Dialogue, held at the IDSA, New Delhi, December 7, 2011.

Ministry of Commerce and Industry, Export-Import Data Bank, http:// commerce. nic.in/eidb/iecnt.asp

Rajya Sabha, Unstarred Question No. 1894, "FTA with Israel", May 13, 2015, http://164.100.47.5/qsearch/QResult.aspx

"India, Israel to Work Towards Signing FTA", PTI, October 12, 2010, http:// www. livemint.com/Politics/1LPlkjLxKhGUOotOeT4xML/India-Israel-to- work-towards-signing-FTA.html

Tani Goldstein, "Israel, India to Sign Free Trade Agreement", Ynetnews, November 25, 2010, http://www.ynetnews.com/articles/0,7340,L-3989862,00.html

Harinder Mishra, "Israel Finance Minister Optimistic on Trade with India", PTI, December 10, 2011, http://www.outlookindia.com/news/article/israel- finance-minister-optimistic-on-trade-with-india/743934

Lok Sabha, Unstarred Question No. 3597, "Indo-Israel Work Plan on Agriculture", August 5, 2014, http://164.100.47.132/LssNew/psearch/QResult16. aspx?qref=3047

Israel Embassy, New Delhi, "New Center of Excellence of Vegetables in Gujarat", August 17, 2015, http://embassies.gov.il/delhi/NewsAndEvents/ Pages/New%20 Center%20of%20Excellence%20of%20Vegetables%20in%20 Gujarat.aspx

Ministry of Tourism, "Nationality-Wise Foreign Tourist Arrivals in India, 2012¬14", http://tourism.gov.in/writereaddata/CMSPagePicture/file/marketresearch/ New/222%20Countrywise%20figure.pdf

Niv Elis, "India's First Travel Convention in Israel Eases Conflict Worries", February 25, 2015, http://www.jpost.com/Business/Indias-first-travel-convention-in-Israel-eases-conflict-worries-392112

PIB, "Reconstitution of Empowered Committee Regarding Setting up of Semiconductor Wafer Fabrication (FAB) Manufacturing Facilities in the Country", January 28, 2015, http://pib.nic.in/newsite/PrintRelease. aspx?relid=115029

Rajya Sabha, Unstarred Question No. 2169, "Waste Water Treatment Plant with Foreign Collaboration", http://164.100.47.5/qsearch/QResult.aspx

NMGC Flyer, http://www.indembassy.co.il/pdf/NirmalGangaFinal.pdf

See "PM's Interview with Saudi Journalists", February 27, 2010, http:// archivepmo. nic.in/drmanmohansingh/press-details.php?nodeid=1024

Ministry of External Affairs (MEA), "External Affairs Minister's Intervention at Ministerial-Level Meeting of the NAM Committee on Palestine", September 26, 2014, http://www.mea.gov.in

See "GA/11319", November 30, 2012, http://www.un.org/press/en/2012/ ga11319. doc.htm

See "A/66/PV.69", November 30, 2011, p. 7, http://www.un.org/en/ga/search/ view_ doc.asp?symbol=A/66/PV.69. Amb. Puri is now a member of the BJP.

MEA, "External Affairs Minister's Interview to Asian Age", January 20, 2013, http:// www.mea.gov.in

Cited in Suhasini Haidar, "India's Official Shift on the Israel-Palestine Conflict Came in 2012", July 23, 2014, http://m.thehindu.com/opinion/blogs/blog- suhasini-haidar/article6241126.ece/?secid=12476

See "UN Member States: On the Record", http://www.un.org/depts/dhl/unms/

See "A/RES/70/141", December 17, 2015, http://www.un.org/en/ga/search/ view_doc.asp?symbol=A/RES/70/141

the list of co-sponsors of the 2014 resolution, See "A/69/487", December 9, 2014, https://documents-dds-ny.un.org/doc/UNDOC/GEN/N14/681/31/PDF/N1468131.pdf?OpenElement; For the list of co-sponsors of the 2015 resolution, See "A/70/488", December 2, 2015, http://www.un.org/ga/search/ view_doc.asp?symbol=A/70/488

See "A/69/PV.61", November 25, 2014, http://www.un.org/en/ga/search/ view_doc.asp?symbol=A/69/PV.61

Ibid.

MEA, "Statement by Mr. Biren Nanda, Ambassador of India to Indonesia and Head of Delegation at New Asia-Africa Strategic Partnership Ministerial Conference on Capacity Building for Palestine at Jakarta", July 14, 2008, http:// www.mea.gov.in

Representative Office of India, Ramallah, "India-Palestine Development Partnership", http://roiramallah.org/pages.php?id=40

MEA, Annual Report 2015-16, p. 66, http://www.mea.gov.in

Ibid., p. xix.

MEA, "Media Briefing on Arrangements for Haj 2006 by Minister of State, Ministry of External Affairs Shri E. Ahamed", May 19, 2005, http://www.mea.gov.in

MEA, "Statement by the Official Spokesman on the Large Scale Demolition of Homes in the Rafah Palestinian Refugee Camp in Gaza by the Israeli Defence Force", May 20, 2004, http://www.mea.gov.in

MEA, "Statement by Shri E. Ahamed, Hon'ble Minister of State for External Affairs on the escalation of violence in Northern Gaza", October 5, 2004, http:// www.mea.gov.in

MEA, "Statement by Official Spokesperson on the Killing of Innocent Civilians in Gaza by the Israeli Defence Forces", June 12, 2006, http://www.mea.gov.in

'Operation Summer Rains', Israel's response to Shalit's kidnapping, was the first

major military intervention after disengagement. However, Israeli military interventions were under a more intense international spotlight in the aftermath of 'Cast Lead'. This monograph therefore covers Indian responses to 'Cast Lead' and the two major interventions subsequent to it in greater depth.

MEA, "Statement by Official Spokesperson on Abduction of Israeli Soldier at Kerem Shalom Crossing Near Gaza", June 27, 2006, http://www.mea.gov.in

MEA, "Statement on the Results of the Elections in Palestine", January 28, 2006, http://mea.gov.in

MEA, "Statement by Official Spokesperson on Developments in Gaza", March 1, 2008, http://www.mea.gov.in

MEA, "Statement by Official Spokesperson on the Terrorist Attack on Mercaz Harav Yeshiva in West Jerusalem", March 7, 2008, http://meaindia.nic.in/ mystart.php?id=550313678

MEA, "Statement by Official Spokesperson on Resurgence of Violence in Gaza", April 18, 2008, http://www.mea.gov.in

MEA, "Statement by Official Spokesperson on the Upsurge of Violence in the Gaza Strip and the Humanitarian Situation", November 17, 2008, http://www. mea.gov.in

"Rocket attacks on Israel from the Gaza Strip", https://www.idfblog.com/facts-figures/rocket-attacks-toward-israel/

MFA, "The Hamas Terror war against Israel", http://www.mfa.gov.il

MEA, "Official Spokesperson's Statement on Situation in Gaza", December 27, 2008, http://www.mea.gov.in

"India Censures Israeli Strikes in Gaza", The Hindu, March 15, 2011, http:// www.thehindu.com/news/the-india-cables/article1538202.ece?mstac=0

MEA, "Official Spokesperson's Statement on Situation in Gaza", December 29, 2008, http://www.mea.gov.in

MEA, "Statement by Official Spokesperson on Situation in Gaza", January 4, 2009, http://www.mea.gov.in

MEA, "Official Spokesperson's Statement on Gaza Situation", January 9, 2009, http://www.mea.gov.in

Lok Sabha, Unstarred Question No. 224, "Israeli aggression in Gaza",

February 18, 2009, http://www.mea.gov.in/lok-sabha.htm?dtl/14004/Q224+Israeli+aggression+in+Gaza

MFA, "Dep FM Ayalon Comments on Human Rights Council Vote", October 17, 2009, http://www.mfa.gov.il/MFA/About+the+Ministry/ MFA+Spokesman/2009/Press+releases/Dep_FM_Ayalon_comments Human_Rights_Council_vote_ 17-Oct-2009

See 'Human Rights in Palestine and Other Occupied Arab Territories', http://www2.ohchr.org/english/bodies/hrcouncil/specialsession/9/docs/ UNFFMGC_Report.PDF

See 'India Express Reservations on Goldstone report', Zeenews, November 2009, http://www.zeenews.com/news576234.html

Richard Goldstone, "Reconsidering the Goldstone Report on Israel and war crimes", April 1, 2011, http://www.washingtonpost.com/opinions/ reconsidering-the-goldstone-report-on-israel-and-war-crimes/2011/04/01/AFg111JC_story.html

MFA, "Behind the Headlines: The Goldstone Report refuted - by Goldstone himself", April 3, 2011, http://www.mfa.gov.il/MFA/About+the+Ministry/Behind+the+Headlines/Behind-The-Headlines-The-Goldstone-Report-Refuted%E2%80%93By-Goldstone-Himself-3-Apr-2011.htm

"Goldstone's continuing value", The Hindu, April 6, 2011, http://www.hindu.com/2011/04/06/stories/2011040650981000.htm

See "Operation Pillar of Defence", https://www.idfblog.com/about-the-idf/ history-of-the-idf/2012-operation-pillar-of-defense/

'A/HRC/22/35/Add.1', n. 1.

MEA, "Official Spokesperson's Response to a Media Question on Violence in Gaza", November 18, 2012, http://www.mea.gov.in

Haidar, "India's official shift on the Israel-Palestine conflict came in 2012", n. 62.

Ibid.

MEA, "Statement Issued by the IBSA Member-States on the Situation between Israel and Palestine", November 22, 2012, http://www.mea.gov.in

Ram Madhav, "We need a new Strategic Culture", November 21, 2012, at http://ram-madhav.blogspot.in/search?q=israel

Ram Madhav, "India needs to develop a Strategic Culture", November 24, 2012, at http://ram-madhav.blogspot.in/search?q=israel

MEA, "Official Spokesperson's Response to a Media Question on Violence in Gaza", n. 99.

MEA, "External Affairs Minister's Speech at Global India Foundation Conference on 'Iran's Eurasian Dynamic: Mapping Regional and Extra- Regional Interests'", February 13, 2013, http://www.mea.gov.in

MEA, "India-Egypt Joint Declaration on the State Visit of H.E. Dr. Mohamed Morsy, President of the Arab Republic of Egypt (18-20 March, 2013)", March 20, 2013, http://www.mea.gov.in

MEA, "5th BRICS Summit: eThekwini Declaration and Action Plan", March 27, 2013, http://www.mea.gov.in

MEA, "IBSA Statement on the Middle East Peace Process", August 23, 2013, http://www.mea.gov.in

MEA, "Prime Minister's Statement in the General Debate of the 68th Session of the UNGA", September 28, 2013, http://www.mea.gov.in

MEA, "Statement by Mr. E. Ahamed, Minister of State for External Affairs, at the International Day of Solidarity with the Palestinian People held at Indian Council of World Affairs, New Delhi", November 30, 2013, http://www.mea.gov.in

Rajya Sabha, Unstarred Question No. 56, "India's Relations with Israel",December 5, 2013, http://www.mea.gov.in/rajya-sabha.htm7dtl/22569/ Q+NO56+INDIAS+RELATION+WITH+ISRAEL

Rajya Sabha, Unstarred Question No. 506, "Israel's Suggestion on Bilateral Relations", August 8, 2013, http://www.mea.gov.in/rajya-sabha.htm7dtl/22036/ Q+506+ISRAELS+SUGGESTION+ON+BILATERAL+RELATIONS

See MFA, "Operation Protective Edge: Israel under fire, IDF responds", August 26, 2014, at www.mfa.gov.il

Ibid.

See Chapter V, "The Threat to Israel's Civilian Population and Israel's Civil Defence Measures", in The 2014 Gaza Conflict: Factual and Legal Aspects, at http://mfa.gov.il/ProtectiveEdge/Documents/Threat_to_%20Home_Front.pdf

MEA, "Official Spokesperson's Response to a Media Question on Escalation of Violence in Gaza and Israel", July 10, 2014, http://www.mea.gov.in

See Lok Sabha, "Regarding Situation in Gaza due to Alleged Attack by Israeli Forces on Palestine Civilians", July 15, 2014, http://164.100.47.132/LssNew/ psearch/ Result16.aspx7dbsl=309 (Ms. Mufti's speech translated from Hindi).

Ibid.

Ibid.

Ibid.

Ibid.

Ibid.

Ibid., Translated from Hindi.

Ibid., Translated from Hindi.

Ibid.

Rajya Sabha, "Rulings by the Chair", July 17, 2014, p. 4, http://rsdebate. nic.in/ bitstream/123456789/631895/2/PD_232_17072014_p1_p12_2. pdf#search=gaza

Rajya Sabha, "Rulings by the Chair", July 17, 2014, p. 314, http://rsdebate. nic.in/bitstream/123456789/631897/2/PD_232_17072014_p311_p321_4. pdf#search=gaza

Ibid., p. 4.

Rajya Sabha, "Rulings by the Chair", July 17, 2014, p. 328, http://rsdebate. nic.in/bitstream/123456789/631893/2/PD_232_17072014_p327_p343_12. pdf#search=gaza

The BRICS Declaration is available at http://pib.nic.in/newsite/PrintRelease. aspx7relid=106712

"South Africa Summons Israel Envoy over Gaza", July 17, 2014, http:// thebricspost. com/south-africa-summons-israeli-envoy-over-gaza-violence/#. VetkSiWqqko

The SD Discussion is available at http://rsdebate.nic.in/ bitstream/123456789/631963/2/PD_232_21072014_p391_p467_8. pdf#search=gaza. Azad's speech translated from Hindi, pp. 392-297.

Ibid., pp. 408-411. Translated from Hindi.

Ibid., pp. 412-413.

Ibid., pp. 414-416. Translated from Hindi.

Ibid., pp. 418-421.

Ibid., pp. 421-422. Translated from Hindi.

Ibid., p. 424.

Ibid., p. 427.

Ibid., pp. 429-430.

Ibid., p. 431.

Ibid., pp. 433-434.

Ibid., p. 435. Translated from Hindi.

Ibid., p. 436.

Ibid., p. 437.

Ibid., p. 439. Translated from Hindi.

Ibid., p. 439.

Ibid., p. 441. Translated from Hindi.

Ibid., pp. 444-445. Translated from Hindi.

Ibid., pp. 446-448. Translated from Hindi.

Ibid., p. 451. Translated from Hindi.

Ibid., p. 451.

Ibid., p. 452. Translated from Hindi.

Ibid., p. 453. Translated from Hindi.

Ms. Swaraj's intervention translated from Hindi, Ibid.. pp. 455-462.

Ibid., p. 459.

Ibid., p. 459. Yechury's interjection translated from Hindi.

Ibid., p. 460. Translated from Hindi.

Ibid., p. 461.

The electoral strength of the two Communist parties, CPI and CPI (M), gradually declined in the 2009 and 2014 general elections. They won 20 seats out of the 138 they had contested in 2009, while in 2014, they contested 160 seats and won just ten. On both occasions, they secured about 4 percent of the total votes polled. See Election Commission of India, www.eci.nic.in.

Fayaz Wani, "Youth killed during anti-Israel protest", July 20, 2014, at http://www.newindianexpress.com/nation/Youth-Killed-During-Anti-Israel-Protest/2014/07/20/article2339676.ece

"Protests Near the Israeli Embassy in New Delhi Over Israel's Gaza Strip Air Strikes", PTI, July 13, 2014, http://www.ndtv.com/india-news/protests-near- the-israeli-embassy-in-new-delhi-over-israels-gaza-strip-air-strikes-587809

"Six anti-Israel protesters detained for demonstrating without police permission", August 25, 2014, at http://indianexpress.com/article/cities/ahmedabad/six-anti-israel-protesters-detained-for-demonstrating-without-police-permission/

"Biggest ever pro-Israel rally in recent times in India", August 17, 2014, http://worldhindunews.com/2014081729801/biggest-ever-pro-israel-rally-in-recent- times-in-india/; See also

Anuradha Chenoy, "Oppose Israel terror in Gaza", July 21, 2014, http://www.newindianexpress.com/columns/Oppose-Israeli-Terror-in-Gaza/2014/07/21/article2340498.ece; Rajesh Rajagopalan, "India, Israel and the Gaza War", July 17, 2014, http://orfonline.org/cms/sites/orfonline/modules/analysis/AnalysisDetail.html?cmaid=69377&mmacmaid=69378. Both the authors are Professors at JNU, New Delhi.

When Dr. Rajagopalan wrote his commentary, about 200 Palestinians had died. Eventually, however, the conflict resulted in the deaths of nearly 2,300 Palestinians.

Ranjit Gupta, "India and the Conflict in Gaza", August 4, 2014, http://www. ipcs.org/article/india-the-world/india-and-the-conflict-in-gaza-4591.html

Ibid.

MEA, "Statement by Permanent Representative of India during the Security Council Open Debate on 'The Situation in the Middle East, including the Palestinian Question", July 23, 2014, http://www.mea.gov.in

See "A/HRC/RES/S-21/1", July 23, 2014, http://unispal.un.org/UNISPAL.

NSF/5ba47a5c6cef541b8025 63e000493b8c/ e3 3 03 790b 3 83 7 6d78 5 2 5 7d2 5 005 4cca2 ?OpenDocument

See "A/HRC/RES/S-9/1", January 12, 2009, http://unispal.un.org/UNISPAL.

See "A/HRC/29/L.35", July 1, 2015, http://unispal.un.org/UNISPAL.NSFZ0/C648528A0DA08FB485257E7A0052C016

Lok Sabha, Unstarred Question No.3739, "Voting on UNHRC Resolution", August 12, 2015, http://www.mea.gov.in/lok-sabha.htim/dtl/25692/Q+NO+3739+VOTING+ON+UNHRC+RESOLUTION

Cited in Judith Bergman, "A Beautiful Friendship", Israel Hayom, July 9, 2015, http://www.israelhayom.com/site/newsletter_opinion.php?id=13111

Editorial, "India-Israel Axis", July 11, 2015, The Jerusalem Post, http://www. jpost. com/Opinion/India-Israel-axis-408668

Efraim Inbar, "Improving Ties between India and Israel", BESA Perspectives Papers, August 6, 2015, http://besacenter.org/perspectives-papers/improving- ties-between-india-and-israel/

Ibid.

Lok Sabha, "Discussion on Indo-Israel Ties", August 18, 2000,http ://164.100.47.132/LssNew/psearch/result1 4.aspx?dbsl = 37

Rajya Sabha, Unstarred Question No. 2514, "Joint development programme with Israel to develop Iron Dome", March 20, 2013, at http://rsdebate.nic.in/bitstream/123456789/621122/2/PQ_228_20032013_U2514_p85_p85.pdf#search=israel

Rajya Sabha, Unstarred Question 1520, "Israel's Offer for Gas Ventures", March 27, 2012, http://rsdebate.nic.in/bitstream/123456789/608465/2/PQ_225_27032012_U1520_p193_p193.pdf#search=israel

Lok Sabha, "Discussion on the Demand for Grant No. 31 under the Control of the Ministry of External Affairs for 2010-11 (Discussion concluded and Demands voted in full)", April 21, 2010, http://164.100.47.132/LssNew/ psearch/Result15.aspx?dbsl=2204

See for instance Rajya Sabha, Unstarred Question No. 1751, "Concern over India-Israel ties", March 29, 2012, http://rsdebate.nic.in/bitstream/123456789/608937/2/PQ_225_29032012_U1751_p87_p87.

pdf#search=israel

Rajya Sabha, Starred Question 372, "Trade Relations with Israel", December 19, 2012, http://rsdebate.nic.in/bitstream/123456789/615386/2/ PQ_227_19122012_ S372_p50_p52.pdf#search=israel

Rajya Sabha, Unstarred Question No. 1582, "Corruption in Defence Deals with Israel", November 24, 2010, http://rsdebate.nic. in/bitstream/123456789/468692/2/PQ_221_24112010_U1582_p41_p41. pdf#search=israel

Rajya Sabha, Unstarred Question 1105, "JV with Israel for Production of Missiles", August22,2007, http://rsdebate.nic.inZbitstreamZ123456789/70799/2/ IQ_211_22082007_U1105_p69_p69.pdf#search=israel

Lok Sabha, "Resolution Placed before the House by the Speaker Regarding Attack on Lebanon by Israel and Killing of Innocent People', July 31, 2006, http://164.100.47.132/LssNew/psearch/result14.aspx?dbsl=5715

Lok Sabha, "Statement Regarding Situation in Lebanon and Evacuation of Indian Nationals", July 27, 2006, http://164.100.47.132/LssNew/psearchZ result14. aspx?dbsl=5608

Rajya Sabha, "Israeli Air Strikes on Gaza and the West Bank', December 10, 2001, http://rsdebate.nic.in/bitstream/123456789/26181/2/ID_194_10122001_15_ p238_ p239_22.pdf

For an analysis of the visit, see Pramit Pal Chaudhuri, "Modi in UAE: India Plays the Gulf Card Against Pakistan", Hindustan Times, August 19, 2015, http://www. hindustantimes.com/analysis/modi-in-uae-india-plays-the-gulf- card-against-pakistan/article1-1381650.aspx. See also Talmiz Ahmed, "India and UAE: A Thali of Prospects", Asian Age, August 20, 2015, http://www. asianage.com/columnists/ india-and-uae-thali-prospects-759.

MEA, "Joint Statement between the United Arab Emirates and the Republic of India", August 17, 2015, at http://www.mea.gov.in

MEA, "Transcript of Media Briefing by Secretary (East) on State Visit of Crown Prince of Abu Dhabi to India", February 10, 2016, http://www.mea. gov.in. While India receives over $70 billion in remittances worldwide, nearly half of this is from the Middle East. The UAE therefore accounts for about 40 percent of the total from the region.

"Sushma Seeks Turkey's Help for Release of Indian Hostages from ISIS Custody", Times of India, March 20, 2015, http://timesofindia.indiatimes. com/world/rest-of-world/Sushma-seeks-Turkeys-help-for-release-of-Indian- hostages-from-ISIS-custody/articleshow/46628425.cms

"Turkey Looking Forward to PM Narendra Modi's Visit: Turkish Ambassador to India', NDTV, June 16, 2015, http://www.ndtv.com/india-news/turkey-looking-forward-to-pm-narenda-modis-visit-turkish-ambassador-to-india-772149

Ministry of Commerce and Industry, Export-Import Data Bank, http://www. commerce.nic.in

PIB, "Israeli Defence Minister Moshe Ya'alon Calls on Union Home Minister Rajnath Singh: Bilateral Cooperation Reviewed", February 19, 2015, http://pib. nic.in/ newsite/AdvSearch.aspx

MEA, "Transcript of Media Briefing by External Affairs Minister on Completing One Year in Government", May 31, 2015, http://www.mea.gov.in

"Address by The President of India, Shri Pranab Mukherjee to the Knesset", October 14, 2015, at http://presidentofindia.nic.in/speeches-detail.htm7441

MEA, "Visit of External Affairs Minister to Israel", January 12, 2016, http:// www. mea.gov.in

MEA, "Remarks by External Affairs Minister at inauguration of India-Palestine Digital Learning and Innovation Centre", January 17, 2016, http://www.mea.gov.in

MEA, "Opening Remarks by External Affairs Minister at the First India-League of Arab States Media Symposium", August 21, 2014, http://www.mea.gov.in

PM Modi's statement is available at http://www.roiramallah.org/pdf/India.pdf

PIB, "Speech by the President of India, Shri Pranab Mukherjee in response to President Abbas' remarks at the state Banquet", October 12, 2015, http://pib. nic.in/ newsite/PrintRelease.aspx?relid=128665

MEA, "Prime Minister's telephonic conversation with King Salman bin Abdul Aziz Al Saud of Saudi Arabia", March 30, 2015, http://www.mea.gov.in

PIB, "'Make in India' Concept Dominates Acquisition Plans of MoD in 2014", December 29, 2014, http://pib.nic.in/newsite/PrintRelease.aspx?relid=114175

PIB, "Year End Review 2015", December 23, 2015, http://pib.nic.in/newsite/

AdvSearch.aspx

Rajya Sabha, Starred Question No. 508, "Technology Upgradation for Law Enforcement Agencies", August 13, 2014, at http://164.100.47.5/qsearch/ QResult.aspx

Israel Embassy, New Delhi, "Israel to enhance cooperation with Andhra Pradesh", December 12, 2014, at http://embassies.gov.il/delhi/NewsAndEvents/ Pages/Israel%20to%20Enhance%20Cooperation%20with%20Andhra%20 Pradesh.aspx

These Working Groups were constituted at the meeting of the India-Israel Joint Steering Committee on HLS in September 2014. MEA, Annual Report 2014¬15, p. 50, http://www.mea.gov.in

Israel Embassy, New Delhi, "26/11: Israel remembers the martyrs", November 26, 2015, at http://embassies.gov.il/delhi/NewsAndEvents/Pages/President- Rivlin-meets-with-US-Secretary-of-State-Kerry-24-November-2015.aspx

Gupta, "India and the Conflict in Gaza", n. 168.

Chinmaya Gharekhan, "Missing Leader Report", Indian Express, January 9, 2015, http://indianexpress.com/article/opinion/columns/missing-leader-report/

Chapter 6

India-Israel Cooperation on Ballistic Missile Defence (BMD)

An Overview

As India becomes a more important player in international politics, its policies on important global security issues also become more important. It's important to remember that India is also making important changes to how it keeps itself safe, which has led to the need for new strategies. Up until recently, Indian policy was driven more by idealism than by practicality and national security. This is no longer the case. One of the areas that has seen a big shift in policy is in the realm of missile defence. India traditionally remained vehemently opposed to missile defence programmes such as the U.S. "Star Wars" programme, opposed militarisation of space and the American and Soviet anti-satellite (ASAT) missile tests. But the growing number of missile threats in India's neighbourhood has made it clear that the country needs to rethink its previous positions and approach. In the early 1990s, China gave Pakistan a lot of short- and medium-range ballistic missiles. This made India think about making a limited missile defence system as a way to protect itself. Since the mid-1990s, India has been working on making its own missile defence system. This is a big change in the country's policy on missile defense.

This chapter outlines in brief the evolution and status of policies as it relates to India's missile defences and then examines the status of the programme. The last part of the chapter talks about what this change in policy could mean for India and for the security situation in Asia as a whole.

India's Policy Approach and Rationale

In the past few years, India's policy towards ballistic missile defences has changed in important ways. While India has never spelt out a policy per se, statements in the United Nations and other multilateral bodies as well as in the Indian Parliament over the years provide a sense of India's policy perspective. India's policy started to change when it gave an official response to US President George W. Bush's National

Missile Defence (NMD) speech in May 2001. Later, India showed interest in making its own ballistic missile defence system, which was another sign of the change. But political opposition at home forced India to go back to its old, safe position of opposing the militarization of space.

But there was a big change: the harsh criticism was replaced by a more nuanced and sometimes unclear response to the new events. India took this nuanced stance because it made sense from a practical point of view. The first was the changing security situation in the region and the use of missile defence to deal with China and Pakistan's growing missile threats. Second, India thought that the US's new plan would take the major nuclear powers away from their usual focus on nuclear deterrence. This was something India didn't want to happen. The third reason was that India thought the US would move away from the old nuclear order (which India wasn't a part of) to set up a new one, and that India could join the new framework in the new global nuclear order that was starting to form. A fourth reason was India's own desire to forge closer ties with the US, a policy articulation that was becoming important in the early 2000s. Still, India's policy changed over time, and the change wasn't always clear if you looked at what the country's political and military leaders said at the time. But, after the Chinese ASAT test in January 2007, the new trends started to catch on.

Need of Missile Defence Shield

As was already said, New Delhi started to think about missile defence options seriously in the mid-1990s. China had long-range missiles that could hit India for a couple of decades, but they were not seen as a big enough threat for India to look into missile defence. In general, Pakistan is a more unpredictable enemy than China. Because of this, India has had to react much more quickly to threats from Pakistan than from China. India's BMD programme shows that this is how they think. India is also worried about China's space capabilities, but mostly about its ASAT weapons.

Changes in the world, especially in the US, with a big focus on missile defence, played a role in Indian policy debates. Also, India was interested in working with the US on high-tech projects, especially since the Bush administration had policies that were good for India.

The politics of the Indian BMD programme are the third and most important factor. The Defence Research and Development Organisation (DRDO), which is in charge of the BMD programme, has a lot of bureaucratic stakes in the programme. This is why they have been against importing BMD systems. Because of the missile defence development programme, the DRDO has also made a case for more money. People don't believe what the DRDO says about what it has done and what it can do because it has a bad track record.

Some people also say that India's decision to work on missile defence systems could be a sign that "India is unable to stop Pakistan from using terrorist proxies." People have said that if Pakistan "resorted to using nuclear weapons," India could respond because it has a BMD system in place. They also said that "an effective Indian BMD could partially, if not fully, stop the incoming attack," which would be followed by "a much stronger nuclear response."

Lastly, changes in India's larger strategic environment made India realise that missile defences could be useful, and in January 2003, the Indian government "decided to integrate missile defence into India's nuclear posture."

Tech Development

India started its missile defence programme in the middle of the 1990s. In 1996, the Ministry of Defence asked Dr. APJ Abdul Kalam, who was then the Scientific Advisor to the Defence Minister, if India could make a missile defence shield to protect itself from Pakistani missiles. Dr. Kalam had moved on from India's civil space programme and was now working on the Integrated Guided Missile Development Programme. He started looking for the systems and parts needed to build the missile defence shield in India. India needed a radar with a range of 300 km so it could detect enemy missile launches from far away. However, India only had a radar with a range of 60 km called Rajendra, which couldn't be used for a missile defence system. India first asked Russia for the radar and then, since Israel already had the Arrow-1 system with the Green Pine radar, asked Israel for it. Due to the fact that Israel and the US worked together on the Arrow system, Israel could not sell the radar to India. Still, Israel decided to work with India and offered to make a Long Range Tracking Radar (LRTR), which is the radar for finding targets and controlling fire. In the same way, India worked with France to make a missile-tracking guidance radar that was made in India. The Electronics and Radar Development Establishment, which is part of the DRDO, worked with the French company Thales. India then made missiles that could stop other missiles, as well as a mission control centre and a launch control centre.

India's first tests of its own BMD were of the PAD (Prithvi Air Defence) and AAD (Advanced Air Defence) missiles in November 2006 and December 2007, respectively. With these tests, India joined a small group of countries, including the US, Russia, and Israel, that have tried to stop ballistic missiles. India did a test in March 2009 with a target that was a ship-launched Dhanush missile, which is the naval version of the Prithvi missile. The missile had a range of 1,500 km. At an altitude of 75 km, a PAD missile was fired at the Swordfish (LRTR) radar to destroy it. Dr. VK Saraswat, who was in charge of the DRDO at the time, said, "This system will be our mainstay until we enter Phase 2." Since then, India has done more tests, and in 2015, the DRDO Chief Controller Dr. Selvamurthy said that the next step is to "move towards multiple target interception." However, the success rate can't be checked on its own. India tested the Prithvi Defence Vehicle (PDV) in April 2014. The PDV is meant to replace the PAD. The PDVs are made to attack targets in the exo-atmosphere, which is above the earth's atmosphere by more than 50 km (31 miles). The last time the PDV was tested, in February 2017, it was a success. However, in 2014, when the target was at an altitude of 120 km, the test was a "near miss," even though the DRDO said it was a success. In February 2017, an Indian warship fired a target missile into the Bay of Bengal, which is more than 2,000 km away from where the interceptor was launched from, which was on Abdul Kalam Island in eastern India. Different reports say different things about how high up the incoming missile was. On March 1, 2017, India did another successful endo-atmospheric test by shooting down an incoming missile from 15 to 25 km up.

The DRDO says that India has finished phase 1 of the project and can now hit targets up to 2,000 km away. It is also making missiles that can hit targets up to 5,000 km away. The DRDO has also made some bold claims that phase 2 of the missile defence system will be similar to the US Terminal High Altitude Area Defence (THAAD) system, but independent analysts are sceptical about these claims. Even though DRDO says otherwise, there have been reports that PAD missiles have trouble intercepting incoming missiles higher than 80 km. Still, Dr. Saraswat, who used to be in charge of the DRDO, said there were problems with dealing with the threat of longer-range missiles. These needs are very important because the second stage of the missile defence shield is almost all about protecting against long-range missiles from China.

Also, India hasn't done any tests with both exo and endo interceptor missiles together in a "integrated mode."

Strategic Implications of India's Missile Defence Programme

India has not yet used its BMD system, but it has already had an effect on Pakistan and the strategic balance between the two countries. But you can't say the same about China. China is not likely to be affected much by India's missile defence system.

Pakistan is worried that India might build or buy an effective BMD shield, which could make Pakistan's nuclear deterrent less effective. Pakistan has taken more than one step to solve this problem. One, it is adding a lot more nuclear weapons to its arsenal. Pakistan has one of the nuclear arsenals that is growing the fastest in the world. One reason for this could be that Islamabad is afraid that India will use a BMD. By adding to its arsenal, Pakistan can throw more missiles at the Indian BMD system in the hopes that some of them will get through. Second,

Pakistan is making a whole set of missiles with different ranges so that India's missile defence shield won't work. Pakistan is making all kinds of ballistic missiles, from ones with a short range to ones with an intermediate range. Even though there are other factors at play, such as the fact that Pakistan seems to be developing TNWs mostly to stop an Indian conventional invasion, one reason could be that Pakistan hopes that these missiles with different ranges will give it more nuclear deterrence in light of India's BMD. Third, Pakistan is also making cruise missiles that can carry nuclear warheads and can't be stopped by Indian BMD systems. In short, India's BMD system may have something to do with why Pakistan's nuclear arsenal has grown so quickly.

The Indian BMD system could also be good for the strategic stability of the area. One reason for making the BMD system is to protect the Nuclear Command Authority (NCA), which is India's national leadership. India's No First Use (NFU) nuclear doctrine is based on the idea that its leaders will be able to order a retaliatory strike even if Pakistan uses nuclear weapons first. If this trust isn't there, the NFU policy can't work. India will stick to the NFU policy if it has a BMD system, even if it's just a small one that protects the NCA in the Indian capital. The stability of nuclear weapons in the area is already in danger because Pakistan won't agree to an NFU policy. If India gives up NFU, as many critics in India want, and moves towards a first-use doctrine like Pakistan's, the region will have two nuclear powers with their fingers on the nuclear trigger. This would make the nuclear balance in the region very unstable. So, an Indian BMD could be good because it would let India keep its NFU policy.

In terms of how China and India get along, most people agree that India's missile defence is not likely to make a big difference. Most of the Chinese missiles that are aimed at India are of intermediate or intercontinental range, which Indian BMD systems cannot stop. Also, India-China dynamics are usually thought to be stable from a strategic point of view. On the other hand, this may be changing because some reports say that India's missile defence plans are now taking China into account as a major factor. In 2014, India and Israel decided to work together to make and use a system to stop conventional and nuclear missiles from China. India's changing worries about China may be mirrored in the way China thinks. China seems to be getting worried about India's growing number of missiles, especially the Agni 4, Agni 5, and Agni 6 long-range ones. The strong reactions in the Chinese state-run media, Global Times, show that India's intercontinental ballistic missiles are making China more nervous (ICBMs). Even so, China does not see India as a major threat or competitor because there is still a "capability gap" between them.

In the short term, India's missile defence system doesn't seem to have a direct effect on China's deterrent posture or its strategic dynamics as a whole. However, it is hard to say for sure how it will affect China in the long term. This is because strategic weapons aren't always seen as very important in the strategic competition between India and China, though this is starting to change on the Indian side. China doesn't think India's missile defence is a big deal because, for Beijing, the US has always been more important than India when it comes to making strategic decisions. But even if China attacked, a successful, limited Indian BMD system would give India more confidence that its leaders could survive an initial nuclear attack by China. This would mean that India wouldn't have to change its NFU.

Naval Barak-8 Missiles

Barak-8 is a long-range anti-air and anti-missile naval defence system developed jointly by Israel Aerospace Industries (IAI) and the Defence Research and Development Organisation (DRDO) of India. The Indian Army inducted a variant of Barak 8 missile to meet its requirement for a medium-range surface-to-air air defence missile. The naval version of this missile has the capability to intercept incoming enemy cruise missiles and combat jets targeting its warships at sea. It would also be inducted into the Indian Air Force, followed by the Army. India has a joint venture for this missile with Israel. Recently developed, India's Akash missile defence system also has the capability to "neutralise aerial targets like fighter jets, cruise missiles and air-to-surface missiles"

Naval Barak-8 is a long-range anti-air and anti-missile naval defence system being developed jointly by Israel Aerospace Industries (IAI) and the Defence Research & Development Organisation (DRDO) of India. Surface-to-air missiles (SAM) can counter attack aircraft, UAVs and incoming anti-ship missiles. The missile is expected to enter service with the Indian Navy in 2013.

In January 2006, India and Israel signed a $350m agreement to co-develop a new generation long-range surface-to-air missile (LR-SAM) for Indian Navy ships.

In April 2009, Israel signed a $1.1bn contract to deliver an upgraded Barak-8 air defence system to India. Deliveries are expected to be concluded by 2017.

Development and Tests of the Long-Range Anti-Air / Anti-Missile

Rafael Advanced Defence Systems and Elta Systems, a wholly owned subsidiary of IAI, were subcontracted for the Barak-8 joint development programme. Rafael provides missile interceptors, while Elta is responsible for the radar system.

The first test of Barak-8 missile took place in Israel in May 2010. The next test is planned to be conducted in Israel in 2012. The weapon qualification programme will involve eight test firings conducted in Israel and India prior to entry into service.

Components of the missile system, including the four-plane MF-STAR radars and shipboard electronic modules were delivered to India for final assembly.

Naval Barak-8 missiles will be installed on the three Project 15A Kolkata Class guided-missile destroyers under construction at the Mazagon shipyard in India. Delivery of the first frigate is scheduled for 2012, and Barak-8 missiles aboard the frigate are expected to become operational in 2013.

Four Project 15B Kolkata Class destroyers will also be armed with extended range surface-to-air missiles (ER-SAM). The extended-range missile can strike targets within the range of 100km.

"In January 2006, India and Israel signed a $350m agreement to co-develop a new generation long-range surface-to-air missile (LR-SAM) for Indian Navy ships."

Naval Barak-8 Design and Features

Barak-8 is a safe carry and launch missile for ships and is based on the small missile and proven vertical launcher concept. It can be easily fitted to existing or new warships, as the installation of the vertical launcher requires small deck space.

The system components include vertically launched missile, a dual-pulse rocket motor, active radar seeker and a two-way data link.

The missile is capable of intercepting supersonic sea-skimming anti-ship missiles and high altitude targets. It can simultaneously engage multiple targets in severe saturation scenarios. The multitarget capability will be achieved by a high performance warhead with an effective hit-to-kill mechanism.

The missile demonstrates exceptional interception characteristics throughout a very wide operational envelope. The same interceptor missile can be equipped with an additional booster motor for increasing the range. An advanced stand alone data link supports multiple simultaneous target intercepts and optimised wide area protection.

The missile will have a length of about 4.5m, diameter of 0.54m and a wingspan of 0.94m. It can travel at a maximum speed of Mach 2, with an operational range of 70km.

"In April 2009, Israel signed a $1.1bn contract to deliver an upgraded Barak-8 air defence system to India."

MF-STAR Radar used on the Jointly developed Naval Defence System

The MF-STAR radar will provide mid-course guidance updates for the missile initially after the launch from the ship. MF-STAR is a multifunction surveillance track and guidance radar for modern naval ships.

The radar uses multibeam, pulse Doppler and electronic counter-counter measures (ECCM) techniques to detect fast moving and low-RCS targets, even in complex environments / conditions and jamming environments.

The radar system provides 360° degree coverage and allows interception of incoming missile as close as 500m away from the ship. During the terminal phase, the second motor will be fired and active radar seeker will be activated to home on to the target.

Propulsion of the Israeli / Indian Surface-To-Air Missiles

Propulsion power for the missile will be provided by a dual pulse rocket motor developed by DRDO. The prototypes were delivered to IAI for final assembly, along with other systems to produce the complete missile.

The rocket motor provides high manoeuvrability at target interception range throughout the wide envelope of the missile.

Conclusion

India wants to put in place a BMD system with many layers. But it hasn't been clear what India's missile defence shield should be aimed at or how it should be built. No matter what the focus is, the delay in making India's missile defence shield work shows that India has a long way to go before it can even deploy a limited missile defence shield. The DRDO had set 2014 as the deadline for making the two-level defence shield work. The Indian government's recent decision to buy 12 batteries of S-400 air defence systems may be a sign of how serious missile threats are in India's neighbourhood, but it also shows that the missile defence shield that has been in the works for more than 20 years may not work. There are also rumours that the S-400s could be equipped with the 40N6 surface-to-air missile. This would make them better than India's PDV at stopping ballistic missiles in the exo-atmosphere. India is making some progress, but it will be a while before it has a system that can be used. Less than ten successful tests can't make sure that India will have a system that works. Comparatively, the US has tested its missile defence about 40 times since 2001. No matter what the final design of the Indian system is, any deployment of BMD will have a mixed effect on the whole. It could make Pakistan less safe, which could lead to a bigger nuclear force from Pakistan, but it will also let India keep its NFU posture, which is good for strategic stability. On the world stage as a whole, more widespread use of ballistic missile defences or even attempts to build them can lead to a technological arms race as different countries try to make sure they don't fall behind in a key area of national security technology. During the Cold War, one reason for the US-Soviet ABM Treaty was the fear that one side might get a technological edge that would help them win. To avoid a bigger arms race in technology, it might be time to look at the idea of making something like an ABM treaty that covers more countries.

References

For a detailed examination of India's opposition to the US and Soviet competition in space including the ASAT tests, see Ashley J Tellis, "The Evolution of U.S.-Indian Ties: Missile Defence in an Emerging Strategic Relationship," International Security, Vol. 30, No. 4 (Spring, 2006), pp. 113-151.

Ashley J Tellis, "The Evolution of U.S.-Indian Ties: Missile Defence in an Emerging Strategic Relationship," International Security, Vol. 30, No. 4 (Spring, 2006), p. 115.

Rajeswari Pillai Rajagopalan, "India's Changing Policy on Space Militarization: The Impact of China's ASAT Test," India Review, Vol. 10 , Issue 4, 2011, pp. 354-378.

Rajesh Rajagopalan, "Missile Defences in South Asia: Much Ado about Nothing," South Asian Survey, 11: 2,2004, pp. 205-217.

Rajeswari Pillai Rajagopalan, "India's Changing Policy on Space Militarization: The Impact of China's ASAT Test," India Review, Vol. 10 , Issue 4, 2011, pp. 354-378.

There are others who have argued that India's decision to pursue missile defence was more of a political imperative than military. See Rajesh Rajagopalan, "India: Largest Democracy and Smallest Debate?," Contemporary Security Policy, Vol. 26, No. 3 (December 2005), p. 606.

Sumit Ganguly, "India's Pursuit of Ballistic Missile Defence," The Non-proliferation Review, Volume 21, 2014 - Issue 3-4, 2015, pp. 373-382.

Sumit Ganguly, "India's Pursuit of Ballistic Missile Defence," The Non-proliferation Review, Volume 21, 2014 - Issue 3-4, 2015, pp. 373-382.

Ashley J Tellis, "The Evolution of U.S.-Indian Ties: Missile Defence in an Emerging Strategic Relationship," International Security, Vol. 30, No. 4 (Spring, 2006), p. 144.

Ajai Shukla, "The Untold Story of India's Missile Defence," Rediff, January 30, 2008, available at http://www.rediff.com/news/2008/jan/30missile.htm

Ajai Shukla, "Anti-Ballistic Missile Defence: Star Wars over India," Business Standard, December 1, 2012, http://ajaishukla.blogspot.in/2012/12/anti-ballistic-missile-defence-star.html

Electronics & Radar Development Establishment (LRDE), a subsidiary of the DRDO and a major player in the Rs. 2,000-crore programme, has developed two types of radars — the long-range tracking radar and the multi¬function fire control radar with two different tie-ups, one with Israel and the other with Thales. Thereafter, the LRDE has indigenized the programme to such an extent that India is in a position to manufacture and meet its needs of radars internally. See Ajai Shukla, "The Untold Story of India's Missile Defence," Rediff, January 30, 2008, available at http://www.rediff.com/news/2008/jan/30missile.htm; and Ashok Sharma, "India's Missile Defence Programme: Threat Perceptions and Technological Evolution," Manekshaw Paper No. 15, 2009, http://www.claws.in/images/publication_pdf/1262760881MP_15 111209.pdf

"40 Cos Involved in Making of Missile Killers," The Hindu Business Line, January 27, 2008, available at http://www.thehindubusinessline.com/todays-paper/tp-economy/article1614356.ece?ref=archive

"India Tests 'Swordfish' Radar with Successful Missile Defence Test," domain-b.com, March 06, 2009, available at http://www.domain-b.com/aero/mil_avi/miss_muni/20090306_successful_missile.html

Vishal Thapar, "India Successfully Tests Missile Defence System," CNN-IBN, March 07, 2009, available at http://ibnlive.in.com/news/india-successfully-tests-missile-defence-system/87057-3.html

Franz-Stefan Gady, "India Successfully Tests Prithvi Defence Vehicle, A New Missile Killer System," The Diplomat, February 15, 2017, http://thediplomat.com/2017/02/india-successfully-tests-prithvi-defense-vehicle- a-new-missile-killer-system/

Smriti Jain, "India's impregnable ballistic missile defence interceptor shield is a strong message to Pakistan," Financial Express, March 2, 2017, http://www.financialexpress.com/india-news/indias-impregnable-ballistic- missile-defence-interceptor-shield-is-a-strong-message-to-pakistan/572233/; and Franz-Stefan Gady, "India Successfully Tests Prithvi Defence Vehicle, A New Missile Killer System," The Diplomat, February 15, 2017, http://thediplomat.com/2017/02/india-successfully-tests-prithvi-defense-vehicle-a-new-missile-killer-system/

https://www.naval-technology.com/projects/naval-barak-8-surface-air-missiles/

"India Starts Work on Phase-II of Missile Defence System," domain-b.com, May 18, 2011, http://www.domain- b.com/aero/mil_avi/miss_muni/20110518_defence_system_oneView.html

Rakesh Krishnan Simha, "India Is Building A Missile Defence System - With Russian Missiles!," Swarajya, November 8, 2015, https://swarajyamag.com/books/missile-defence-erecting-an-iron-dome-over-india

Sandeep Unnithan, "DRDO Readies Shield against Chinese ICBMs," India Today, March 09, 2009, http://indiatoday.intoday.in/site/story/DRDO+readies+shield+against+Chinese+ICBMs/1/31874.html

Sandeep Unnithan, "DRDO Readies Shield against Chinese ICBMs," India Today, March 09, 2009, http://indiatoday.intoday.in/site/story/DRDO+readies+shield+against+Chinese+ICBMs/1/31874.html

"India's Ballistic Missile Defence system: All you need to know," Times of India, February 12, 2017, http://timesofindia.indiatimes.com/india/indias-ballistic-missile-defence-system-all-you-need-to- know/articleshow/57105516.cms

Sumit Ganguly, "India's Pursuit of Ballistic Missile Defence," The Non-proliferation Review, Volume 21, 2014 - Issue 3-4, 2015, pp. 373-382.

Vivek Raghuvanshi, "India, Israel to Build Anti-Missile System," Defence News, February 6, 2014, http://www.defensenews.com/article/20140206/DEFREG03/302060025/India-Israel=-Build-Anti-Missile-System

"India needs to cool its missile fever," Global Times, January 4, 2017, http://www.globaltimes.cn/content/1027113.shtml

Xiaoping Yang, "China's Perceptions of India as A Nuclear Weapon Power," Regional Insight, Carnegie Endowment for International Peace, June 30, 2016, http://carnegieendowment.org/2016/06/30/china-s-perceptions-of-india-as-nuclear-weapons-power-pub-63970

Rajesh Rajagopalan, "India: Largest Democracy and Smallest Debate?," Contemporary Security Policy, Vol. 26, No. 3 (December 2005), p. 609.

It is not clear whether 40N6 has become operational even in Russia in addition to the emerging complexities in India-Russia relations. For details, see Franz-Stefan Gady, "India Successfully Tests Prithvi Defence Vehicle, A New Missile Killer System," The Diplomat, February 15, 2017, http://thediplomat.com/2017/02/india-successfully-tests-prithvi-defense-vehicle-a-new-missile-killer-system/

Chapter 7

A Look at India and Israel: From West Asia

An Overview

The way people in West Asia see ties between India and Israel has been tied to both the region's negative view of Israel and Israel's changing position in West Asian geopolitics. In the last 20 years, India's economic and political power has grown, and its economic ties with countries in West Asia have grown stronger. This has brought new factors into play. This point of view, along with the hope that India can play a positive role in West Asian affairs, has changed how Arabs see India-Israel ties. The Arab point of view is getting more complex because Israel is against what the Islamic Republic of Iran and its allies and proxies are doing in the area.

The Arabs thought that Israel was a foreign body that had been transplanted onto Arab land. They also thought that Israel's creation was a continuation of Western imperialism and colonialism. Even though Jews are a people of the Book, Israelis were seen as oppressors and usurpers of Arab land. As Israel made it harder for Muslims to visit holy places in Palestine, these views became even stronger. The repeated defeats of the Arabs by the Israelis, even though the Arabs had more people, were very hard on the Arabs' minds and made their wounds worse. Seven decades after the creation of the state of Israel, many people in the Arab world feel like they can't do anything to change the situation.

In 1948, when Israel became a country, people in the Arab world couldn't believe it. Arab pride was severely hurt by the fact that they couldn't stop this by force of arms. Even though the Suez crisis didn't do much damage to Egypt, it showed how the West could use Israel in the region. The complete defeat of the Arab armies in 1967 and again in 1973, along with the peace treaties that Egypt and Jordan signed with Israel afterward, shattered Arab hopes that they could get rid of Israel. Still, new actors keep coming up to talk about the pain, anger, and frustration of Arabs, which shows up as violent opposition to the state of Israel. The Palestine Liberation Organization (PLO) did become a serious non-traditional threat to the Israeli state, but it wasn't able to change anything except for some spectacular acts of terrorism. The Islamic Revolution in Iran created another enemy sworn to destroy Israel.

The fact that the Palestinians and the rest of the Arab world can't do much to stop what Israel is doing has made them feel even more frustrated. Some of these Israeli actions are the destruction of Sabra and Shatila by Israel's allies, the Phalangists, in 1982; Israel's brutal response to the First (1987–1993) and Second (2000-2005) Intifadas; the Lebanon Conflict (2006); and the Gaza wars of 2007, 2008–2009, 2012, and 2014. Even though violent opposition to Israel has moved on from the PLO to other groups like Hamas and Islamic Jihad, the rhetoric has stayed the same, both in the West Bank and in Gaza, and from one generation to the next. Even though the Palestinians have been fighting for decades, there has been no real change on the ground. On the contrary, Israel's plans to take over more land and its settlements keep growing.

This history has gotten different responses from the four most important groups in the Arab World: the ruling regimes, the clerics, the media and opinion leaders, and the general public, or "street." Arab regimes were united in their strong opposition to Israel's creation at first, but as time went on, they became more and more frustrated because they couldn't make any real changes. The strategic situation in the region has changed, and so has the way Arabs think about things. In 1979, the Islamic Revolution in Iran added a new factor to regional politics: the Islamic regime, which wanted to change the way things were in geopolitics. Many regimes in the area, especially monarchies, saw this as a new threat. During the first Gulf crisis, when Iraq occupied Kuwait, many Gulf Cooperation Council (GCC) countries were upset that the Palestinians stood by Saddam Hussein.

After the Second Gulf War, the Shia crescent formed, and in recent years, the Obama administration has been trying to reach a nuclear deal with Iran. This has brought Arabs together in a way that means Israel is no longer their main enemy. The "Arab Spring" made people think about more pressing problems. Even though many Arab regimes say they support the Palestinian cause and will listen to the people, they don't plan to do much to back up their words.

In Sunni states, the clerical establishment mostly takes its political cues from the ruling establishment. With the exception of the Al-Aqsa issue, it doesn't care more about the Palestinian issue than the ruling regimes do. Arab leaders, especially those on the left, and the media are still very against Israel and what it does. Most likely, this won't change. They have a lot of power in the Arab street, but with so much chaos in the region right now, they have other things on their minds.

Even though people are very against Israel, public opinion changes quickly. One day, the Palestinian issue might be the most important thing to them, and the next day, it might be something else. Iran and its allies and proxies are always there to remind them of this and the geopolitical threat that is coming. So, the region's view of Israel is shaped by the above-mentioned four groups: the regimes, the clerical establishment, the opinion-makers, and the people on the street. Their views are not all the same, but they are all against Israel's place in the region. So, it's not surprising that after 70 years, only two of the 22 countries in the League of Arab States have recognised Israel.

India–Israel ties and the West Asia

In order to understand how India and Israel are seen from West Asia, it would be helpful to look at how India's views on Israel and its ties with it have changed over time. Indian policy has been shaped by many things in the past and continues to be shaped by many things today. India just got its independence in 1947, so it was against all kinds of colonisation and could understand the Palestinians' situation as another colonised people. It saw the creation of Israel as a different way of continuing the colonisation of Palestine. Having been through the pain of a divide between communities, it was very against religion being used to create states. It was also worried that Pakistan would use Muslim sympathy to get Muslim countries to fight against India. It fought back against Pakistan's bad propaganda by being "more loyal to the Palestinian cause than the King." Also, as a country that wants to be in charge of the third world, India couldn't ignore Arab feelings.

During the Mandate (1922–1948), the Indian government spent a lot of time and money on Muslim issues and the Arabs' fight in general and in Palestine in particular. They also gave them both material and moral support. Some important Muslim leaders, like the Ali brothers, worked hard to get people in India to support these causes. At first, they were part of the Indian National Congress and influenced how the Congress and Gandhiji thought about the problem. Gandhiji, who, when he was asked, admitted that he didn't know much about the issue, said that Palestine should be for the people of Palestine. Mohammad Ali Johar was a well-known leader of the Khilafat movement. He was close with the Grand Mufti of Jerusalem, Haj Amin al-Husseini, and he strongly supported the Palestinian cause. Shawki, an important Egyptian poet, wrote a poem that praises what he did. In January 1931, Johar died in London and was buried in Jerusalem. People say that the Grand Mufti had him buried in Jerusalem so that Indian Muslims would support him at the 1931 General Islamic Congress in Jerusalem.

India opposed the splitting of Palestine and the creation of the state of Israel at the United Nations because of all of these different reasons (UN). When Israel was founded in May 1948, the most powerful people in India's government had two very different ideas about it. Maulana Abul Kalam Azad was in charge of the group that didn't want to recognise a state based on religion. On the other hand, some people, like Sardar Vallabhbhai Patel, pushed for this new reality to be accepted. Prime Minister Jawaharlal Nehru said that since the UN had recognised Israel,

India should do the same, but it shouldn't make diplomatic ties with Israel because that would go against its values. On September 17, 1950, India made it official that it recognised Israel. India's stand was welcomed by all sections of Arab opinion-makers.

Diplomacy Involved

India helped the Arab nationalist movements in Egypt and Algeria because it believed and stood for the same things. In 1955, Nehru brought Gamal Abdel Nasser, the president of Egypt, to Bandung to strengthen ties between Africa and Asia. During the Suez crisis in 1956, Egypt got help from India. It's interesting to note that Israel wasn't invited to Bandung. This may have been because Arab countries threatened to boycott the event. Egypt, on the other hand, didn't let Portuguese ships use the Suez Canal when India kicked them out of Goa. This was because many Arabs believed that India and Indians were against colonialism and on the side of the oppressed people of the world.

During the India–Pakistan War in 1965, the relationship between India and the Arab world was put to its first real test. The Gulf States and Pakistan's partner in the Central Treaty Organization (CENTO), Iran, made it clear that they were on Pakistan's side. The Arab press also said that Israel was giving India weapons, which is not true. Arab Republics, on the other hand, helped India. In 1967, after the "Naqba," in which Israel badly beat the Arab armies, India helped the Arabs. The government, the people, and the media all liked this a lot. But when Pakistan asked India to leave the meeting in Rabat that created the Organization of Islamic Cooperation in 1969, India didn't get much help (OIC).

Again, the Arab world did not help India during the 1971 Bangladesh War, except for Oman, Syria, and Iraq. Algeria remained neutral. India, on the other hand, did get help from Israel. India didn't expect this negative response from the Arab world, and it knew that it would have to change how it helped the Arabs. After the Arab-Israeli War of 1973, some Arab countries had a very different view of the world. Egypt changed its mind and began to work with Israel. It also switched its allegiance from the Soviet Union to the United States. As a result, it was kicked out of the Arab League. Jordan also did what Egypt did. Arab countries, Arab streets, Arab media, and Arab regimes were all divided. India's main partner in the Arab world, Egypt, was no longer as friendly as it used to be, and India's policy towards Palestine in this situation started to lose some of its importance.

India's Support in maintaining Peace

In 1974, when Yasser Arafat spoke to the UN General Assembly, he became known around the world. India supported the UN giving Arafat this platform at a time when many countries thought the PLO was a terrorist group. Arafat had a lot of influence on India's political system. In 1975, the PLO opened an office in the city of New Delhi. India was the first country that wasn't Arab to agree that the PLO was the only legitimate representative of the Palestinian people in 1977. The Arab world was happy about these moves.

India was also aware of the First Intifada, which began in 1986. India was one of the first countries to recognise the state of Palestine after it was declared on November 15, 1988, at an extraordinary conference in Algiers. Indira Gandhi's sympathy for the Palestinians and the close relationship she and Arafat were able to build helped the Indian support for the Palestinian cause as well. Rajiv Gandhi followed in her steps as well. During the 1970s and 1980s, India had a very positive reputation in the Arab world because of this.

The Iraqi invasion of Kuwait in 1990 divided the Arab world. At the beginning of 1991, the First Gulf War began. The US completely destroyed the Iraqi Army and grew its power in the Arab world. The US started the Arab-Israeli peace process again after winning the Gulf War. From October 20 to November 1, 1991, Israelis and Palestinians met at the Madrid Conference. This caused a split within the Palestinian camp, with the people who didn't want peace coming together under the name Hamas. Relations with Israel, or the lack of them, were no longer the litmus test for whether or not you had good relationships with the Arab world.

Recognition and The Results of It

By the end of 1991, the Soviet Union had fallen apart. This created a moment of unipolarity and a very different world in which the US was the only hegemon. The Non-aligned Movement (NAM) and solidarity with the third world, as well as the voices of NAM countries like India, became less important. India had to change its policies to deal with the US, and its relationship with Israel was a big part of that because of the Jewish lobby in the US. Because of this, India's policy towards Israel since 1947 needed to be looked at again, and any changes needed to be made.

The next logical step was for India to start diplomatic relations with Israel in January 1992. This set the relationship between India and Israel on a new path. It's interesting that China took a similar path. Before making diplomatic ties with Israel, India worked closely with the Palestinian leadership. Arafat went to India and agreed that it was India's sovereign right to have diplomatic relations with Israel and that Palestinians had no right to question this decision, especially since they were also in talks with Israel. Two states living in peace next to each other was important to the Palestinians. The relationship between India and Israel would help India's efforts to help set up a Palestinian state. This would make the peace process bigger than just the United States.

The Arab world as a whole did not like the fact that India had diplomatic relations with Israel. Arab people were shocked, and Arab news outlets were very critical. The Arab leaders, on the other hand, were not too worried. Aside from the Iranian clerical regime, most people didn't pay much attention to the change. Iran, which wanted to become the leader of the Muslim world, was working to build strong ties with the Palestinians who were against peace. Yet, when President Ali Akbar Hashemi Rafsanjani was in charge, it had a pragmatic approach and didn't criticise the Indian initiative too much. During this process, India kept the Arab regimes informed by briefing their envoys in Delhi and sending special envoys to their capitals to explain the next step.

The Oslo Accords, which were made between Israel and the PLO in 1993 and 1995, were a result of the Madrid Conference. They were a way for the PLO to recognise Israel as a state. This led to the creation of the Palestinian National Authority (PNA), which has only a small amount of freedom. Also, India started making changes to its economy and building up its own strengths in the 1990s. It kept up its policy of supporting the Palestinian cause, but at the same time, it slowly and steadily got closer to Israel. Both of these policies stayed the same, and relations with Israel got better while staying under the radar. People in the Arab world could see that India had changed.

The PLO and PNA were still grateful for India's help, but Arabs on the street and in the media were not convinced and thought India had changed its traditional role. At the same time, Pakistani propaganda was going strong. The OIC has often criticised India on the issue of Kashmir and how it treats Indian Muslims, citing things like the destruction of the Babri Masjid in 1992 and the Mumbai riots in 1994. This was mostly because of what it did. Even though OIC member countries told India one-on-one that they did not agree with the criticism, they did nothing to stop it. India, which had always been a strong supporter of Arab causes, especially the Palestinian cause, saw this as a bad thing.

Shifts in India's Israel Policy

As India's economy got stronger, it was ready to try something new and be less cautious about its relationship with Israel. In 1997, Israel's President Ezer Weizman was the first head of state to visit India, and in 2000, India's Foreign Minister Jaswant Singh was the first to visit Israel. India already thought of Israel as a strategic partner because of its help during the Kargil War with Pakistan in 1999. This process came to an end in 2003 when Prime Minister Ariel Sharon went to India. This got a lot of criticism from West Asia, but it wasn't anything India couldn't handle. China, on the other hand, didn't get the same kind of criticism because it wasn't a traditional supporter and so couldn't be seen as a traitor.

The Israeli-Palestinian peace process kept going, and after the Second Intifada began in 2002, the Middle East Quartet was formed. In 2002, at the Beirut Summit of the Arab League, the Arab world came up with its own peace plan. It was based on an idea from Saudi Arabia and said that the Arab world would recognise Israel if it met certain conditions. When Yasser Arafat died in 2004, India lost its main contact in Palestine, someone who knew how hard India had worked to help the Palestinian cause.

The Second Intifada, the Lebanon war, and the Gaza wars really split the Palestinians into two groups that are at odds with each other. The PNA was the only group that talked to Indians. These events made it even less important for India to keep its relationship with Israel in a delicate balance while openly criticising how Israel treats the Palestinians. But because India became less important to the Palestinian cause, Arabs had less reason to criticise its actions in a harsh way.

Conclusion

India's importance in the Arab world has grown as the world has changed and its economy has grown quickly over the past 20 years. Today, India stands on its own in the world, and Palestine is no longer a big part of relations between India and the Arab world. In the eyes of the Arab world, India and Pakistan became one country when King Abdullah of Saudi Arabia came to India in 2006 as the Republic Day's chief guest. Pakistan's propaganda is no longer as effective as it used to be. The relationship between India and Israel has moved into a new phase in which it is becoming less tied to the Palestinian issue and, more importantly, the relationship between the US and India.

The relationship has grown by leaps and bounds and now stands on its own, with high-level visits and more and more talks about security and defence. In 2014, Prime Minister Narendra Modi met with Israeli Prime Minister Benjamin Netanyahu at the UN General Assembly. India has also changed how it feels about resolutions that criticise Israel. Pranab Mukherjee was the first Indian president to go to Israel. He did this in 2015. He was also the first head of state to stay as a guest of the PNA in Ramallah. Some people said that he did this because he still cared a lot about how Indians felt in the past. In November 2016, Israeli President Reuven Rivlin became the second Israeli head of state to visit India. His trip may have been noticed mostly in India and Israel.

The "Arab Spring," the civil wars in Syria and Yemen, and the nuclear deal between Iran and the P5+1 (the US, UK, France, Russia, China, and Germany) have all changed the political landscape of the region, which is now dealing with the effects of the rivalry between Saudi Arabia and Iran. Reports say that China has offered to be a go-between for these two rivals in the area, and they are thinking about it. This competition, along with the Trump administration's mixed feelings about the two-state solution and the status of Jerusalem, and the fact that Europeans are tired of hearing about refugees, have pushed the Palestinian problem to the back of the news. The fighting between Palestinians in their own camp also doesn't help their cause.

All of this has made it possible for Netanyahu to stop peace talks and even skip events like the January 2017 Paris Palestine–Israel conference. The Arab street is also more focused on problems in their own countries right now. In this new setting, the region pays little or no attention to the relationship between India and Israel. In the region, Prime Minister Modi's trip to Israel in July 2017 won't make much of a splash, except maybe in Iran. But it could hurt the positive feelings that people still have about India. India will become another important but not loved country in the area, like China.

References

Singh Sanjay (2017), India-Israel http://dx.doi.org/10.1080/09700161.2017.1330940

Chapter 8

The Modi Government's Policy on Israel

The Rhetoric and Reality of De-hyphenation

Historical links

Background

In January 1992, India's government, which was run by the Congress party and led by Prime Minister Narasimha Rao, made full diplomatic ties with Israel. This event was a turning point in the diplomatic history of both countries. It happened soon after India voted to overturn a United Nations resolution from 1975 that said Zionism was the same as racism.

Several things helped Rao end India's four-decade-long reluctance to work with Israel. With the end of the Cold War and the fall of the Soviet Union, economic liberalisation began, and Rao looked to the West as India's most important partner. Full diplomatic relations with Israel showed the West that New Delhi was officially giving up the ideological rigidity that characterised India's foreign policy for much of the Cold War, when the Non-Aligned Movement (NAM) was at its peak.

Changes in the Israeli-Palestinian peace process happened quickly, which also made India change its mind. The Palestinian Liberation Organization (PLO) changed its traditional strategy of armed struggle against Israel to include political engagement. It not only acknowledged that Israel existed, but it also supported the steps that led to the start of peace talks between the US and the USSR in Madrid in October 1991. These talks were attended by Israel's four closest neighbours: Egypt, Lebanon, Syria, and Jordan. Even though nothing big came out of the conference, it showed that everyone involved in the conflict was willing to work towards a political solution.

India worked hard to make friends with the Arab world by avoiding getting closer to Israel. However, when Israel's Arab neighbours started negotiating, New Delhi couldn't be blamed for trying to get along with Israel. Even so, the Organization of Islamic Cooperation (OIC) passed resolutions in support of Pakistan, which was the one who started the armed conflict in Kashmir. In India, people's calls for policy changes got louder. China just started full diplomatic relations with Israel, which made it easier for the Indian government to do the same. Israel was a great place to get advanced military technology and equipment, and India could learn from Israel's experience in fighting terrorism in its own struggles in Punjab and Jammu and Kashmir (J&K). So, New Delhi's pragmatic policy towards Israel was driven by India's security and strategic needs.

Even after India and Israel made up in 1992, the Indian government didn't want to be seen as trying to court Israel. When Sharad Pawar, who was the Defence Minister at the time, talked about working with Israel to stop terrorism, some Muslim politicians told him he was wrong. When Israeli President Ezer Weizman went to India in December 1996, it was a sign that relations were getting warmer. With the formation of the National Democratic Alliance (NDA) government led by Atal Bihari Vajpayee, India's policy changed in a clear way. Because the Hindutva-leaning Bharatiya Janata Party (BJP) is pro-Israel, government leaders were more willing to talk about how friendly India is with Israel. Even when the second intifada started and the rest of the world criticised Israel for how it treated the Palestinians, the Vajpayee government kept getting closer to Israel. There was a big jump in how much the US and Israel worked together on defence, especially when it came to sharing information. By the time Israeli Prime Minister Ariel Sharon made his historic trip to India in 2003, the two countries had become major trading partners.

After the 2004 general elections in India, which led to the formation of the Congress-led United Progressive Alliance (UPA) government, there were some worries about whether the good relations with Israel that had been built up under the previous BJP-led NDA government would continue. Even though the UPA government led by Manmohan Singh needed the support of left-leaning parties, it couldn't change the policies set by the previous government. So, relations between India and Israel got a lot better during the two terms of the UPA government, from 2004 to 2014. But there weren't many important trips, especially from India to Israel. Israel's military operations in the Gaza Strip and the Second Lebanon War are said to have stopped Pranab Mukherjee from going on a trip he had planned for 2006. In January 2012, External Affairs Minister S. M. Krishna made a symbolic visit. It was the first time an Indian foreign minister had been there in more than a decade, and it was done to mark the 20th anniversary of the two countries' first diplomatic ties.

Under Prime Minister Narendra Modi's nationalist government multilevel and multi-dimensional relations between Israel and India are intensifying. Israel's Prime Minister, Benjamin Netanyahu, welcomed the Indian Prime Minister Narendra Modi on his maiden arrival in Israel at Tel Aviv Airport in on July 4, 2017. The two countries have developed strong strategic, military, and technology partnerships.

Moreover, there have been ideological sympathy between the Bharatiya Janata Party (BJP) and Israel for a long time. It helps to advance the ambitions of both sides. However, if we look at history, we will find that the relationship between Israel and India has not always been as friendly as it is today.

Dynamic Strategic Equations and a New Era

India's foreign and security policy has been rethought from the ground up because of the recent change in government. Over the last two and a half years, India's policy has changed in a number of areas. For example, India's relationship with the US has changed in a big way, its relationship with Israel has gotten much better, it has tried carefully to change the nature of its relationship with China, and it has been working hard to make inroads into Southeast Asia. Since Narendra Modi came to power in 2014, it seems that India's diplomatic goals towards Israel have become more important than those towards other West Asian countries. Modi can be credited with making the relationship between India and Israel more strategic by bringing it out from "under the carpet." So, strategic relations between India and Israel are at a turning point in history. At the same time, the relationship will need to be cared for for a few years before it is fully developed.

Pranab Mukherjee's trip to Israel in October 2015 was the first time an Indian President had been there. It was also a big step forward in the relationship between the two countries. Usually, foreign trips by the Indian president don't get much attention. However, Mukherjee's six-day tour of Jordan, the Palestinian Authority, and Israel was seen as a warm-up for Prime Minister Modi's much-anticipated trip to Israel. In a special move that showed how close relations are between India and Israel, President Mukherjee spoke at a special session of the Knesset and said that his "visit to Israel is happening at a time when relations between our two governments are going in a very good direction." Israeli Prime Minister Benjamin Netanyahu said, "I talk to my dear friend Modi quite often. We are getting closer and closer together." When we met once, he told me, "India wants Israel," and I told him that I thought our two countries were very close. In January 2016, India's Foreign Minister Sushma Swaraj went to Israel. Her trip was part of New Delhi's ongoing efforts to not only make India's relationship with Israel stronger but also more well-known.

In November 2016, Israeli President Reuven Rivlin spent a week in India. This was a good sign for the relationship between the two countries and showed that India didn't feel bad about its growing ties with Israel. After President Weizman's visit, Rivlin is the first Israeli head of state to go to India in 20 years. During his meeting with the Israeli President, Indian Prime Minister Modi called India's relationship with Israel "multidimensional and wide-ranging." He also stressed the need to "build on convergences and commonalities" in agriculture, science, technology, research and innovation, defence, tourism, education, and culture. President Rivlin also said, "Our relationship is not just something we talk about. This partnership is making a difference in the water we drink, the food we eat, the technology we use, and many other important parts of our lives. Rivlin used his speech at Agro Tech 2016 in Chandigarh to try to connect the Hindi word jugaad to the Jewish State of Israel and its way of thinking, inventing, and working. He said, "Jugaad is how we think, how we invent, and how we work."

During Modi's time in power, India was able to keep its strategic and defense partnership with Israel without causing any chaos. It did this by taking a strong political position in favor of Palestine and voting in favor of Palestine at the United Nations. It was important that India kept friendly relations with the oil-rich Arab states in the Gulf region. In 2015, India was one of five countries that didn't vote for a UN Human Rights Council resolution that supported a report on war crimes committed by Israel during Operation Protective Age. Modi was the first Prime Minister of India to go to Israel in 2017. He chose not to visit the Palestinian Authority at that time, which was a clear sign that he had changed sides. Netanyahu said to Modi when he arrived in Israel, "Welcome, my friend. We really like India. We like how much you care about culture, history, democracy, and progress. Modi's enthusiasm comes from the fact that Hindu nationalists in India have always been very supportive of Israel. In the 1920s, Vinayak Damodar Savarkar wrote, "If the Zionists' dreams come true and Palestine becomes a Jewish state, we will be almost as happy as our Jewish friends."

When the Modi government passed the controversial Citizenship Amendment Act (CAA) in December 2019, which makes it harder for Muslims to become citizens, it was criticized around the world. But Dana Kursh, the Israeli Consul General for South India, said, "India has the right to pass CAA because it is a sovereign country." India should not be told what to do or not do by the European Parliament. India's right to be independent must be respected, and the country knows how to keep its people safe. When Turkish President Recep Erdogan was criticizing the Citizenship Amendment Act (CAA) in front of the rest of the world, it was important for a strong lobbying country like Israel to say that it was an internal matter of a sovereign nation.

From another point of view, India and Israel have some of the same strategic goals. For example, they both want to have qualitative (and in some cases quantitative) military dominance over their rivals and be able to choose their own technology and weapons. India has also taken advantage of the fact that Israel is known around the world for improving old weapons systems and military hardware from the Soviet Union. India now has all of Israel's missiles, rockets, radars, communication equipment, ships, assault weapons, sniper rifles, night-vision devices, and equipment for watching the border. Israel has sold motion detectors and other surveillance gear to India and Pakistan in the Jammu and Kashmir region to keep track of people who sneak across the Line of Control (LoC) between the two countries. Israel also sold India unmanned aerial vehicles (UAVs) for high-altitude surveillance and offered to train Indian forces in the region to fight back against insurgencies. Several Indian police officers who work in Kashmir, which is ruled by India, went to the Israel National Police Academy to learn more about their jobs. But people think that when it comes to international politics, countries care more about how they look than how they do. Arms diplomacy helped Israel build military and strategic ties with several Arab and Asian states so that diplomatic ties could be normalized. However, arms diplomacy alone can't build long-term relationships.

In the same way, top Israeli leaders said in 2017 that Israel would never "back Pakistan on the Kashmir issue." On January 26, 2021, the anniversary of the Republic of India, Netanyahu wrote a letter to Prime Minister Narendra Modi that said, "To my great friend, Prime Minister Narendra Modi. On India's 72nd Republic Day, I want to wish you and the rest of the country well. Every year, our friendship gets stronger. On Republic Day, Yariv Levin, a member of Netanyahu's Likud Party and the Knesset, praised "India's strong commitment to the ideals of the Constitution's rights and values." Israel's problem is not Islamist extremism, but the people whose land it is militarily occupying. Israel doesn't see a problem with giving Jewish people citizenship in Palestine by taking it away from Muslim and Christian Palestinians. In the end, Israel takes its territorial sovereignty more seriously and with more care than Islamic terrorism.

When he became prime minister in May 2014, it was expected that Narendra Modi would be the first Indian prime minister to visit Israel since he took office. Netanyahu went to India in January 2018, while Modi went to Israel in July 2017. In 2017, Netanyahu broke protocol and met Modi personally at the airport. In the same year, Netanyahu also met Modi personally. Modi feels a special attachment to Israel. When Narendra Modi was chief minister of Gujarat, Israel put a lot of money into the state. Modi is sure that Israel can also play a big part in making his "Make in India" program a success. In the events that came before, President Pranab Mukherjee was the first Head of State from India to visit Israel in October 2015. In January 2016, External Affairs Minister Sushma Swaraj went to Israel. In February 2018, Modi also made a trip to the West Bank. Modi was the first Indian Prime Minister to visit both Israel and the Palestinian territories. During Modi's time in power, New Delhi's relationships with both Israel and Palestine have improved.

The Bharatiya Janata Party (BJP) has always liked Israel because of how militaristic and nationalistic it is. At one of its meetings in October 1991, the BJP called for full diplomatic ties to be made with Israel. As External Affairs Minister, BJP leader Atal Bihari Vajpayee set up a secret trip to India for his Israeli counterpart, Moshe Dayan, in 1977-1978. As Prime Minister of India in September 2003, Vajpayee also hosted Israel's Prime Minister, Ariel Sharon. During the two UPA governments that Manmohan Singh led, the two countries' strategic ties stayed the same as before. But when it comes to how he deals with Israel, the BJP-led government and the Congress party-led government have very different views. Unlike the BJP government, which openly explains why it wants to get closer to Israel, the Congress made sure that its leaders were never seen in public with Israeli leaders or officials. In 2012, S.M. Krishna, who was the External Affairs Minister, and A.K. Antony, who was the Defence Minister, both put off their trips to Israel and asked the Israeli Defence Minister Ehud Barak to do the same.

The Congress thinks that India's relationships with the Islamic Arab world, including Palestine, which gets "theoretical support" from India, will be hurt by India's open and honest relationships with Israel. Another thing is that he has to share the stage with the "racist" who ran Israel and that the Indian Left and Muslims are against him. The second way that Modi's approach to Israel is different from that of his predecessors is that he has tried to show that India's relationship with Israel is different from its relationship with Arab countries and Iran. Both relationships are important to him, and he has been able to get the message across that they are not at odds with each other and can move forward without hurting each other. India wants to have different kinds of relationships with each Arab country. For instance, India's relationships with Saudi Arabia and the UAE are not related. And Iran is no different. Modi's trips as prime minister to the UAE, Turkey, Saudi Arabia, Qatar, Iran, and other places should be seen as part of this plan.

In 2020, Israel signed normalization agreements with Morocco, Oman, Bahrain, and the United Arab Emirates (UAE). But these agreements are not just a sign of a big change in politics in the area. They also get rid of the bad reputation of making diplomatic ties with Israel. And the changing political situation in the Middle East gives India a chance to strengthen its ties with Israel without hurting its relationships with other countries in the area.

In the later years of Benjamin Netanyahu's rule, India and the UAE are working together to find a new way to strengthen diplomatic and political ties in the region. External Affairs Minister S. Jaishankar spent three days in Israel with another important ally, the UAE. Nearly 4 million Indian immigrants live in UAE, which has diplomatic ties with Israel thanks to the Abraham Agreement, which was signed on August 13, 2020. After Jordan did it in 1994, the UAE is the second country to have good relations with Israel. In fact, the name "Indo-Abrahamic understanding" refers to the fact that the Jewish and Islamic religions have the same roots. Both Jews and Muslims believe that Abraham, or Ibrahim, was a prophet. Because of the spirit of the Abrahamic deal, after Bahrain, the UAE, Sudan, and Morocco have also signed the Abrahamic Agreement and want to make things better with Israel. Egyptian scholar Soliman thinks that the three-way relationship between Prime Minister Narendra Modi, the UAE, and Israel could be the center of a bigger regional alliance. People think that this new multilateral agreement could fill the void left by the United States in the Middle East and could change the region's geopolitics and geoeconomics. Jaishankar met with Sheikh Abdullah bin Zayed, the foreign minister of the United Arab Emirates, Antony Blinken, the secretary of state of the United States, and Yair Lapid, the foreign minister of Israel. After Japan, the United States, India, and Australia met to talk about security, Indian media said that the meeting was a step toward forming a "New Quad." Harsh Pant, an expert on international politics, said that India, Israel, and the UAE show how India's diplomatic profile is changing in the "New Quad" area.

The government of India thinks that Israel's "homeland security" methods, which may include mass punishment and torture, can teach them a lot about how to fight domestic terrorism, such as what happened in Mumbai after the 2008 attack, or how to deal with large-scale protests against projects that the States or the Centre want to move forward; and, of course, how to deal with militancy in Kashmir.

Gradual De-Hyphenation

Aside from the anti-colonial part of the NAM's position, the main reason India supported the Palestinian cause without question was to make a lot of India's Muslim minority happier. In the same way, India has always tied getting closer to Israel to progress in the conflict between Israel and the Palestinians. Now, when the Modi government has decided to show what used to be behind-the-scenes ties with Israel, there are more and more calls for India to stop involving Israel in the Palestinian issue. Still, the first steps towards getting rid of the hyphen were not taken until 1992, when Narasimha Rao was in charge and his government established full diplomatic relations with Israel. Since then, India's relations with Israel have slowly gotten better, but they are still limited by ideas and domestic politics.

Top Indian leaders have visited both Israel and the Palestinian Authority as part of the same tour. In 2000, Union Home Minister L. K. Advani and External Affairs Minister Jaswant Singh, as well as External Affairs Minister S. M. Krishna in 2012, went on trips that were called "regional" because they included meetings with both Israeli and Palestinian leaders. But Union Home Minister Rajnath Singh's visit to Israel in November 2014 was a big deal because it was only in Israel. The fact that

Rajnath's tour didn't include the Palestinian Authority was seen as a sign that the Modi government wanted to break with the tradition of including the Palestinian Authority and Jordan on high-level official visits to Israel. This also meant that some of the ties between India and the PA would have to be loosened. But when the old policy came back, it was clear that there was a need to balance different domestic political demands. In October 2015, President Pranab Mukherjee went to Jordan, the PA, and Israel. He was the first foreign head of state to spend the night in Ramallah. In January 2016, Sushma Swaraj, who is the minister of external affairs, also went to the Palestinian Authority (PA) and Jordan, as well as Israel. While she was in Ramallah, she said that India was still "steadfastly committed" to "the Palestinian cause" and "to Palestine's efforts to build its nation and its capacity."

Prime Minister Modi hasn't been shy about how much he wants to get along with Israel. As a sign of how much things have changed between the two countries, India bought more arms from Israel in the first nine months of the Modi government than the Manmohan Singh government did in the three years before. As C. Raja Mohan pointed out, the UPA government leaders didn't want to be seen with Israeli leaders in public, but Prime Minister Modi's "immediate instinct" has been "to flaunt India's special relationship with Israel and his own personal bonhomie" with his Israeli counterpart. Prime Minister Benjamin Netanyahu officially invited Modi to visit Israel when they met at the UN General Assembly in September 2014. During this meeting, which was the first between the Prime Ministers of Israel and India in more than a decade, Netanyahu said, "We are very excited about the possibility of getting closer to India." We think anything is possible. Modi said that India is the only place where anti-Semitism has never been tolerated and Jews have never been hurt.

Moshe Ya'alon was the first Israeli Defence Minister to go to India since full diplomatic ties were made in 1992. He went there in February 2015. The next month, Modi met Israeli President Reuven Rivlin at the funeral of Lee Kuan Yew in Singapore. There, he told Rivlin that he still wanted to go to Israel. When President Rivlin met Modi in India in November 2016, Modi was there on a trip, and Rivlin told him, "It will be our honour to welcome you to Jerusalem, the capital of Israel."

Overall, the situation in West Asia is pretty good for Israel, which is not seen as the main cause of instability in the area. The chaos caused by the Islamic State has taken the focus off of the Israel-Palestine conflict and given India a lot of room to move. Most of the other countries in the region are too busy fighting each other and dealing with the jihadist juggernaut to care about the first visit to Israel by an Indian Prime Minister. Modi will definitely go to Israel, but he hasn't said when. This is true even though it may not be possible for a prime minister to go there alone for a number of reasons.

Even though some things are going well in India and the region, there are some things that the Modi government can't ignore before separating India's policy towards Israel and Palestine. Some people have said that Modi's solo trip to Israel could seriously weaken India's traditional support for an independent Palestinian state. This is because India has always supported an independent Palestinian state. India has been able to keep a sensible balance between the major regional players in West Asia. India can't ignore its energy ties with Iran and the Gulf states, which are just as important as its strategic ties with Israel. Also, since relations between the two countries are already strong, it's not clear what new results Modi's solo visit would be able to bring about. There is always a chance that this move could be used against the Modi government during important state assembly elections in Uttar Pradesh, where most of India's Muslims live. Elections in Uttar Pradesh in early 2017 could be a big problem for the Modi government, as both regional and national opposition parties would be tempted to use ideological rhetoric against it. The government doesn't want to hear that the Palestinian cause has been completely given up as part of the BJP's plan to get rid of Muslims.

Another problem caused by India's move towards Israel is that New Delhi wants to become a permanent member of the UN Security Council (UNSC). India needs the Arab countries, which make up a large group in the General Assembly, to back its bid for membership. A group of angry Palestinians might try to stop India's work if they are upset. In July 2015, India was one of five countries that didn't vote during a United Nations Human Rights Council (UNHRC) vote that criticised Israel for "alleged war crimes" in Gaza. This was the first time that India didn't vote on a UN resolution that criticised Israel. It was also said that Netanyahu had talked to his Indian counterpart and asked India to stay out of the vote. Adnan Abu Alhaija, the Palestinian ambassador to India, said that India's decision was wrong and that New Delhi's new position on Palestine would make it hard for other UN members to understand what India's role would be if and when it became a permanent member. So far, India's strong support for Palestinians hasn't stopped it from building a partnership with Israel that is good for both countries. But weakening or changing India's support for the Palestinians would have some clear effects on India.

Most likely, the Modi government would move slowly to protect important strategic, economic, and energy interests while also improving India's relationship with Israel. The government may say in public that India's policy towards Israel and Palestine will stay the same, even though it has become weak and unstable. India used to vote against Israel at important international forums, but now it doesn't vote on Israel-related issues. This shows that the government is determined to make a major change in India's policy towards Israel. In April 2016, India and more than 30 other countries on the general board of the United Nations Educational, Scientific, and Cultural Organization (UNESCO) criticised Israel for its policies of digging up the al-Aqsa mosque and al-Haram a-Sharif/Temple Mount and keeping people out. But when a similar resolution came up for a vote in October 2016, India decided not to vote. Since the text of the UNESCO resolution was almost the same, Israeli officials may have been surprised when India didn't back the Palestinian draft. The only way to explain the change is that the Modi government made a subtle shift in policy. What happens in UN forums over the next few years is likely to have a big impact on India's policy towards Israel and Palestine. Even though nothing is certain in international politics, India has already shown that it can go in a different direction under Modi's leadership.

In October 2016, Modi said at a public event in Himachal Pradesh that the Indian army's "surgical strikes" against terrorist launch pads across the Line of Control (LoC) in Pakistan-occupied Kashmir were similar to Israel's policy of assassinations and military action against specific people. He was quoted as saying, "These days, people all over the country talk about how brave our army is. We used to hear that this is what Israel did. The country has seen that the Indian Army is just as good as anyone else's. Most of the time, prime ministers use metaphors and symbols in their speeches. These are used at national and international events to build national identity and help shape strategic culture. By using an Israeli military action as a model and putting it into the larger story of Indian military strategy, one can see that there is an ideological connection that plays a big, if subtle, role and justifies some policy options over others. This shows how important geopolitical and geopsychological factors are in the foreign and security policies of the Modi government, which are about to change in a big way. Modi's attitude towards the Jewish state is different from that of his predecessors because he talks positively about it in public. There seems to be a link between these events and a change in India's policy towards Israel.

Counterterrorism Cooperation and Defence Cooperation

During the Cold War, India's close ties to the Palestine Liberation Organization (PLO) and its unwillingness to condemn the terrorist acts done by the PLO made the West and Israel suspicious of India. People thought that New Delhi had two different sets of rules because it was quick to condemn terrorism when its own people were hurt, but slow to do so when Israelis were hurt. Still, India and Israel have been able to agree on a number of things. Israeli leaders showed that they understood the limits of India's political and diplomatic support for the Palestinians. This is because New Delhi is worried about Pakistan's efforts to get the Arab states to side against India over the Kashmir issue. Since 1992, the relationship between the two countries has gotten better, which can be seen in the way they work together on defence, share intelligence, and fight terrorism.

India gets the second most of its military equipment from Israel. Daniel Carmon, who is the Israeli ambassador to India, said that defence cooperation between the two countries is one of the "central pillars" of their relationship. India and Israel are working together on important defence projects. For example, India's DRDO and Israel's IDF are making the Barak-8 surface-to-air missile defence system and the Spike anti-tank guided missile (ATGM). In October 2016, India gave the go-ahead for the Indian army to buy Israeli combat radio sets. This was one of the most recent defence purchases from Israel.

Even though the roots and nature of the terrorism they face are different, both India and Israel have to deal with jihadist terrorism. Terrorism against both countries is backed by people who live nearby. India has found it helpful to learn from Israel's way of dealing with terrorism, because Israel's fight against cross-border terrorism has given it amazing technological and operational skills.

Repeated attacks across the border on Jammu and Kashmir, as well as a growing sense of danger from the area, have pushed Indian policymakers to work more closely with Israel on security. India's internal conflict theatre is made up of many different types, such as sub-conventional war, low intensity conflict, proxy war, insurgency, and non-combat operations. This means that the Indian military and the Israeli military need to work together more on counterterrorism.

The 2008 terror attacks in Mumbai showed once again how badly the Indian government can't control its borders, turn intelligence into actionable information, and stop or stop terrorist attacks before they happen. The urgent need to fix the Indian security system, which is very weak and broken, led to a growing interest in Israeli methods for fighting terrorism. For the purpose of fighting terrorism, Israel has given India satellite photos, unarmed vehicles (UAV), hand-held thermal imagers, night vision devices, long range reconnaissance and observation systems (LORROS), and detection equipment. India has already used some Israeli methods and techniques to deal with terrorist threats from Pakistan. A group called the Joint Working Group, which was set up in 2000, has helped New Delhi and Tel Aviv talk about how to fight terrorism. Even when President Rivlin met with Prime Minister Modi in November 2016 in New Delhi, India, one of their main goals was to work together to fight terrorism.

India's ruling party, the BJP, has always been a strong advocate for closer ties between India and Israel. Its leaders, both in the government and in the opposition, have always praised Israel's policies for fighting terrorism and protecting national security. The Modi government has made it clear that India wants to focus on counterinsurgency and counterterrorism operations, especially in Jammu and Kashmir, by carrying out surgical strikes in Pakistan-occupied territory. In the same way that Modi compared India's surgical strikes against terrorism to Israel's successes, India is likely to put the development of elite special forces like Israel's Sayeret Matkal at the top of its list of priorities. These changes are likely to lead to more cooperation with Israel to fight terrorism. P. R. Kumaraswamy says, "India's efforts to modernise its technology and Israel's efforts to cut costs in defence research are complementary and should be the basis for a long-term partnership." David Malone also thinks that the security partnership between India and Israel is not the only thing that brings the two countries together, but that it is the most important thing as long as terrorism is a threat to both countries.

Even though the Modi government is steadily increasing the size and scope of its cooperation with Israel in fighting terrorism and sharing intelligence, this can only go so far because India and Israel are not directly fighting the same enemy. India can't completely agree with Israel's idea of what terrorism is. In the same way, the Indian government can't use the same kind of forceful tactics against terrorism that Israel has used. Counterterrorism is usually the job of the government, but expanding efforts to include think tanks and academic institutions could be a unique way to encourage honest conversations about what both sides have learned from past counterterrorism and counterinsurgency campaigns and to bridge the gap between the Indian and Israeli views on terrorism.

Israel's main goals were security, survival, and economic growth. The country didn't have natural resources like oil and gas, or even enough water to drink. One way to solve this problem was to improve technology and become self-sufficient economically. Arms diplomacy has become a good way for Israel to build relationships with other countries. Security and defense cooperation have always been and still are the most important parts of relations between the two countries. Israel sent arms to India during the Indo-China war in 1962, which was 30 years before the two countries became official allies. India also used Israeli weapons in the 1965 and 1971 wars between India and Pakistan. When India's foreign intelligence agency, the Research and Analysis Wing (RAW), was set up in 1968, former spy chief RN Kaw was asked by Prime Minister Indira Gandhi to make contact with Israel's Mossad.

Israel has also become India's most reliable source of arms, and it is willing to keep a supply line open without any political requirements. Even though the Clinton administration had to deal with economic sanctions and a ban on weapons and military technology because of the Pokhran-II nuclear tests in 1998 and the Kargil War in 1999, Israel had already built strategic relationships with India and given them surveillance systems.

India buys the most weapons from Israel right now, and Israel is India's second-largest arms supplier. Between 2015 and 2019, the amount of imports went up by 17.5%, and annual sales are now more than a billion dollars. Israeli Aerospace

Industries (IAI) and India's Defence Research and Development Organisation (DRDO) are working together to make surface-to-air missile systems for the Indian Armed Forces. The Stockholm International Peace Research Institute (Sipri), which keeps track of global defense sales, says that between India and Israel, defense trade has been worth more than $1 billion a year for the last five years. It is said that India will soon sign a $2.5 billion deal with Israel Aerospace Industries to buy a medium-range surface-to-air missile defense system for its military.

Economic, Trade and Multi-dimensional Cooperation

When it comes to relations between India and Israel, military-security cooperation or deals on arms often take center stage. During the high-level visits, there wasn't much talk about other areas of cooperation, but both sides are now paying more attention to improving cooperation in other areas. But things are changing now, and the two countries are also working on tripartite and multilateral partnerships with countries that share their values and want to find new ways to work together in all areas of their bilateral relationships. The head of Israel's Economic and Trade Mission, Sagi Itchar, said that trade between India and Israel is getting better and should reach USD 4 billion in 2021. In 2020, the two countries traded about $3.4 billion worth of goods and services with each other. Long ago, the groundwork for the economic cooperation we have now was set. Shri Kamal Nath, the Minister of Commerce and Industry, went to Israel in November 2005. While there, a Joint Study Group (JSG) was set up to increase trade between the two countries from $2 billion to $5 billion by 2008. From April 2000 to March 2021, Israel invested $224.76 million directly in India. In September 2019, India's total ODI earnings were USD 118.24 million.

India and Israel have many different kinds of relationships with each other today. From April 2020 to February 2021, trade between the two countries (except for defense) was worth $4.14 billion. There are more and more Indian software companies in Israel. In 2006, the two countries signed a comprehensive agreement to work together in the agriculture field. Right now, the fifth part of the agreement is being carried out. In 1993, India and Israel also signed an agreement to work together on science and technology. In 2017, a $40 million Industrial R&D and Innovation Fund between India and Israel was set up.

In December 2020, the two countries signed a deal to work together more on health and medicine issues. At the height of the COVID-19 epidemic, Indian and Israeli officials also worked together to make COVID-19 test kits that can be used quickly. In March 2021, it was said that Premas Biotech of India and Oramed of Israel had made a COVID-19 oral vaccine together. In the past few years, there have also been more cultural exchanges, tourists, and people-to-people contacts.

During his trip to India in 2018, Benjamin Netanyahu, who was then the Israeli Prime Minister, held an event in Mumbai called "Shalom Bollywood." Some of the most famous people in the Hindi film industry were there.

Israel's economy is a developed free market economy, and the World Bank's Ease of Doing Business Index ranks it 35th in terms of how easy it is to do business there. In fact, after the United States, Israel is the country with the most new businesses. The most important parts of the country's economy are technology and making things. The diamond industry in Israel is known all over the world, and just cutting and polishing diamonds makes up 23.2% of the country's total exports. India is also a big player in the diamond trade around the world. India is Israel's third-biggest trading partner in Asia and seventh-biggest worldwide. Even though diamonds and chemicals make up most of the trade between the two countries, trade in areas like electronic machinery and high-tech products, as well as communication systems, medical equipment, etc., has grown in recent years. India is still a top priority for the Israeli government as it works to expand trade.

Israel is one of the top 10 countries that export military equipment. In 2007, Israel's exports made up 10% of the world's total exports. Many Israeli companies, like Elbit Systems, Israel Aerospace Industries, and Rafale Advanced Defence Systems Ltd., are on the list of the top 100 arms manufacturers and military service providers in the world. India is also a big market for Israeli arms, and it is still the country where Israel sells the most weapons in the world. According to the Stockholm International Peace Research Institute, 40% of the surveillance and strategic drones in the world are made by Israeli defense companies.

The world might have trouble in the future if there isn't enough fresh water to go around. India already has water shortages and other problems in a lot of cities and areas. Israel has made a lot of progress in this method of getting water from the sea (extracting salt from seawater and making it usable for daily human consumption). The Israel-based company IDE has been helping businesses in Greater Mumbai and West Bengal with their water problems. They have also built three desalination plants in India, in Nemili Taluk in Ranipet district, Chennai in Tamil Nadu, and Jamnagar in Gujarat. In August 2020, the governments of Israel and Uttar Pradesh signed a deal to work together to deal with the lack of water in the Bundelkhand region.

The two countries also seem to be trying to get closer to each other in the areas of culture and tourism. India is one of the few places where people with Jewish roots have never been treated unfairly or been persecuted. Both cultures are also important to both countries. To do this, the tourism industry also needs to be pushed, and more and more Indian tourists are going to Israel.

Conclusion

The relationship between India and Israel has changed a lot in the last 25 years. India officially recognised Israel in 1950, but full diplomatic relations didn't start until 1992. This freed New Delhi's West Asia policy from ideological rigidity, moral sentimentalism, and self-doubt. Even though relations with Israel have been normalised for almost 25 years, they still get a lot of attention in India. Israel's policies towards the Palestinians still spark a lot of debate in India, but that doesn't stop people from seeing the benefits of being friends with Israel. Cooperation in agriculture, the transfer of technology, foreign investment, and working together on security have all helped make people feel good about Israel. Cross-border terrorism and jihadist extremism have happened in India and Israel's area, and this has brought them closer together. Even though things moved slower than expected, ties have grown.

At the same time, India's long-standing ties with the Palestinians and the rest of the Arab world are a big problem when it comes to building stronger ties with Israel. The Modi government has said again how important it is to have good relations with Israel. They have also said that India will continue to support the Palestinian cause. But since 2015, India's votes at the UN on issues involving Israel and the Palestinians have changed in a noticeable way. People have seen New Delhi's decision to not vote on resolutions that condemn Israel in some UN agencies as a change from India's past support for the Palestinians. India leans towards Israel because New Delhi hasn't gotten much support from Arab countries for its position on Kashmir. Also, Arab countries haven't really tried to put pressure on Pakistan to stop terrorism across the border in Kashmir.

The leaders of India have realised that it's important to keep close ties with both Israel and the Arabs, but it's not helpful to hide the growing friendship with Israel. In fact, there is an urgent need for India to strengthen its ties with Israel because jihadist radicalization is creating a violently chaotic political climate in West Asia, which is hurting regional security. Even though it's hard to predict how future events in the region will affect Indo-Israeli relations, it doesn't seem likely that they will end what has been a very productive partnership between the two countries. With Narendra Modi in charge, it's clear that India's foreign policy is ending a certain era. The way the Modi government used diplomatic energy, strategic creativity, and political courage to build a new relationship with Israel shows that India's foreign policy is changing in a big way.

Some people have said that Modi's trip to Israel and his friendship with Netanyahu were caused by the Hindu right and the Likud party in Israel, which have similar ideas. But this is not the right way to argue or think about it. How would these critics explain Modi's high priority for countries like Iran, Qatar, Saudi

Arabia, and the United Arab Emirates if a right-wing anti-Muslim agenda was the driving force? In no way are these places less important to India than Israel. Modi plans to see all Arab and non-Arab states in the Middle East as possible partners in his plan to grow the economy and trade. During a trip to Israel in October 2021, External Affairs Minister Subramanian Jaishankar said that India sees Israel as "perhaps its most trusted and innovative partner in many ways." Ron Malka, who used to be the Ambassador to India and is now the Director General of the Ministry of Economy, said that Israel's relationship with India is "our biggest international achievement with any country." Yuval Steinitz, who used to be the finance minister of Israel, called for the Free Trade Agreement to be finished in 2012. "Our special ties with the US may be the only ones stronger than those with India." India and Israel have come to this point in their relationship after a lot of diplomatic work. If the US is Israel's most important country after India, then India's most important diplomatic ally is also Israel.

References

Bagchi, Indrani. "'India-Israel Ties No Longer Just a Close Friendship' - Times of India." The Times of India, 27 Dec. 2021, timesofindia.indiatimes.com/india/india-israel-ties-no- longer-just-a-close-friendship/articleshow/88527673.cms. Accessed 3 Jan. 2022.

Jangid, Khinvraj. "Arms Diplomacy Was Israel's Legacy to Earn Diplomatic Wins. But Pegasus Got It a Bad Image." The Print, 28 Dec. 2021, theprint.in/opinion/arms-diplomacy-was-israels-legacy-to-earn-diplomatic-wins-but-pegasus-got-it-a-bad-image/789319/. Accessed 10 Jan. 2022.

Nanda, Prakash. "India-Israel Ties: Under Modi, Congress Tradition of Being Apologetic about This Relationship Ends-India News, First post." First post, 7 Mar. 2017, www.firstpost.com/india/india-israel-relations-under-modi-congress-tradition-of-being- apologetic-about-this-relationship-ends-3318896.html. Accessed 20 Dec. 2021.

Sen, Somdeep. "India's Deepening Love Affair with Israel." Www.aljazeera.com, 9 Sept. 2021, www.aljazeera.com/opinions/2021/9/9/indias-deepening-love-affair-with-israel. Accessed 10 Jan. 2022.

Gupta, Shishir. "New Chapter in India-Israel Relations: Jaishankar to Cement Post-Netanyahu Ties." Hindustan Times, 16 Oct. 2021, www.hindustantimes.com/india-news/jaishankar-to-firm-up-political-ties-with-israel-via-dubai- 101634361927560.html. Accessed 2 Jan. 2022.

Baba, Moyuru, Takeshi Kumon. "India, Israel Aim to Boost Ties through Defence Tech and Trade." Nikkei Asia, 28 Nov. 2021, asia.nikkei.com/Politics/International-relations/India-Israel-aim-to-boost-ties-through-defense-tech-and-trade. Accessed 10 Jan. 2022.

Vanaik, Achin. "How India Has Moved with Israel: A Timetable of Milestone Events." The Wire, 26 May 2021, thewire.in/diplomacy/india-israel-palestine-history-diplomatic- relations. Accessed 10 Jan. 2022.

Ningthoujam, Alvite. "India-Israel Ties: New Opportunities in the Middle East." Thediplomat.com, Oct. 2021, thediplomat.com/2021/10/india-israel-ties-new-opportunities-in-the-middle-east/. Accessed 10 Jan. 2022.

"India-Israel Bilateral Trade Likely to Reach $4 Bn This Year." The Financial Express, 15 Dec. 2021, www.financialexpress.com/economy/india-israel-bilateral-trade-likely-to- reach-4-bn-this-year/2381046/. Accessed 06 Jan. 2022.

Embassy Of Israel in India. "India-Israel Relations." Embassies.gov.il, 2021, embassies.gov.il/delhi/AboutTheEmbassy/India-Israel-Relations/Pages/default.aspx. Accessed 9 Dec. 2022.

Miglani, Sanjeev. "Netanyahu Pushes for India-Israel Free Trade Agreement." Theweek.in, The Week magazine, 15 Oct. 2018, www.theweek.in/news/biz- tech/netanyahu-pushes-for-india-israel-free-trade-agreement.html. Accessed 10 Dec. 2022.

Embassy of India, Tel Aviv. "Welcome to Embassy of India, Tel Aviv, Israel." Www.indembassyisrael.gov.in, 22 June 2021, www.indembassyisrael.gov.in/pages?id=nel5a&subid=7ax9b.

Kumaraswamy, P. R. "The Maturation of Indo-Israeli Ties." Middle East Quarterly, Spring 2013, vol. 20, no. 02, 2013, p. pp. 39-48, www.meforum.org/3494/india-israel-ties. Accessed 10 Jan. 2022.

Pate T. Re-(Modi)fying India's Israel Policy: An Exploration of Practical Geopolitical Reasoning Through Re-representation of 'India', 'Israel' and 'West Asia' Post-2014. Journal of Asian Security and International Affairs. 2020;7(1):7-35. doi:10.1177/2347797020906647

Kumaraswamy, P. R. "Modi in Israel." The Cairo Review of Global Affairs, 12 Nov. 2017, www.thecairoreview.com/essays/modi-in-israel-2/. Accessed 3 Jan. 2022.

"History & Overview of India-Israel Relations." Jewishvirtuallibrary.org, 2014, www.

jewishvirtuallibrary.org/history-and-overview-of-india-israel-relations.

Embassy of India, Tel Aviv. "Welcome to Embassy of India, Tel Aviv, Israel." Www.indembassyisrael.gov.in, 22 June 2021, www.indembassyisrael.gov.in/pages?id=nel5a&subid=7ax9b

P. R. Kumaraswamy, India's Israel Policy (New York: Columbia University Press, 2010), p. 156.

Tanvi Madan, "Why India and Israel are Bringing their Relationship Out from 'Under the Carpet,'" Brookings, February 11, 2016, https://www. brookings.edu/blog/order-from-chaos/2016/02/11/why-india-and-israel-are- bringing-their-relationship-out-from-under-the-carpet/.l

Ministry of External Affairs, "Visit of Minister of External Affairs to the State of Israel," January 10, 2012, http://mea.gov.in/press-releases.htm7dtl/17905/Visit+of+Minister+of+External+Affairs+to+the+State+of+Israel.

Madan, "Why India and Israel are Bringing their Relationship Out from 'Under the Carpet.'"

Stanly Johny, "Ties with Israel on Upswing: Pranab," The Hindu, October 14, 2015, www.thehindu.com/news/international/president-pranab-mukherjee- sixday-trination-tour-ties-with-israel-on-upswing-pranab/article7762301.ece.

Declaring Indo-Israel relationship as "very unique," "much much deeper," and beyond buyer-seller mode, Israeli Ambassador Daniel Carmon said that bilateral ties were being constantly updated on account of a "changing world, changing parameters, changing needs." See PTI, "Indo-Israel Ties 'Unique and Special': Envoy Daniel Carmon," Economic Times, January 13, 2016.

"President Rivlin Meets Prime Minister Modi of India," Website of the President of the State of Israel, November 15, 2016, http://www.president.gov.il/English/Presidential_Activities/Press_Releases/Pages/news_161116_03.aspx.

IANS, "I Fell in Love with this Word: Israeli President Rivlin on 'jugaad,'" Hindustan Times, November 20, 2016, http://www.hindustantimes.com/ india-news/i-fell-in-love-with-this-word-israeli-president-rivlin-on-jugaad/ story-ZNcTf56FqytJKCuI2AGmBJ.html.

IANS, "India for Enhanced Political, Economic Engagement with Palestine: Sushma," Deccan Herald, January 17, 2016.

Natalie Obiko Pearson and N. C. Bipindra, "Israel Next to Consider Making Arms in India as Ties Improve," Bloomberg, February 17, 2015, https://www. bloomberg. com/news/articles/2015-02-17/israel-next-to-consider-making- weapons-in-india-as-ties-improve.

C. Raja Mohan, "Raja-Mandala: Re-imagining the Middle East," Indian Express, January 19, 2016, http://indianexpress.com/article/opinion/ columns/raja-mandala-re-imagining-the-middle-east/.

Israeli Ministry of Foreign Affairs, "PM Netanyahu Meets with Indian PM Narendra Modi," September 29, 2014, http://mfa.gov.il/MFA/ PressRoom/2014/Pages/PM-Netanyahu-meets-with-Indian-PM-Narendra-Modi-28-Sep-2014.aspx.

Dipanjan Roy Chaudhury, "Make in India: Israeli Defence Minister Moshe Ya'alon Meets PM Narendra Modi, Promises Technological Support," Economic Times, February 20, 2015, https://goo.gl/o2ibkt.

Nicolas Blarel, "Modi's Visit to Israel: Political Blunder or Calculated Gamble?" The Wire, June 9, 2015, http://thewire.in/3411/modis-visit-to- israel-political-blunder-or-calculated-gamble/.

Israeli Ministry of Foreign Affairs, "President Rivlin Meets Indian PM Narendra Modi," November 15, 2016, http://mfa.gov.il/MFA/ PressRoom/2016/ Pages/President-Rivlin-meets-Indian-PM-Narendra-Modi- 15-November-2016. aspx.

Shubhajit Roy, "Gaza Conflict: UNHRC Adopts Resolution as India Abstains," Indian Express, July 4, 2015.

Siddharth Varadarajan, "Netanyahu's Phone Call to Modi, Not ICC Reference, Changed India's Israel Vote," The Wire, July 5, 2015, https:// thewire.in/5515/ netanyahus-phone-call-to-modi-not-icc-reference-changed- indias-israel-vote/.

In an interview to The Hindu, Alhaija said that India's decision to abstain was influenced by its security relationship with Israel. See Suhasini Haidar, "Palestine 'Shocked' at Indian Abstention," The Hindu, July 7, 2015.

United National Educational, Scientific and Cultural Organization, Executive Board, Hundred and ninety-ninth session, 199 EX/33, PARIS, April 14, 2016, http:// unesdoc.unesco.org/images/0024/002444/244481e. pdf.

Raphael Ahren, "Outrageous as it May Be, UNESCO's Jerusalem Vote has a Silver Lining," Times of Israel, October 14, 2016, http://www.timesofisrael. com/ outrageous-as-it-may-be-unescos-jerusalem-vote-has-a-silver-lining/.

Dhrubo Jyoti, "Modi Praises Indian Army for Surgical Strikes, Compares it to Israel," Hindustan Times, October 18, 2016, http://www.hindustantimes. com/india-news/modi-praises-indian-army-for-surgical-strikes-compares-it- to-israel/story-eTqN4s5a3Y70KVv4DRMfWM.html.

Bahukutumbi Raman, "Indo-US Counterterrorism Cooperation: Past, Present, and Future," in US-Indian Strategic Cooperation Into the 21st Century: More Than Words, eds. Sumit Ganguly, Brian Shoup, and Andrew Scobell (New York: Routledge, 2006).

Richard A. Bitzinger, "Israeli Arms Transfers to India: Ad Hoc Defence Cooperation or the Beginnings of a Strategic Partnership?" Policy Brief, April 2013, https://www.rsis.edu.sg/wp-content/uploads/2014/07/PB130401_Israeli_Arms_Transfers_to_India.pdf.

PTI, "Indo-Israel Ties 'Unique and Special.'"

IANS, "India Successfully Test-Fires Barak-8 Missile," Business Standard, September 20, 2016, http://www.business-standard.com/article/news-ians/ india-successfully-test-fires-barak-8-missile-116092001021_1.html.

Rahul Bedi, "India Completes Price Negotiation for Israeli Spike ATGMs," IHS Jane's Defence Weekly, May 25, 2016, http://www.janes.com/ article/60741/india-completes-price-negotiation-for-israeli-spike-atgms.

Sanjib Kumar Baruah, "India to Buy Israeli Combat Radio," Asian Age, October 22, 2016.

Harsh V. Pant, Contemporary Debates in Indian Foreign and Security Policy (New York: Palgrave Macmillan, 2008), p. 134.

Ritu Sarin, "From Israel, Lessons on Fighting Terror," Indian Express, July 21, 2009.

Efraim Inbar and Alvite Singh Ningthoujam, "Indo-Israeli Defence Cooperation in the Twenty-First Century," Begin-Sadat Center for Strategic Studies, January 1, 2012, http://besacenter.org/mideast-security-and-policy- studies/indo-israeli-defense-cooperation-in-the-twenty-first-century-3-2/;

Neville Teller, "India and Israel: Strengthening the Bonds," Jerusalem Post, January 5, 2016, http://www.jpost.com/Blogs/A-Mid-East-Journal/India- and-Israel-strengthening-the-bonds-439427.

Kumaraswamy, India's Israel Policy, p. 257.

David Malone, Does the Elephant Dance: Contemporary Indian Foreign Policy

(Oxford: Oxford University Press, 2012), p. 191.

Nicolas Blarel, "Redefining India's Grand Strategy? The Evolving Nature of India's Israel Policy," in India's Grand Strategy: History, Theory, Cases, eds. Kanti Bajpai, Saira Basit, and V. Krishnappa (New Delhi: Routledge, 2014), p. 479.

Author's interaction with security experts and academics in Tel Aviv and Herzliya during an official visit to Israel in September 2016.

Index

C

D

www.ingramcontent.com/pod-product-compliance
Ingram Content Group UK Ltd.
Pitfield, Milton Keynes, MK11 3LW, UK
UKHW021321020826
14184UKWH00003B/19